For Nancy & Joe,

Mega-Thinking for 21st Century Success

Uniting Brain Science and Thinking Skills

Friends who love Florida North as much as we do.

Mary Fennessey Ferron, Ph.D.

Mary Fennessey Ferron

Published by FastPencil

This book is dedicated
In loving memory of my Parents,
John and Jennie (Coviello) Fennessey
and
To the loves of my life who
inspire me and bring me joy
My husband, Don
My children,
Matthew, Jen, and Laura
My grandchildren and future Mega-Thinkers,
Cam, Ryan, Cassidy, Braeden, Sam, Connor, and Katelin

❧

Contents

Acknowledgements

I gratefully acknowledge the contributions of the people and organizations that helped make this book, <u>Mega-Thinking for 21st Century Success,</u> a reality. My deepest thanks and admiration go to my husband Don for his love, support, patience, and confidence in me. He also provided indispensable editing services. Very special thanks go to my sister, Elaine Fennessey Casey, for being my cheerleader. Her phone calls, emails, cards, and visits provided continuous energy boosts to keep me going. A heartfelt and loving thank you is sent to my children, Matt, Jen, and Laura, and to my grandchildren, Braeden, Ryan, and Cam LaMothe, Sam and Cassidy Ferron, and Katelin and Connor Walsh. They inspire me to want to make the world a better place. My hope is that in some very small way, this book will help towards achieving that goal.

Thank you to the following organizations: The Learning and the Brain Society [http://www.learningandthebrain.com], The Association for Supervision and Curriculum Development [http://www.ascd.org], The National Center for Teaching Thinking [http://www.nctt.net], The Waters Foundation [http://www.watersfoundation.org], and isee systems [http://www.isseesystems.com] for offering the workshops and conferences that are responsible for making me aware of the need for Mega-Thinking in the 21st century. I am so very thankful for the brilliant people who presented at the workshops, spoke at the conferences, and wrote the books that influenced my thinking. Many of you are included in this book.

Thank-you to Dr. Robert Swartz, Founder of the National Center for Teaching Thinking, for identifying a "thinking school" that became the heart of my doctoral dissertation. It became the impetus for the intellectual journey that led me to this point. A special thank you to the Principal, Dr. Lawrence Aronstein, and the teachers who were passionate advocates for developing the thinking ability of *all* students. A special thank you to my professors and dissertation advisers at the University of Connecticut for stimulating my thinking about the development of young minds: Dr. Thomas Weinland, Dr. Deborah Burns, and Dr. Arthur Roberts. Thank-you to Dr. David Sousa, who has influenced my thinking about learning and the brain since 1995 when I first attended one of his workshop presentations.

Finally, I wish to express my great appreciation for permission to use the following material:

- Thank you to neuroscientist Bruno Dubuc at McGill University for allowing me to use the image, the "Pleasure Center of the Brain". It is from the outstanding free resource, "The Brain from Top to Bottom [http://www.thebrain.mcgill.ca]".
- Thank you to the Waters Foundation [http://www.watersfoundation.org], an outstanding free resource to bring Systems Thinking into Schools, for granting me permission to use "The Habits of Systems Thinkers" (HOST Image), the "Visualization Tools" image, and the "Iceberg Image".
- Thank you to Kathy Schrock, an educational technologist, who allowed me to use "The COGS of the Cognitive Process [http://www.schrockguide.net]" to depict Bloom's Revised Taxonomy.

Introduction

...success is defined not by where you are born, how smart you are, or how much money you have — or even by dumb luck. Success is attained by using your brain's faculties to respond to the circumstances and challenges you face in life.
— Brown and Fenske with Neporent

You are your own Chief Executive Officer — your personal CEO. In order to create a more successful future for yourself in the 21st century, you need to sharpen your thinking skills, so you can cope with change, make informed decisions, and solve complex problems. This book, <u>Mega-Thinking for 21st Century Success: Uniting Brain Science and Thinking Skills</u>, will help you reach your goals. As you read it, you will acquire the three essential characteristics of a Mega-Thinker: 1. You will learn how your brain works; 2. You will learn to think skillfully in the following six categories of thinking: common-sense thinking, critical thinking, creative thinking, systems thinking, self-control thinking, and school success thinking, and 3. You will learn how to maintain a healthy brain.

There are many books available today in all of these areas, but that's part of the problem that I see as an obstacle to skillful thinking. People today live very busy lives, so many of them do not have the time or energy to study these topics in depth. A major value of this book is that it summarizes key information from many books into one convenient source that provides you with a firm foundation for building your thinking ability. I am hopeful that this one book acts as a springboard for you to learn more about the brain and thinking skills and to read some of the books that I have cited.

Thinking Comes Naturally

Let's be clear from the start. I am not trying to teach you "to think", because the thinking process comes naturally. Thinking is "the business of the brain".[1] You are born with the ability "to think", but you are not born with the ability to think skillfully. That needs to be learned and it can be.[2] Most of your thinking skills develop within the complex environment in which you live your life. However, since mental discipline and skillful thinking are not gifts of nature, society often looks to the field of education to train the mind and develop the habits of skillful thinkers.[3] Sometimes schools are successful at developing thinking and sometimes they are not. The fact that you are reading this book indicates that you perceive a gap between where you are now and where you want to be as a "thinker". As your own CEO, you are taking action to fill that gap. Congratulations!

The Journey Begins

To help you become a Mega-Thinker, you and I will take a journey into the worlds of brain science, thinking skills, and brain health. You will access the abundant knowledge base that currently exists in these fields. However,

I am not a scientist, and this is not a science book. I am an educator, a teacher. I taught at the elementary, middle school, high school, and college levels. I was also a school administrator who specialized in curriculum and instruction, particularly in the development of thinking skills. With my background, I want you to think of this book as an independent study project, a do-it-yourself activity, and I am your personal instructor. My goal is to help you become a Mega-Thinker by explaining, simplifying, and consolidating a vast amount of complex information into a format that is readable, non-threatening, informational, practical, understandable, and useful for you.

The Missing Link

In the days that I was an active educator, developing skillful thinkers included many components including the following: dispositions, skills, strategies, school environment, and classroom climate. Teachers focused on the conditions within the classroom that would maximize the development of the brain including an atmosphere of "relaxed alertness" where safe risk-taking in thinking was fostered by combining high challenge activities with low threat evaluation.[4] A big debate centered on whether to teach thinking skills directly or to infuse them into the curriculum. However, there was no focus or debate about the role of the brain. It simply was assumed that the brain was part of the whole process of developing thinking. As a result, at the time I was working in schools, few people grasped the critical role that the physical brain plays in developing thinking skills.

It wasn't until my beloved mother developed Alzheimer's that I began to focus on the brain. My personal breakthrough came when I attended a lecture about memory and the brain given by Dr. Erik Kandel at the Marine Biological Lab in Woods Hole, Massachusetts. During his lecture, Dr. Kandel talked about his book, In Search of Memory: The Emergence of a New Science of Mind. His lecture and his book fascinated me. It hooked me on the topic of memory and the brain. It was the spark that led me to a new way of thinking about developing thinking skills. It dawned on me that the missing link in all efforts to develop and improve thinking ability was a focus on the brain itself. Lack of knowledge about how the brain works is a huge obstacle to skillful thinking.

The Mysterious Human Brain

There is a good reason why I did not focus on the brain and how it worked, when I was working as a teacher and administrator. I simply knew very little about the brain. Very few people knew how the brain worked when I was growing up and going to school. Very few people today know how the human brain works. Your amazing brain may be the most powerful tool in the universe, but it has been a mystery throughout most of human history. Scientists have known for a long time what the brain looks like; they just didn't know how it worked. It still has many secrets left to reveal. According to scientists who study the brain and nervous system, they are in the early stages of learning about the complex human brain.[5]

It is only in the last 50 years that scientists have begun to unravel its secrets. Major advances took place when brain-imaging technology was introduced including CAT scans (Computerized Axial Tomography) and fMRIs (functional Magnetic Resonance Imaging). Scientists can now look inside a live human brain in real time and see what is happening as the brain is actively engaged in various mental activities. They are exploring how people think, feel, act, learn, and remember.[6] As a result, the brain's secrets are being revealed at an increasingly furious pace. This means that the 21st century will see fascinating breakthroughs about the brain that will affect your life in ways no one can imagine today. Nevertheless, even though knowledge about how the human brain works is limited, the information that is available now in 2014 can change and improve your life.

Neuroeducation

Dr. Kandel's lecture and book stimulated my interest in learning more about the brain and its connection to thinking, learning, and memory. I started attending conferences including those offered by "The Learning and the Brain Society [http://www.learningandthebrain.com]". These conferences are co-sponsored by universities and organizations that include the McGovern Brain Research Institute at MIT, The Mind, Brain, and Education Program at Harvard, the Comer School Development Program at Yale, Boston University, John Hopkins University, The Neuroscience Research Institute at the University of California at Santa Barbara, the National Association of Secondary School Principals, the National Association of Elementary School Principals, and the Dana Alliance for Brain Initiatives. These conferences bring together neuroscientists, clinicians, educators, and policymakers. Together, they are forming a new field of study called Neuroeducation. The scientists, particularly neuroscientists, and the clinicians study and conduct research on learning and the brain. The teachers and policymakers use the results of their studies and research findings to solve educational problems.

Educators from across the United States and from many countries around the world attend these conferences. The first conference that I attended in 2009 nearly blew my mind! The speakers provided a goldmine of information. Among them were the following and their topics: Gary M. Small, M.D., *Digital Brains and Memory: Surviving the Technological Alteration of the Modern Mind*; Patricia Greenfield, Ph.D., *New Media, Multitasking, and Education: The Effects of Technology on Learning*; Richard Restak, M.D., *Think Smart: Improving Brain Performance in the Modern Age*; Edward Hallowell, M.D., *Crazy Busy: Dealing with an Overstretched, Overbooked, Distracted Life*; John Ratey, M.D. *Countering the Cyber Life: Getting in Touch with our Hunter-Gatherer Genes,* and Judy Willis, M.D. M.Ed., *The Neuroscience and Strategies for Maximizing Children's Long-Term Memory and Brain Potential.* I bought many of their books and became immersed in the links between thinking and the brain. It was after one of these conferences that I decided to write this book. I wanted to unite what I learned about brain science with what I already knew about developing thinking skills and share the knowledge. I wanted the powerful messages presented at conferences like these to reach a wider audience. I realized that the way I could make a difference was to write a book for people like you.

Personal Change Process

People like yourself recognize the need to take personal action to improve your thinking ability, so you are ready to engage in a change process. As you can see in Figure 1, I adapted Fullan's Model of the educational change process[7], to represent the change process for becoming a Mega-Thinker. In a change process, there are five regular and predictable phases: starting point; initiation; implementation; continuation, and outcomes. The research on change has found that for real change to occur, a person needs to be aware of the need to change. Regarding thinking ability, many people are not aware that they have a problem with their thinking. They would be at the starting point.

The Change Process

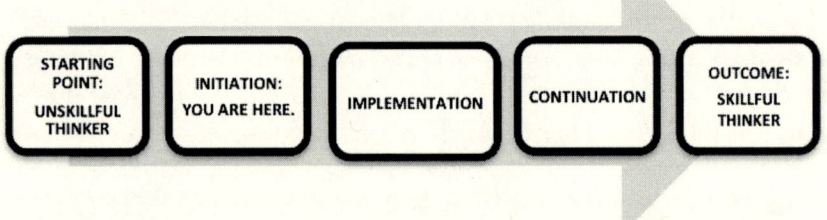

Figure 1. Change process for developing Mega-Thinking- adapted from Fullan, Michael (2007). The New Meaning of Educational Change, 4th ed.

Since you are aware that you can improve your thinking ability, you are already in the initiation phase. In this phase, you will learn how your brain works. You will move on to the implementation phase as you learn about and practice some skills and strategies for the six different categories of thinking. As you continue to practice them, your mental habits and behaviors will begin to change. By the time you finish this book, you should be on your way to becoming a Mega-Thinker.

Organization of the Book

Mega-Thinking for 21st Century Success is organized into three sections: Part 1. Know Your Brain; Part 2. Train Your Brain, and Part 3. Maintain Your Brain. In order to make the most sense of this book, you should read the four chapters in Part 1 in order. Part 1 provides the foundation for your knowledge about the brain, and I refer to that knowledge throughout the book. Since I also frequently refer to the content of Chapter five, Common Sense Thinking from Part 2, that chapter should be read right after Part 1. After that, it does not matter in which order you read the chapters.

However, as simplified as I tried to make it, the content of these chapters may still be challenging for you. In that case, use a strategy to get the main ideas. I recommend SQW3R which stands for Survey, Question, Write, Read, Recite, Review. It is particularly helpful for reading textbook type material. A full description of this technique is found in Chapter 10, School Success Thinking.

Part two focuses on six categories of thinking skills: common-sense; critical; creative; systems; self-control, and school-success thinking. To make it easier to remember them, I made up a formula: C^3S^3. The formula and the image of the atom on the cover are designed to make you understand that all kinds of thinking are connected. Although I listed the types separately, they are not separate. As a "thinker", you do not have a separate compartment for each of these categories of thinking. You may acquire skills at different times that sharpen your ability to work well in each area, but these skills are fluid. Your brain is continually working; it is not limited to one-at-a-time thinking processes. However, the more skills and strategies you acquire means your brain has more to select from, and the more skillful your thinking will be.

Part three provides information about taking care of your brain and keeping it healthy. You will learn how nutrition, exercise, rest, and stress affect your brain. You will learn how technology affects your brain in positive and negative ways. Finally, everything will be put together so you understand the "big picture" of Mega-Thinking.

Guide to Reading This Non-Fiction Book

There are a few strategies that you can use to get the most out of reading this book. I already provided one strategy, SQW3R. These useful strategies will help to keep your brain awake!

1. Use Graphic Organizers

Before you begin to read a book or study any new topic, you will be more successful as a learner if you activate your brain. It will help you to remember things if you use graphic organizers as you read. I recommend an advance organizer like a "KWL" before you begin reading each of the three main parts of this book. The KWL activity is a very simple and useful strategy for any learning activity. Perhaps you have used it already, since it is a very common learning tool. Take a piece of paper set it up in three columns like the following KWL example.

K	W	L
What I Know	What I Want to Know	What I Learned

K stands for "What I Know". W stands for "What I Want to Know", and L stands for "What I Learned". To use the tool, you write down what you know about a topic in the "K" column. You then write down what you want to know about a topic in the "W" column. Finally, after studying the topic, you go back and write down what you learned in the "L" column. What you are doing is putting your brain to work. You are activating your prior knowledge. Learning becomes more meaningful when you can make connections with what you already know and make predictions about what you will learn. Filling out the form does not have to be a major production. Use abbreviations or any shortcuts you know to fill in the columns. Keep it simple. The goal is to engage your brain.

2. Change Location

I recommend that you read each chapter in a different location. This does not have to be difficult, since the changed location could be a different part of the same room. This simple strategy will help your memory, because it provides some novelty, and your brain loves novelty! In addition, as you will learn, your brain stores information in different areas. Before it is stored, the new information travels along mental pathways. One pathway involves your experiences in time and place, and it is called the "episodic" pathway. When you try to recall something you learned, your brain acts like a detective to locate the information in its memory storage areas. It searches through the multiple pathways. If each chapter is read in a different location, then it makes it easier for the brain to retrieve what you learned.

3. Use Color

If you plan to highlight this book, try to use different colored highlighters. Again, this small action provides the novelty your brain likes which makes memory retrieval easier.

4. Take Breaks

Have you ever read a book, and when you finished you had no recollection of what you just read? That happens to many people. I want you to remember what you read here, so I suggest that you take breaks. Your brain pays attention to information at the beginning and at the end of a learning experience. It pays less attention to the middle, so you need to increase the number of beginnings and endings.[8] It can be a quick break. Stand up and walk around; take some deep breaths to get more oxygen to your brain, or take a water break. It may sound crazy, but taking breaks every 20 to 30 minutes will help you remember.

5. Reflect on what you are learning.

Stop and think about what you are learning. Take a few moments to reinforce the new knowledge. Reinforcement of new concepts helps strengthen brain connections, so it enhances learning. You can practice reinforcement as you read a chapter. Break time is a good time to reflect. At a minimum, you should reflect on what you learned at the end of a chapter by asking yourself the following questions:

1. **Head**: What did you learn? Imagine that you belong to a Book Club that is reading this book. Summarize the key points that you want to highlight during discussion.
2. **Heart**: How do you feel about what you learned?
3. **Action Step**: What are you going to do now? Suggestions: learn more about the topic; share what you learned, or practice what you learned.

I'll list these questions at the end of each chapter. Take a few minutes to reflect on what you learned and to answer the questions. Think about how you could use what you have learned.

6. Watch a Video

The image of an atom on the cover provides a clue to its importance in developing thinking. The entire world inside of and outside of your body is made of atoms—mainly oxygen, carbon, hydrogen, and nitrogen. The interactions of all these atoms play a key role in forming your perceptions of the world. Your perceptions make you the unique person that you are.

I think that a basic comprehension of the minuscule size but awesome power of an atom will help you grasp the amazing power of your magnificent yet small brain. The fascinating yet brief video, *Powers of 10,* will get this message across—especially the final minute, which focuses on the human body. Therefore, take nine minutes and watch *"Powers of 10 [http://www.powersof10.com]"*, a video which demonstrates the relative size of things in the universe.

Limitations

I want you to know that I recognize that this book has limitations. It includes my biased personal selection of research-based content from diverse fields including neuroscience, molecular biology, cognitive psychology, behavioral economics, organizational development, education, and the literature on thinking skills. Considering the scope of the topics, the length of this book, and my background, it was necessary for my personal choice to prevail.

My creative contribution primarily resides in the way I put together many puzzle pieces to display the "big picture" needed for you to improve your thinking ability. The bulk of the book is assembled and adapted from the work of many experts. I am exceedingly grateful for the insights I have gained from them, and I hope this book helps to spread the word about their work.

Get Ready

As you read this book, you will be developing an intellectual toolbox filled with knowledge, dispositions, skills, and strategies that you can use on a regular basis at work, at school, at home, and in the voting booth. I passionately believe that the requirements of democracy, the demands of the workplace, the responsibilities of adulthood, and the survival of our planet depend on human brains that don't just think, but think skillfully. The world needs people who can use their brains wisely to solve the "Big E" global problems that humans face today: energy, equity, environment, education, and economy.[10]

Overall, I am hopeful that this book will serve as an action-oriented, self-development guide that assists you on the road to success in the 21st century. By the time you complete this book, I want you to feel empowered to say, "I am a skillful thinker. I'm on the road to becoming a Mega-Thinker". Let's begin.

CHAPTER 1

The Power of Perception

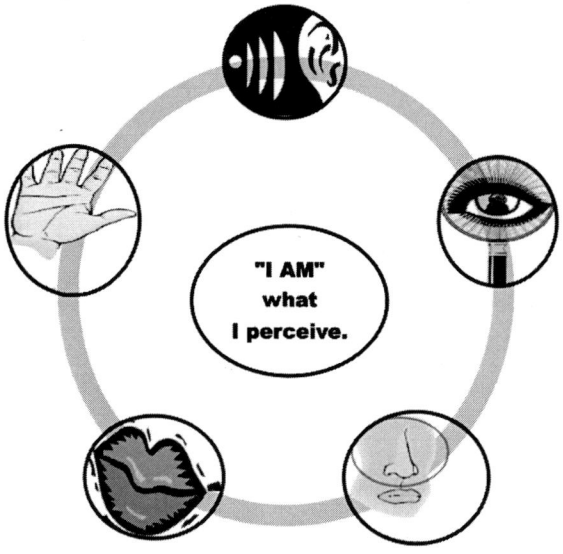

Figure 1.1: This central idea graphic organizer shows you how your sensory experiences contribute to the central idea—they form your perceptions and your personal identity.

Outside highly technical matter, perception is by far the most important part of thinking. Perception is how we look at the world, what things we take into account, how we structure the world.
— Dr. Edward deBono

Making Sense of the World

How do you know—anything? How did you learn about the world and make sense of it? You learn because of the activity of your brain. Your brain is always working and you are always thinking. You could plaster a "Brain at Work" sticker to your forehead, and it would be true twenty-four hours a day. Every experience of every moment of every day is processed by your brain in an effort to make sense of the world for you. You learn about the outside world from information that stimulates your senses, and then travels to your brain, and your brain makes meaning out of it. Therefore, you are what you perceive.

Your brain searches for meaning as it rapidly scans all the millions of bits of outside sensory data that continuously bombards you in the forms of atoms and molecules. As this happens, some of these atoms and molecules from the outside world connect with the sensory receptors inside your body including photo-receptors in your eyes for sight, chemo-receptors in your nose for smell and on your tongue for taste, and mechano-receptors in your ears for hearing and on your skin for touch. Perception is the name of this powerful mental processing, and as the quote at the beginning of this chapter states, "perception is by far the most important part of thinking". That's why learning about perception is the first step in learning how your brain works.

Fundamental Brain Information

Consider this question: What do a frog and your brain have in common? They both leap! You know that frogs leap, but why do brains leap? Your brain leaps into action when it experiences a perception of danger. First and foremost, your brain is biologically designed for you "to survive".[1] As unbelievable as it may sound, your brain is not primarily designed to enable you "to think" in a conscious way that involves reasoning, reflecting, judging, and deciding. Although you have in your possession the most powerful tool in the universe—a human brain, you are not in control of it. You probably think you are, but you are not. That's why you need to learn how your brain works.

Survival is Job #1

Your brain is constantly on guard to protect you. It is always working, 24/7, even when you are sleeping. In some ways, it is like a wild animal which acts on instinct. Nile crocodiles in Africa, boa constrictors in the Amazon rain-forest, and frogs in a local pond do not gather information, evaluate evidence, or consider consequences before they act. They cannot. They have small, primitive, "survival" brains. Instead, they strike out at an enemy (fight) or flee (flight) in order to survive. Sometimes, like a deer in the headlights, they freeze. Your brain is also wired with this fight, flight, or freeze ability. As soon as bits of sensory data enter your brain, they are processed. If the information your brain receives is threatening, either physically or emotionally, your brain LEAPS into action immediately and automatically.

You as a rational, conscious, and thoughtful human being are not involved in the decision to take this action. Let me repeat that, because it is very important for understanding how your brain works. You as a rational, conscious, and thoughtful human being are not involved in the decision to leap. Your brain makes survival decisions while working at the unconscious level! Why? It is due to the design of your brain. If you stop to think consciously, you'd be dead. Times have changed, but the design, the structure of your brain has not. You need to understand the brain's structure and how it functions. Although you no longer need to be afraid of saber-toothed tigers, you will face saber-toothed choices in your life. You need to be prepared to make wise decisions and to take wise actions. What determines how you decide and how you act? Your brain does.[2] That's why you need to know how it works.

Your Unconscious Brain in Action

Let's return to perception, the most important aspect of thinking, and get some answers to the following questions. How does your brain decide which sensory data has meaning for you? What data is admitted? What data is kept out? Remember that you as a conscious human being are not involved in the decisions.

In forming your perceptions, your brain acts as a "self-organizing information system", according to Dr. Edward deBono, one of the world's authorities in creative thinking and the direct teaching of thinking skills.[3] Every human brain self-organizes the sensory information in its own way, based on its own experiences. That means that your brain organizes the information it receives from the environment in a way that has meaning and makes sense for you and only for you. Your brain is not concerned about how other brains make sense of the world. As a result, every brain sees the world differently.

Finding Meaning

What determines "meaning"? How does your unconscious brain know what has meaning for you? How does it decide what data to admit and what to delete? Remember, survival comes first. At the moment of initial sensory awareness, your brain kicks into action to keep you alive. As it scans the data, your brain seeks information that may threaten you. It could be a putrid smell, a hidden hiss, an unexpected touch, a rancid taste, or fast approaching footsteps in the dark. The major point is that there are millions of bits of sensory information, but your brain's main focus is on the bits of data that threaten you, because your survival is job #1. After scanning for survival needs, it searches for meaning in other areas that are important to you.

How does your brain know what is important to you? It has learned what has meaning for you based upon your past experiences. It knows what you care about and pay attention to. How does it know this? Your brain cells communicate and connect and form mental pathways for things it cares about. You will learn how your brain cells work in chapter two, Neurons Rule.

After scanning, your brain reviews the sensory information with everything it already knows about you, and it admits and organizes the information according to your personal needs and desires. It then connects new information to your existing memories in order to create some mental order that makes sense to you, and only you. In this process of mixing incoming information with already stored information, your brain is organizing your personal, unique life experiences into your "perceptions" of the real world.

This is one of the most important, if not the most important messages of this book. Because your perceptions are unique to you, you see the world in ways that no other human being does. Do you remember Dr. deBono's quote: "perception is by far the most important part of thinking"? Perception plays a powerful role in the quality of your thinking. It shapes your mental habits and behaviors. Perception is so important, you are reading about it in Chapter 1. Once you have a basic understanding of perception, future information about your brain will make more sense.

Living in Two Worlds

David Brooks writes in his book, The Social Animal that "…the act of perception is a thick process. It is not just taking in a scene but, almost simultaneously, weighing its meaning, evaluating it, and generating an emotion about it".[4]

Although it is a complex process, forming perceptions is part of your brain's natural behavior. As you can see in the graphic above, your brain uses the information it receives from your five senses to create a world view that is one-of-a-kind and uniquely yours. No two people, not even identical twins raised in the same environment, have identical world views. [5] No one else makes sense of the world exactly as you do. No one else sees the world the way you do! This means that every person alive is also building-a-world, their own world, based upon what their own brain perceives.

As a result of how people form their perceptions, every person on earth is actually living in two separate worlds. World #1 is the "real world". It is the external, physical world that exists outside of your body. Everybody lives in the real world. World #2 is your "personal world". It is the internal, perceived world that exists inside of your body, specifically inside your brain. Only you live in that world. Stop right here. This is important.

KEY POINT:

YOUR PERCEPTIONS = ONLY YOUR VIEW OF THE WORLD

You have now hit the bulls-eye of the problem with trying to develop skillful thinking. To make sense of the world, the brain uses its perceptions to take in new information, make meaning, and adopt beliefs. There are two major problems. The first is that your senses are so limited in how much they can perceive. Second, even the sensory signals you do receive can be weak. Weak signals form weak patterns. When the brain receives weak signals and patterns, it is difficult to make "meaning" for you, so it becomes creative. It guesses! According to the world renowned neuro-scientist, Dr. Eric Kandel, the brain has neural pathways with built-in "complex rules of guessing". He calls the brain an "ambiguity-resolving machine par excellence!" When patterns are weak, the brain turns them into meaningful pieces of information by guessing![6]

Does this information make you wonder how accurate your perceptions are? I hope so. In general, people do not usually test, question, or thoroughly examine their perceptions. However, people use their perceptions to form conclusions and beliefs about the world. Without realizing it, these perceptions become very comfortable and very familiar mental pathways for them. Even though the perceptions may be incorrect, people become stuck in them. As a result, people see the world through self-imposed bars.

They have become prisoners of their own beliefs, and they don't know it. People then make decisions and act on these beliefs. As a result, perceptions become a huge barrier to skillful thinking. Perceptions are barriers because every individual's unique perceptions of the world are not true! Mine are not true and neither are yours. In his book, The Fifth Discipline, Peter Senge explains that people see the world through their assumptions, their "mental models", and mental models never hold the "truth" because they are always incomplete. They may even be based on guesses. No one person has the absolute truth about how the world works, because people only see snapshots of the real world based on their personal perceptions.[7]

Creating Perceptions

When are perceptions formed? The answer is so simple and innocent. You begin to develop your perceptions as a baby. You were forming your perceptions of the world as you lived your life in your home, neighborhood, schools, churches, stores, and playgrounds. That's how everyone learns. You learn the rules and customs of "my world", and you use this information to make sense of the world "out there". When you are developing a position on an issue, you may ask: What do my friends think? What about my relatives, my co-workers, my union, my political party, my clubs, my teams, my favorite "talking heads" on television or radio, my favorite editorial writers or bloggers, etc.? What is their opinion and why? What about the books, magazines, newspapers, and websites you read? What about the tweets you receive and the information shared on places like Facebook? They influence your perceptions. How diverse is your community? What is your neighborhood like? All of these social factors of "group think" influence the formation of your unique perceptions of the world— your perceived world.

However, much of the information an individual receives as a child is not an accurate picture of the "real" world. After all, how can you really know what the world is like for other human beings who do not share your country, language, religion, ethnic group, culture, sex, style, socio-economic status, etc.? Their perception of the outside "real world" is just as real to them as yours is to you. It is also as inaccurate as yours is. Each world view is most likely biased and prejudiced towards "our world", and people like "us", but people don't realize it. In your youth, you developed unconscious attitudes and perceptions that impact your life today. Every person on this planet did the same. Who is right?

Seeking the Truth

In their book, <u>Revolutionary Wealth</u>, world- renowned futurists, Alvin and Heidi Toffler address this issue. They state that part of the problem in finding "the truth" is based on the fact that every chunk of knowledge eventually becomes obsolete. They call this obsolete knowledge— "obsoledge". However, people, organizations, and government entities around the world base many decisions on obsolete knowledge and assumptions that are no longer true. How can this be? It all goes back to how perceptions were formed. Why do you believe what you do? You know that you began to develop your perceptions as an innocent child. The Tofflers identify six different sources of information that influence people throughout their lifetime and assist them in determining the truth as they perceive it: consensus, consistency, authority, revelation, durability, and science.

- Consensus: This is conventional wisdom where you follow the crowd, because even if you find out eventually that your thinking is wrong, you are not embarrassed. "Everyone" else believed it too.

- Consistency: The facts as you know them fit with other facts that you believe are true based on your unique experiences.
- Authority: You accept something as true because your family or another authority figure told you it was true.
- Revelation: Many religious groups are based on divine revelations that are not questioned by mortal humans. The source itself is the truth.
- Durability: This is truth that is old. It is accepted because it comes from the past and has stood the test of time.
- Science: This truth is always changing. Scientists believe that the current truth is just the foundation for new research and new scientific discoveries.

Are these sources of truth all equally valuable? That is for you to determine, but not according to the Tofflers. They make it clear that, in their opinion, science is the most valuable source of information because it is self-correcting. Science uses the scientific method to engage in a process that involves rigorous testing in an effort to find the truth. As a result, they hold the scientific method in great esteem as you can tell by the following statement:

The invention of the scientific method was the gift to humanity of a new truth filter or test, a powerful meta-tool for probing the unknown and—it turned out—for spurring technological change and economic progress. [8]

The scientific method is an important tool for a Mega-Thinker as well, so it is included in Part 2, Train Your Brain. However, do you think society-at-large agrees with the Toffler's opinion of science as the most effective truth filter? Not necessarily.

Discomfort Zone

You already learned that no one has an accurate perception of the "real" world. Seeking the "truth" requires people to be open to new knowledge. It means you may need to change your mind, and many people are not comfortable doing that. It's a tough message for people to accept. As a result, some people remain in their comfort zones. They choose not to engage in the change process to become a skillful thinker. They remain at the starting point—unskillful thinker. There is too much discomfort with change. They cling to the truth they have been told, and they maintain their perceived view of the world. The tendency to behave that way is captured by Dr. Daniel Kahneman, a behavioral economist and the winner of the 2002 Nobel Prize in Economic Sciences, in this statement:

An unbiased appreciation of uncertainty is a cornerstone of rationality — but it is not what people and organizations want. Extreme uncertainty is paralyzing under dangerous circumstances, and the admission that one is merely guessing is especially unacceptable when the stakes are high. Acting on pretended knowledge is often the preferred solution. [9]

People who are unable to appreciate uncertainty will not accept the fact that their world view is flawed. Sadly, flaws in perception are the crux of the problem with trying to solve many of the problems in today's world. Well-intentioned people may be coming to the table to address common problems, but they have different perceptions leading to pretended knowledge of the "real" world. They are unaware that what they know may be "obsoledge" or perhaps not true. They choose to remain comfortably folded within the warmness of their own personal reality, their own perceived world.

Getting Unstuck

Could people change their perceptions if they wanted to? Yes. That's one of the purposes of this book. Once you know how your brain works, you will understand that you have immense personal power. You have the power to reshape your brain, so you can reshape your perceptions, your own mental models. You can become unstuck from them by eliminating old brain pathways and creating new ones.

Two types of skills are needed for this to happen: 1. reflection and 2. inquiry. With reflection, you learn to slow down your thinking and try to become aware of the sources of your perceptions. With inquiry, you ask questions and share views about perceptions-yours and others. You learn to bring mental models into the open and challenge them.[10] This is especially important when the conversation is about a "hot-button" topic. As you read this book, you will acquire some mental tools, so you can effectively engage in reflection and inquiry. Once you are unstuck from old perceptions, you can be more open-minded as you view the real world. You will be able to engage in more skillful and more powerful thinking, so you can develop a more realistic picture of the real world. Before going into the details about how your brain works, I want to make it very clear what I mean by perception.

Perception by Any Other Name...

There are many names that are used for the concept of perception. The following chart depicts some of them.

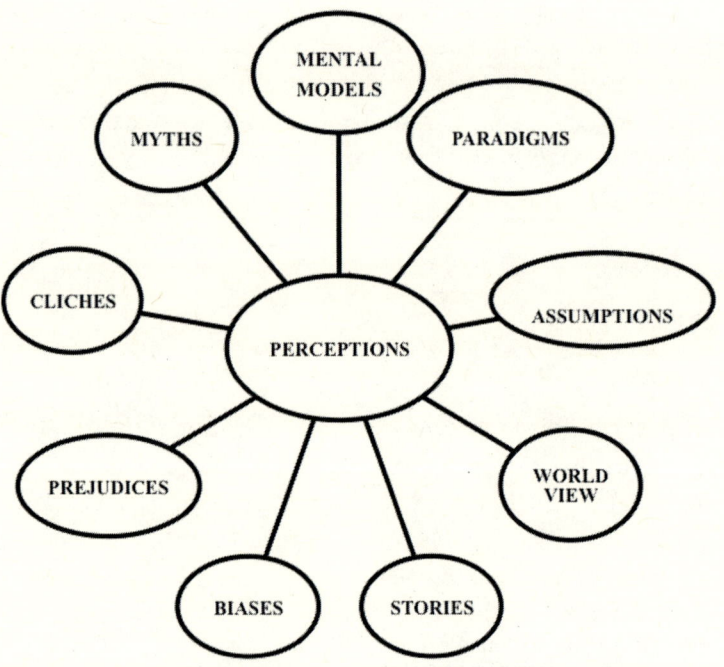

Figure 1.2: Synonyms for "perception". This basic radial graphic organizer, or "star" diagram , depicts the relationship between the central topic and the outside circles.

Perception has many aliases. The name itself is not that important. What is important is that as a result of your experiences and your brain's hard work, you walk around, usually unknowingly, with a set of "perceptions" or "mental models", or "paradigms", or "assumptions" that obstruct your ability to think clearly. You may actually stop thinking, because you believe that you have the "truth". Without realizing it, you then become stuck in a brain rut. Peter Senge, one of the most respected people in the world in the field of systems thinking, believes one of the biggest problems with mental models is that they are often hidden. People do not realize that they have mental models, so they do not understand how their perceptions influence their behavior.[11] Is this a problem? Yes! One of the dangers of being stuck in your perceptions or mental models is that they hide from you from what is real and true. How can society truly solve problems and make decisions if citizens do not have accurate and true information?

I recently visited the John F. Kennedy Presidential Library near Boston, and during the orientation film, the following text from a speech President John Kennedy gave at Yale University in 1962 played on the screen:

Too often we hold fast to the clichés of our forebears. We subject all facts to a prefabricated set of interpretations. We enjoy the comfort of opinion without the discomfort of thought. Mythology distracts us everywhere. For the great enemy of the truth is very often not the lie—deliberate, contrived, and dishonest—- but the myth—-persistent, persuasive, and unrealistic.

I think that this statement, made over fifty years ago, recognizes the power and danger of perceptions. Although President Kennedy did not use the word "perception", by using the words cliché, opinion, and myth, he describes the problem that persists today. In his book, to think, Frank Smith also acknowledges the impact of perceptions on today's problems. However, instead of perception, he uses the word "stories".

The great problems of the world today—political, environmental, social, and economic—are not due to lack of facts, and probably not to lack of thought either. They reflect the values of people and governments, the stories they believe. There will be no solutions if we constantly wait for new skills and knowledge; what is required is an ability to recognize and understand the stories that are currently being played out, their consequences, and how they might be changed in ourselves and others. [12]

Remember, you do not see the world as it really is, you see it through your own personal point of view—your perceptions and the stories you believe. Take a moment to think about the enormous challenges facing this world, and the tremendous variation in perceptions of reality that exist across this great planet. The importance of recognizing, questioning, challenging, and understanding the stories that form perceptions cannot be underestimated.

Make Perceptions Visible

Although developing perceptions is a natural part of being human, they can hinder your thinking ability. It's difficult for you to see the world through someone else's eyes. It is also difficult for other people to see the world through your eyes. More than ever before in the history of the world, in the global environment of the 21st century, people need to make the effort to identify perceptions and make them visible. Perceptions need to be examined and questioned. If ever human beings are going to solve worldwide problems, they must make the effort to understand perceptions that differ from their own. People need to be open-minded and to really listen with understanding and empathy to the perceptions of others. This is the most important skill of Mega-Thinking. As you read this book, you will be acquiring dispositions, skills, and strategies that will enable you to pause and examine perceptions. Your journey towards the goal of becoming a Mega-Thinker has begun.

Visible Perceptions

The following version of a famous Hindu parable helps to summarize and to clarify the concept of perception. This version, which is in the common domain, is by John Godfrey Saxe, an American poet:

The Blind Men and the Elephant

It was six men of Indostan
To learning much inclined,
Who went to see the Elephant
(Though all of them were blind),
That each by observation
Might satisfy his mind.

The First approached the Elephant,
And happening to fall
Against his broad and sturdy side,
At once began to bawl:
"God bless me! but the Elephant
Is very like a wall!"

The Second, feeling of the tusk
Cried, "Ho! what have we here,
So very round and smooth and sharp?
To me 'tis mighty clear
This wonder of an Elephant
Is very like a spear!"

The Third approached the animal,
And happening to take
The squirming trunk within his hands,
Thus boldly up he spake:
"I see," quoth he, "the Elephant
Is very like a snake!"

The Fourth reached out an eager hand,
And felt about the knee:
"What most this wondrous beast is like
Is mighty plain," quoth he;
"'Tis clear enough the Elephant
Is very like a tree!"

The Fifth, who chanced to touch the ear,
Said: "E'en the blindest man
Can tell what this resembles most;
Deny the fact who can,
This marvel of an Elephant
Is very like a fan!"

The Sixth no sooner had begun
About the beast to grope,
Than, seizing on the swinging tail
That fell within his scope.
"I see," quoth he, "the Elephant
Is very like a rope!"

And so these men of Indostan
Disputed loud and long,
Each in his own opinion
Exceeding stiff and strong,
Though each was partly in the right,
And all were in the wrong!

Moral:

So oft in theologic wars,
The disputants, I ween,
Rail on in utter ignorance
Of what each other mean,
And prate about an Elephant
Not one of them has seen!

Summary

This fable tells the story of the power of an individual's perception. Each blind man was certain that his experience was real and true. Each one was able to make his perception visible and explain why he believed what he did. However, each one was also rigid and unable to even consider the alternatives. Communication shut down. They were stuck in their unique, personal perceptions. As a result, they argued and they never got to the truth. This brief fable delivers the powerful message that I have spent many pages trying to deliver. Most people are stuck inside their own perceptions and are unwilling to recognize that the perceptions of others may have some truth. Recognizing the role of perception as a huge barrier to Mega-Thinking is the most important first step to your goal to become a Mega-Thinker.

In the next chapter, you will learn about the most basic component of your brain—the mighty but minuscule neuron. It is the basic building block of your brain. It is also the key to getting unstuck.

Questions for Reflection

1. **HEAD**: What did you learn? Imagine that you belong to a Book Club that is reading this book. Summarize the key points that you want to highlight during discussion.
2. **HEART**: How do you feel about what you learned?
3. **ACTION STEP**: What are you going to do now? Suggestions: learn more about the topic; share what you learned, or practice what you learned.

CHAPTER 2

Neurons Rule

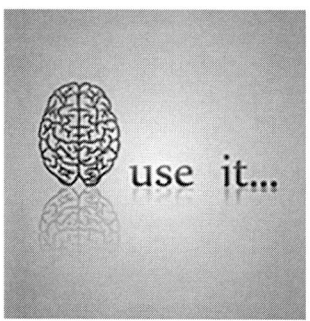

…what the brain can do depends on whether or not it is used.
It is the ultimate use-it-or-lose-it machine, and it is eager to learn new skills.
— Ronald Kotulak

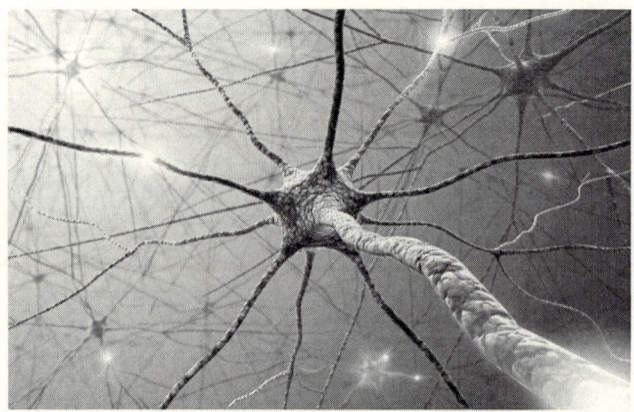

A neuron is a brain cell, and it is the key to understanding how your brain works. Its primary function is communication with other neurons. It is the basic building block of the brain, but unlike a solid block, a neuron is alive with activity. If you saw a picture of a living neuron cell, it would appear to sparkle and glow from the lively activity inside.

The activity is caused in part by electricity! You are not plugged into an electrical outlet, but your brain cells create electricity. The electricity travels through your neurons at a blinding speed of over 250 miles per hour. Electrical signals are required for your brain cells to communicate, and they communicate with other neurons all the time. In fact, they are very outgoing. It is typical for one neuron to have ten thousand connections with other neurons[1].

In your brain right now, your neurons are making more than a trillion connections with each other. If they didn't make connections, then you would not be able to learn anything. All the mental activities you engage in like perceiving, remembering, and learning take place because these brain cells, the neurons, connect and communicate or "talk" with one another. At this moment, because your neurons are communicating, you have enough electricity surging through your brain to light a 25 watt light-bulb.[2]

Neurons at Work

In order to understand how your brain works, you need to understand how a neuron works. Until the 1950s, no one knew how they worked, so you will be learning about something that very few people in the history of the world ever knew. You already know that although all brains have the same basic design, no two brains are exactly alike. You know that brains are different because of the different life experiences that people have. What you probably don't know is that as you engage in your life experiences, it is the action of your neurons making connections that makes you and your brain unique. Let's learn how a neuron works.

Neuron Design and Activity

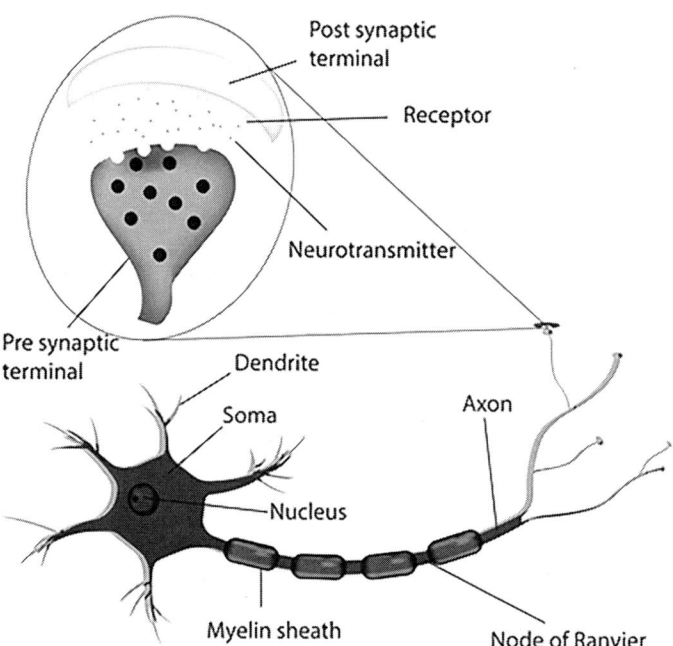

This chapter started with an image of a neuron. The image above identifies its parts. You need to understand its parts to learn how it behaves. Neurons are tree-like structures. Just as nutrients flow one way in a tree from roots to trunk to branches, communication signals flow one way in a neuron from dendrites to the cell body to the axon to the axon terminals and to the synapse (the gap between neurons). If a connection is made, then this one-way flow of action is repeated on the connecting neuron with the signal starting at the dendrite.[3]

Every neuron has four main parts: 1. Many dendrites (the tree roots part) with a dendrite terminal at the end of each dendrite to accept incoming chemical messages. This is the "input" location of the brain cell or neuron. 2. The main cell body which contains a nucleus. 3. One axon, a long thread-like structure (the tree trunk part). It is the cell part that gets covered with a substance called myelin. Myelin is a white fatty substance that develops around some neurons to protect them and to speed up communication. 4. Multiple axon terminals (the tree branches part). Each axon terminal is an "output" location for chemical messages. Beyond the axon terminal is a miniscule space called the synaptic gap.

As you can see in the previous image of a neuron, the axon terminal (in the enlarged area) is a knob-like structure. Inside the knob at the end of an axon terminal are small sacks (represented as large dots in the image above) that are called synaptic vesicles. Inside these sacks are many different and powerful brain chemicals called neurotransmitters. This is the "output" location of the brain cell where neurochemicals (represented by small dots) are released into the gap, the synapse. There is always a synaptic gap between neurons; they never touch each other. Touching would interfere with the communication process.[4]

For neurons to connect and communicate there is a lot of exciting activity taking place within your brain. Let's begin with the "input" area. Brain chemicals are released from the sacks in the axon terminal into the synaptic gap. Thousands of dendrite receptors are waiting in the synaptic gap for the right chemical to be released. The process operates like a "lock and key" system.[5] Different dendrite receptors accept different chemicals. The correct chemical, or key, must be used to gain entry into a dendrite. As you read, try to picture the activity. Imagine flash fires, chemical explosions, and dramatic searches!

Input area: FIRE! When a chemical (a neurotransmitter) is accepted by a dendrite, it creates a SPARK in the dendrite. The spark creates an electric signal that travels to the nucleus in the cell body and down the axon to the axon terminal.

Output area: At the axon terminal, the little sacks containing different chemicals await. When the electric signal reaches the end of the axon there is an EXPLOSION as the electric spark causes the chemicals (neurotransmitters) to be released into the synapse, the synaptic GAP.

SYNAPTIC GAP area: SEARCHING! Dendrites are locked. Chemicals (the keys) are searching for the right dendrite receptors to connect with, so the neuron's message can continue to be communicated. If a KEY (chemical) finds the right LOCK on a dendrite, it unlocks the opening to the dendrite and the chemical enters the "input" area and sets off a SPARK. If chemicals do not connect to a dendrite, they return to the sacks in the axon terminal.

Let's repeat. The input of a chemical into a dendrite causes a spark which sends an electric signal to the cell body and down the axon. From there, the electric signal is directed to an axon terminal where it triggers the synaptic vesicles, the sacs that hold the brain chemicals, to release neurotransmitters into the synaptic gap. Dendrites await... the right chemical unlocks entrance to dendrite...which triggers an electric spark... the spark travels through the cell body... down the axon...the spark triggers synaptic vesicles to release chemicals into the gap...and on and on.[6]

Fire and Wire

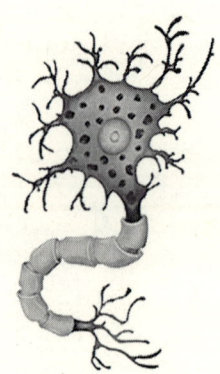

The decision of neurons to send signals or not to send signals is what controls your actions and behaviors, your perceptions and your memories. This is very important. Ronald Kotulak states a well-known fact in neuroscience when he says that "Cells that fire together will wire together."[7] Neurons communicate and link together when they have something in common. Connecting is not random. The neuron is scanning incoming information and looking for patterns. If it makes an association, then it connects, it "wires" and then it fires the electrical signal.

However, this action does not always take place. Sometimes the nucleus in the cell body doesn't receive the right signal from its dendrite. In that case, it won't fire the electric signal down the axon, so no connections are made. If neurons stop "firing" they will eventually be "pruned" or deleted, then the connections and pathways will cease to exist. That's how you forget things!

The repeated wiring and firing action of neurons, the process of making connections among neurons, is how you learn. It is also how you develop and sometimes get stuck in thoughts and behaviors. As you are continually exposed to the same information and behaviors, you learn them. Your neurons keep firing and wiring along the same pathways, so they become fast and deep. That's usually a good thing, but it is also how you remain trapped in the same thoughts. It is easy for your brain to leap to a conclusion as it receives the same message again and again. However, you can become "unstuck" by exposing yourself to different information, different perceptions, and different behaviors. The new learning creates new mental pathways and prunes old mental pathways. New learning helps you become unstuck from your ingrained and perhaps incorrect mental models.

Remember that your brain is paying attention to what has meaning for you. If you start to develop new interests, you stop paying attention to your old interests and start paying attention to the new ones. You are training your brain as it learns what is important and has meaning for you now. The old connections become weaker and eventually they are deleted. Remember, that's how you become unstuck. It's almost like having a new pet. You need to train it. You can consciously work to become unstuck when you make a deliberate effort to change your thoughts and behaviors by exposing yourself to new ones.

Partners at Work

Before continuing with information about neurons, I want to mention another type of brain cell. It is the glial cell which is sometimes simply called glia. I need to mention it now, because you will be learning about how the brain works, and it may seem as if the neurons are doing all the work, but they are not. A neuron's main job is communication, but it needs support in carrying out its job.

Glia do not communicate, but they protect neurons and clean up after them. You know that neurons have myelin on them. A glial cell produces the myelin. You know that neurons can be pruned or deleted. There is no "delete" button on a neuron to make it disappear. It physically decays, so glial cells are like the brain's janitors, and they remove the dead neurons.[8] I won't mention a glial cell again, but be aware that neurons have partners that help them do their work.

Physically Demonstrate Neuron Activity

An easy way to review neuron activity is to use your hands and arms to model the actions of a neuron. Hold out your right hand with your fingers spread apart. The center of you hand, your palm, represents the cell body; your fingers are the dendrites, and your forearm is the axon. You need to imagine the axon terminals streaming out below your elbow. Remember that electric signals travel only one way, so the signal has traveled through the dendrites in your right hand to the cell body, then down the axon to the axon terminals. Now imagine that the electric signal triggered the synaptic vesicles to release brain chemicals into the synaptic gap.

These neurotransmitters are swimming around and trying to communicate with another neuron. They are searching for the right dendrite receptor. Be that dendrite. Take your left hand and make another neuron. Stretch out those dendrites, I mean fingers. Now move your left hand near, but do not touch, the axon terminals which are coming out below your elbow. Now a neurotransmitter can cross the synaptic gap, find the right dendrite, unlock the entrance, enter the dendrite and create a spark to keep the communication going. You have created your own model of neurons making connections and communicating.[9] Now that you have a basic understanding about how neurons work, you will better understand the experiments that led to solving the mystery of the neuron.

Core Knowledge about Brain Communication

How did scientists learn about the activity WITHIN neurons? How was this mystery revealed? CURIOSITY is the hallmark of science, and it was curiosity about a traumatic early life experience that led Dr. Eric Kandel, a neuroscientist and molecular biologist, to ask questions and conduct research that profoundly influenced the world of neuroscience. As a young scientist in the 1950s, Dr. Kandel wanted to know why we have memories. He felt compelled to study memory because he could not forget the horror he experienced in 1938 when Hitler was on the rise. At the time, he was a young boy living in Vienna, Austria with his parents and his brother. His family owned a little toy store. Shortly after his ninth birthday, the Nazis came to his family's apartment and forced them to leave. He and his mother and brother were ordered to go to a stranger's apartment. His father was working at the toy shop at the time, and he did not join them. He was missing for days.

Eventually his father returned and his family was allowed to return to their home, but it had been vandalized and everything of value was taken. In his book, In Search of Memory, Dr. Kandel wrote that he could never forget the fear, humiliation, poverty, and bewilderment that he experienced. He wondered what biological processes enabled him to review his own history with such emotion. What enabled him to engage in a form of "mental time travel"?[10] Because of his life experiences, Dr. Kandel focused his scientific work on the brain to find out why we remember.

Studying Neurons

Dr. Kandel's goal was to understand how memory is stored in the brain. To do this, he planned to study the simplest example of a memory being created and stored. Therefore, he needed to study neurons. He decided it was important to study one neuron at a time; therefore, in order to conduct his experiments, he needed to find an animal with large neurons. Humans were not considered, because our neurons were too small to study using the technology of the time.

It didn't matter which animal he selected, because the neurons in all living things are the same. They have the same parts, and they work in the same way. That's a bit humbling, but it's a fact.[11] Dr. Kandel needed to find an animal with a simple nervous system (not too many cells), so he could trace the information flow of the signals in the brain cells. Aplysia, the California sea slug, met his criteria. It is more than a foot long and weighs several pounds. Dr. Kandel described it as, "a large, proud, attractive, and obviously highly intelligent beast — just the sort of animal one would select for studies of learning!"[12]

More importantly, Aplysia's cells are among the largest in the animal kingdom, and its brain has a very small number of cells, about 20,000, compared to a human brain with 100 billion! Dr. Kandel needed large cells so he could insert microelectrodes into them in order to record the brain's electrical activity. Aplysia's brain cells are grouped into nine separate clusters or ganglia. For his research, Dr. Kandel studied one ganglia with about 2,000 cells to find out how we learn and remember. The results were phenomenal, and they led to his winning the Nobel Prize.

What Should Aplysia Learn?

First, Dr. Kandel had to decide what Aplysia would learn. He examined past research and chose Ivan Pavlov's experiment with the behavior of dogs to develop his framework. You can Google "Pavlov and dogs" if you want to learn about it. Dr. Kandel framed his experiment with Aplysia around the three procedures for learning described by Pavlov in his experiment: Habituation, Sensitization, and Classical Conditioning. However, he changed them from procedures to study **behavior and learning** to procedures that would study **biology and learning**. Kandel planned to study the changes that occurred inside Aplysia's neurons as sensory information flowed through them. He wanted to see what occurred in the synapse area, the gap area, and what happened to the target neuron when it experienced three different patterns of carefully controlled electrical stimulation which was administered by the scientist.

The experiments involved studying Aplysia's simplest behavior, the way its gill behaved in different situations. Since Aplysia breathes through its gill, it is normally relaxed. However, if it feels threatened, it reacts by withdrawing or hiding the gill. That's a basic survival instinct called a gill-withdrawal reflex. The experiments involved a weak touch to Aplysis's siphon and a shock to its tail. Originally, the weak touch to the siphon made the gill withdraw. Eventually, Aplysia "learned" that the gentle touch was not a danger and the gill stayed relaxed. Then the game changed. The weak touch to the siphon was followed by a shock to its tail. Naturally, Aplysia withdrew its gill. Eventually, the shocking stopped. However, whenever it received a weak touch to its siphon now, this smart sea slug withdrew its gill. It was taking no chances. It had "learned" to connect the weak touch with the strong shock.[13]

Findings

While performing the experiments on Aplysia to see how well it "learned", Dr. Kandel could actually see, at the molecular level, the flow of information moving electrically through the neurons and chemically across the synapses. He saw the physical changes in the structure of the neuron while Aplysia's brain was learning and making memories. As a result, the study of Aplysia's very large neurons dramatically increased scientific knowledge about the biology of brain cells, and how they communicate. Dr. Kandel clearly demonstrated **neuroplasticity**, the ability of the brain to change and reorganize itself based on the activity of neurons. Dr. Kandel discovered that memories are indeed formed at the molecular level. His research on neurons supported findings that emerged during the first half of the twentieth century. These finding led to the "Neuron Doctrine".[14]

The Neuron Doctrine

The following three principles about neurons are sometimes called the Neuron Doctrine. They are the core of scientific understanding about the organization and function of the brain.

1. The neuron is the fundamental building block and signaling unit of the brain.
2. The neuron can generate electrical signals that can travel great distances within the nerve cell, along its axon. Electrical action stops at the synapse.
3. Nerve cells communicate by releasing chemicals called neurotransmitters. The electrical signal triggers chemicals to be released, and they travel across the synapse to another nerve cell.

Biology of Mind

Dr. Kandel calls the work that is being done today to understand how the brain works, "biology of mind". He defines "biology of mind" as the conversion of behavioral psychology, cognitive psychology, neuroscience, and his area of molecular biology. He believes that "the biology of mind will be to the 21st century what the biology of the gene was to the 20th century".[15] The tools of science are so different now from when Dr. Kandel started his study of neurons. At this moment, no one knows what mysteries of the brain that these new tools will reveal in your lifetime, but they will be amazing.

Brain Growth

Dr. Kandel demonstrated that neurons have the ability to communicate, connect, change, and reorganize. He saw neuroplasticity in action. This means that your brain is not fixed; it is not static. No matter what kind of brain you were born with, neuroscientists are finding that you can make your brain smarter and more skillful by making new connections and growing new pathways. Brain cells are living and dynamic. Every time you learn something new, your brain makes new connections and grows. With every new experience, whether it is good or bad, your brain changes. It is making new connections and physically reshaping itself all of the time as a result of your experiences. Whether you want it to or not, your brain is changing.

Your brain is like the Transformer toys that can change their structure. Instead of "Optimus Prime" you have "Brainius Prime". Connections occur when brain chemicals cross the synaptic gap and unlock dendrites. The number of dendrites on a neuron is not fixed. New connections create new dendrites! The more you learn, the more connections and dendrites you have. As you continue to learn, your dendrites increase in number.[16] By continuing to learn new things and to make new connections, you automatically grow your brain. In his book, Think Smart, Dr. Richard Restak explains that your brain is capable of change until the day you die. Whether or not it changes depends in large part to the challenges you set for it.[17] It is up to you to make sure you challenge and use your brain to learn new things!

Starting Point

You now know that neurons are the building blocks of your brain, and when they make new connections and grow, your brain grows! Did you ever imagine that you had the power to grow and change your brain? Now you do know! When does the process start?

It starts when you are an embryo in your mother's womb. There are two main ways in which brains develop: 1. through the pre-programmed instructions, like a set of blueprints that are built into your genes, and 2. through your experiences in the outside world. The "blueprints" provide your brain's foundation. For example, they are responsible for your being born with survival skills. Your brain naturally goes through four stages of brain growth as you grow from infancy to adulthood. Let's review them.[18]

1. During fetal development
   After several months, a human embryo has approximately 200 billion brain cells. Half of these brain cells die by the 20th week of fetal life because they did not make connections with the embryo's growing body, but this is normal. The overproduction of brain cells is critical to the embryo's development, since it guarantees that there are plenty of cells for new skills to develop. This is the first window of opportunity for growing a healthy brain. If a mother eats well and avoids tobacco, alcohol, and drugs, then a baby is off to a good start. However, serious damage to the growing baby's brain cells can occur if she does not avoid these things. Brain care must start early.
2. After birth until age 3

The early years of a child's life, especially the first three years, are a very important learning period. Connections are being made at an amazing rate, and this is when the foundation is set for many personal charac- teristics including thinking, language, attitudes, and behaviors. By age 1, a baby's brain is 60% of adult size. By age 3, a child's brain has reached 90% of its full adult size. The brain adds or deletes connections among brain cells based upon individual experiences— especially touching, hearing and seeing. Lots of enriched, stimulating experiences lead to brain growth by increasing the number of connections, and lack of stimulation leads to decay or pruning, which eliminates inactive neurons and decreases the number of connections. Therefore, whether or not a child, by the age of three, grows up in an enriched or an impoverished environment makes a huge difference in brain structure. It is important to note that enriched and impoverished environments have absolutely nothing to do with wealth. The quality of the environ- ment is based on the kind of interactions that a child has with people, things, sounds, images, tastes, and smells. Play and joy have a huge role in enriching the mental growth of a child. An interesting fact is that the hippocampus, the part of the brain that is most important for memory, is not fully developed until ages two or three. That may be the reason that most people do not have memories before then.

3. Between 4 and 12

    These years provide a second chance for lots of brain growth. For example, these are the best years to learn a foreign language. Until the age of twelve, a child's brain is a "Super-Sponge" that is actively absorbing knowledge, skills, and dispositions from its environment. By age 12, the brain's basic architecture is complete and new learning becomes more difficult.

Years after 12

No other organ in the body takes as long to fully develop as the brain. Legally, you may be considered an adult at age 18, but it is most likely that your brain is not fully developed by then. Your left, pre-frontal cortex, the part of your brain behind your forehead, is also called the "executive function" area. It is responsible for decision-making, problem solving, judgment, and emotional control. This area isn't fully developed until as late as age 25, when the axons on the neurons in the PFC are finally coated with myelin, the white, fatty substance that insulates and protects them. Although scientists did not know this until the end of the 20th century, auto insurance companies must have had some statistics to inform them of this fact. As everyone who pays car insurance knows, rates go down at age 25!

Effort Leads to Intelligence

How can this information about the brain impact your life? It can give you the confidence to know that as your brain changes, so does your intellectual ability. You have the power to grow your intelligence. Once upon a time, as recently as the 1970's, scientists believed that the intellectual ability of individuals was limited by the genes they inherited from their parents. Either you were born with a "smart" brain or you were not, and the brain you were born with did not change.

These two expressions, "The apple doesn't fall far from the tree", or "You plant corn, you get corn", capture the idea that your DNA determined your destiny. That belief is now known to be false. One of the most important findings in neuroscience is that intelligence is not limited by biology. You can increase your intelligence. Yes, you have it within your own power to improve your intelligence, but improvement requires deliberate effort on your part.

The Flynn Effect

One of the most well-known studies that found evidence of the fact that you can improve your intelligence comes from a 1998 report, "IQ Gains Over Time: Toward Finding the Causes", written by James R. Flynn, Emeritus Professor of Political Studies at the University of Otago in New Zealand. He is world famous for what is known as "the Flynn Effect".[19]

As a political and social scientist, he studied IQ (intelligence quotient) scores from 18 of the world's industrialized countries that kept records of IQ tests since 1930. His research identified a large increase in IQ scores in these countries. Scores on IQ tests were going up about three points per generation. Flynn was astonished by these findings. Based on his research, Flynn concluded that genes alone could not be responsible for such large IQ gains, because it did not seem possible that genetic factors could cause such significant change in such a relatively short time.

According to Flynn, genes account for 36% of the IQ variance, with 64% coming from environmental differences. Imagine that! 64% of the difference in IQ scores, almost 2/3s of the difference, is because of the environment in which a person lives.

Importance of Enriched Environment

What does this mean? It means the totality of the conditions or circumstances that surround a person influences his intelligence. That means not only physical conditions but also social, cultural, emotional, educational, religious, and political traditions. If you grow up in a safe, enriched environment with lots of mental stimulation, your intelligence will grow. If you grow up neglected in an impoverished environment with little mental stimulation, then your intelligence may not grow. Even if you have the "genes" to be highly intelligent, your environment can cripple your potential.[20]

In other words, Flynn did not believe that people were being born smarter. His findings suggest that your "intelligence" depends not only on inside factors—biological genes, but also on outside factors—environment, experience, and personal effort. As Dr. Richard Restak states, "The environment will always be the principal determinant of whether or not a particular genetic predisposition gets fully expressed."[21] It is important for you to realize that the experiences you have every day, as you live your life, might impact the development of your intelligence by 64%! What happens at home, in school, in the neighborhood, at work, and in social groups impacts your IQ in either a positive or negative way.

What is Intelligence?

Let's step back a moment and clarify what intelligence is. There are many definitions, but I'll use only one. It is a classic definition from Dr. David Weschsler, the psychologist who developed several widely used intelligence tests including the Weschsler Adult Intelligence Scale (WAIS) and the Weschsler Intelligence Scale for Children (WISC). He states that intelligence is "...the global capacity of the individual to act purposefully, to think rationally, and to deal effectively with his environment".[22] Based on all of the information in this chapter so far, intelligence can be depicted in a four factor formula.

Your Intelligence =

Genes + Effort + Knowledge + Environment.

The only factor that is outside of your control in this formula is the genetic factor which contributes only about 36% to your full intellectual ability. YOU have the power to increase your own intelligence with the other three factors! The fact that you can grow your intelligence is a powerful finding.

What can you do if you are not living in an enriched environment? Just as you are learning to become a better thinker on your own, you can improve your intelligence on your own. Make the effort to stay curious, pay attention, explore new intellectual activities, love to learn, and perhaps make a public library your second home. Try to find and enter an environment, however small, that supports the development of the mind, especially your mind. Try to find an environment that celebrates you, and wants you to be the best you can be.

The fact that people can grow their intelligence is verified by studies about the accomplishments of students who are leaving troubled schools and attending schools with supportive and stimulating mental environments. Factors like socio-economic status, sex, religion, ethnicity, nationality are not important in these schools. The factors that matter include an environment that helps you to achieve your potential plus your own determined effort to learn and succeed.

Summary

In this chapter, you learned about neurons, the building blocks of your brain. You learned about Dr. Kandel and his experiments with Aplysia that were scientific breakthroughs in understanding how brain cells are designed and how they communicate. You learned that you have a lifelong window of opportunity to grow your brain. Right now electrical signals are lighting up your brain and bursts of brain chemicals are enabling brain cells to communicate, so you are learning and your brain is growing. You also learned that your intelligence is not fixed. You have the power to increase your intelligence.

In the next chapter, you will learn more about your brain as you take a tour of the brain and learn about its basic parts. You will meet the cast of characters responsible for learning and memory and emotional control. Get ready to meet Miss Amy G Dala, your amygdala! She is the drama queen within your brain, and if you let her, she'll be your brain's boss!

Questions for Reflection

1. **HEAD**: What did you learn? Imagine that you belong to a Book Club that is reading this book. Summarize the key points that you want to highlight during discussion.
2. **HEART**: How do you feel about what you learned?
3. **ACTION STEP**: What are you going to do now? Suggestions: learn more about the topic; share what you learned, or practice what you learned.

CHAPTER 3

Brain Basics and the Cast of Characters

Part 3: CEREBRUM—forebrain;
Job #1: THINKING

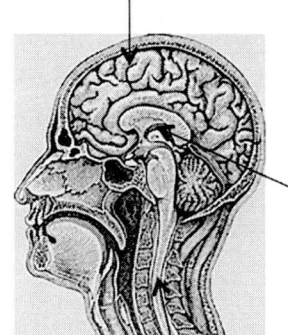

Part 2: Limbic System—midbrain;
Job #2: FEELING

Part 1: Brain Stem—the oldest part; hindbrain;
Job #3: SURVIVING

With modern parts atop old ones,
the brain is like an iPod built around an eight-track cassette player.
— Sharon Begley

To drive a car, you need to know a few of its parts, like the gas pedal, the breaks, the steering wheel, and the ignition. For you to skillfully operate the most powerful tool in the universe, the human brain, you also need to know a few of its parts. As I stated in the Introduction, lack of knowledge about how the brain works is a huge obstacle to skillful thinking. The purpose of this chapter is to help you overcome this obstacle by learning the basics about how your brain works. Don't worry. This isn't a biology course, and there is no test. It's an educational overview, a practical look at the design and function of your brain in one chapter. Although you are going to read about brain parts, I'll only emphasize the ones that I think are most important for developing your thinking ability. A neuroscientist might gasp at what I have left out, but my goal is simply to provide you with a "big picture", so you can understand why you think the way you do.

The important message in this chapter is that the design of your brain, its structure, impacts the quality of your thinking, so you need to understand how your brain is designed. The quote that introduced this chapter provides a clue to its design—new parts do not replace older parts. Instead, they are put on top of the older parts. Your brain has three main parts, and each has a unique job to do. However, your thinking process must go through the older parts to get to the new parts! As a result, it is not surprising that humans have some problems with their thinking ability.

The Triune Brain: Three Distinct Jobs

The "triune brain theory" was developed by Dr. Paul MacLean, a neuroscientist, in the 1960s. It is one of several models that scientists use to describe the structure of the human brain.[1] Dr. MacLean described the architecture of the brain as having three distinct parts, basically three distinct brains, based upon evolutionary development. Since the 1960s, however, neuroscientists have discovered so much interconnectedness in the brain that this theory has been challenged.

Although it may be an oversimplification of an incredibly complex and still mysterious process, I think this theory remains useful because of its simplicity. As you can see in the following chart, each part of the triune brain has a major and unique job to do. The jobs are 1. Surviving, 2. Feeling, and 3. Higher-order Thinking.

TRIUNE BRAIN			
	1.BRAIN STEM	**2.LIMBIC SYSTEM**	**3.CEREBRUM**
MAJOR JOBS INCLUDE...	JOB #1: SURVIVAL	JOB # 2: FEELINGS	JOB #3: HIGHER-ORDER THINKING
MAJOR STRUCTURES	BRAIN STEM CEREBELLUM	AMYGDALA HIPPOCAMPUS THALAMUS	BRAIN LOBES NEO-CORTEX
OTHER NAMES	HINDBRAIN, PRIMITIVE BRAIN, R- COMPLEX, REPTILIAN BRAIN, LIZARD BRAIN	MIDBRAIN, LIMBIC SYSTEM, OLD MAMMALIAN BRAIN, LEOPARD BRAIN	NEO-CORTEX, FOREBRAIN, CEREBRAL CORTEX, HUMAN BRAIN, LEARNER BRAIN
LOCATION	TOP OF SPINAL CORD, CENTER OF BRAIN	INSIDE BRAIN AND WRAPPED AROUND #1	OUTSIDE SURFACE, WRAPPED AROUND #2
AWARENESS LEVEL	UNCONSCIOUS	OUTSIDE OF CONSCIOUSNESS	CONSCIOUS

According to the triune brain theory, the earliest brain, the "hindbrain" which is also called R-complex, carries out job 1, which is to help you survive. The "midbrain" houses the limbic system, the second brain to develop and it carries out job 2 which focuses on your emotional feelings. The third brain is the "forebrain", the Cerebrum which carries out job 3, which is to help you do your planning, decision making, and problem solving. Job 3 is also where you control your impulses. The mental activities involved in job 3 are called higher-order thinking skills. **Many people believe that their brains are always working at the job 3 level, when in fact, they are not.**

This brief summary of the triune brain theory helps to clarify the brain's design with its "modern parts atop old ones".[2] The chart helps you to understand not only the brain's design, but also the importance of its different functions, and the sequence in which they occur. Today the three parts are recognized as distinct yet integral components of **one whole brain**. Let's now explore some brain basics.

Brain Parts

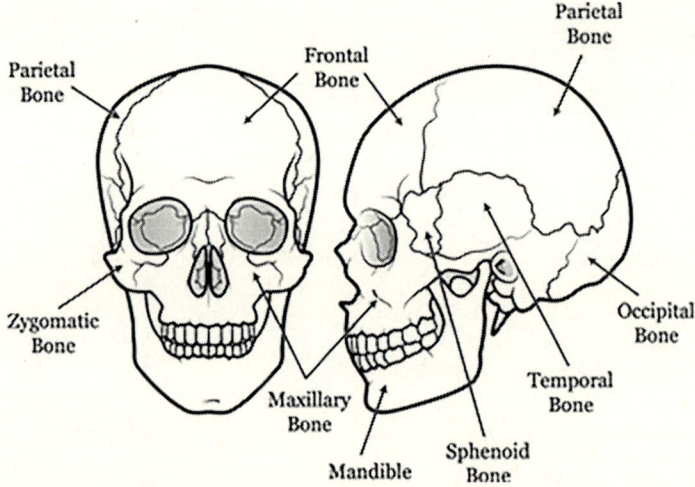

Let's start with your skull, your "brain box".[3] Your head has layers. You are familiar with your scalp. It is the skin covering your head and your hair grows out of it. Beneath your scalp is your skull. It is made of separate bones that bind together after you are born. Have you ever been told to be very careful of the "soft spot" on a baby's head? It's soft because the bones have not fused together yet. Your skull acts like a helmet to protect your brain. As you can see by looking at the skull above, the names of the bones are the frontal bone (forehead area), the parietal bone (top of your head), the temporal bone (side of your head) and the occipital bone (back of your head). The bones protect different sections of the brain called lobes which are parts of the cerebrum, your thinking brain. The lobes get their names from the skull bones that protect them. Each lobe has a special function.

Functions of Brain Lobes

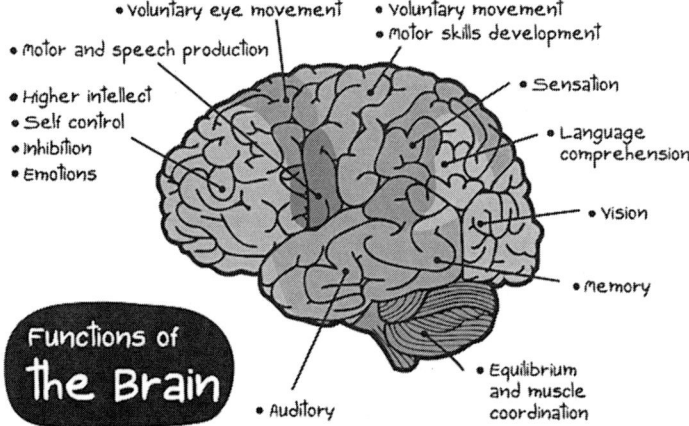

- **Frontal Lobe:** (touch your forehead area) — It is responsible for higher-order thinking. Your pre-frontal cortex (PFC) is located on the left side of your frontal lobe. Your PFC is your brain's CEO.[4] It is the "executive function" area that carries out executive functions like problem-solving, decision-making, judging, goal-setting, predicting, planning, and emotional/impulse control.
- **Temporal Lobe:** (touch the sides of your head, below your temples and near your ears)—It is like a Band Leader because it specializes in speech, language, and sound. It is responsible for your understanding and use of language, especially hearing and speaking.
- **Parietal Lobe:** (touch the top of your head) — It processes information coming into your brain from your senses through the sensory neurons in the area called the primary somatosensory cortex area. It also carries the instructions for movement going out from your brain to your body through the motor neurons in the area called the primary motor cortex area. There are specific locations in the parietal lobe for your different body parts. It is like a Masseuse because it specializes in touch and movement.
- **Occipital Lobe:** (touch the back of your head) — This lobe is like a Cameraman. It is responsible for your vision.

Insular Lobe

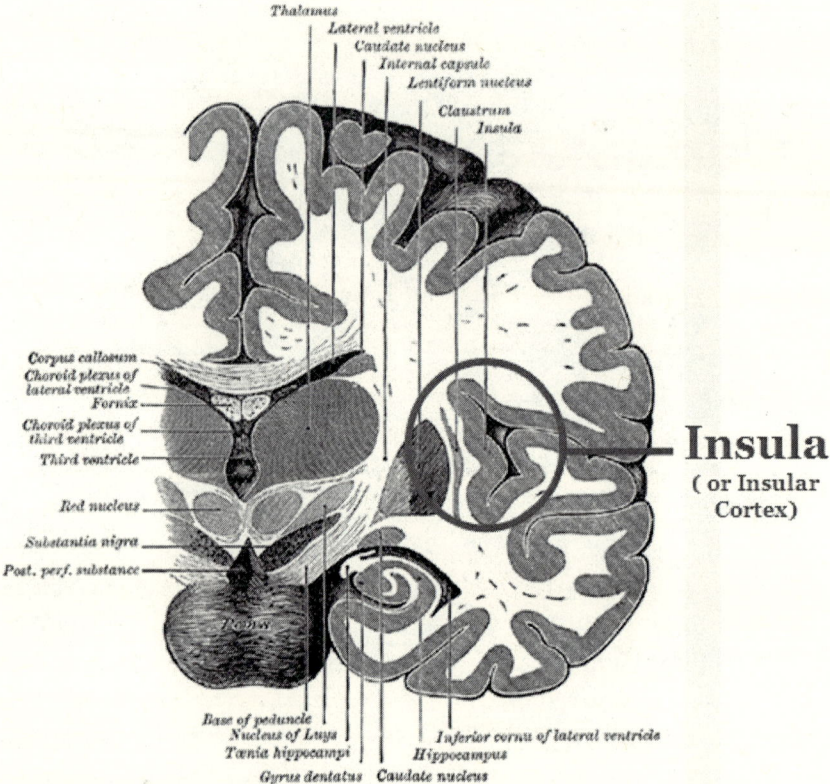

Insula
(or Insular Cortex)

- **Insula Lobe:** the hidden lobe. This is the fifth brain lobe and the only lobe not visible from the outside of the brain. It does not have a bone to protect it, because, as you can see, it is folded within the brain itself. It is located below the parietal lobe, beside the temporal lobe, and beneath the frontal lobe. Many people don't know about it. It went unrecognized as a brain lobe for many years, but it is receiving great attention today as a result of brain imaging. Neuroscientists now think that the insular lobe plays a role in perception, self-awareness, intuition, interpersonal life, and consciousness as well as taste and some motor control. Neuroscientists are investigating whether this is the area that gives you your "human feeling".[5] This is an area to watch in the future.

If you damage any one of the brain lobes through accident or disease, you interfere with its ability to function. This means you can damage your ability to see, hear, smell, taste, touch, and think. How do scientists know this is a true fact? Until brain imaging became available, scientists learned about the brain by studying lab animals like Aplysia and real people either alive or dead (cadavers). They learned a lot about the lobes of the brain from real people like Phineas Gage.[6]

Phineas Gage and the American Crowbar Case

Phineas was a railroad foreman working in Vermont in 1848. He and his crew were working on clearing an area so they could put down railroad tracks. To clear the rocks, they needed to drill holes in them, fill them with dynamite, then use a long iron rod to make sure the explosive was packed in tightly. It was Phineas' job to do the packing. As you can probably guess, on the day that changed his life, the dynamite exploded as he packed it into the rock with a rod that was 3 feet and 7 inches long. As a result of the explosion, the rod pushed right through his head. It entered through his left cheek, passed behind his left eye, drove through his brain, and came out of his head. Witnesses were sure he was dead, but he wasn't. Fortunately, he actually recovered; however, he was not the same. His personality and behavior had changed.

Before the accident Phineas was smart, calm, and professional. After the accident, he had difficulty making decisions; he became violent, and he lost his job because of his lack of professionalism. Although he looked almost the same, he had changed dramatically. No one could explain why. When he died, his mother gave doctors permission to have his skull and brain, so they could be studied. Doctors discovered that the accident destroyed much of his left frontal lobe. They concluded that the change in Phineas' behavior was connected to the damage to this part of his brain, which we now call the executive function area. Phineas' story attracted lots of medical attention in the 19th century. It helped doctors recognize that an injury to a specific part of the brain could change a person's behavior and personality. It led to more research on the structure and function of the brain. Seatbelts, bicycle helmets, and hardhats are some of the protective gear in widespread use today to protect your brain.

Cerebrum

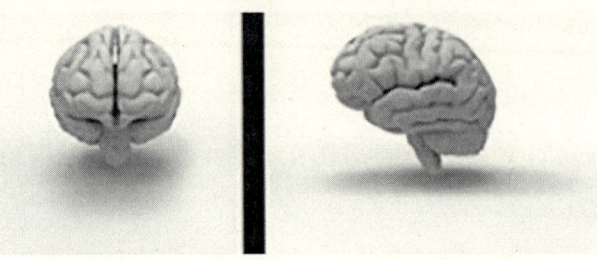

Do you think the brain inside your head looks like the familiar looking brain in the images above? No, it doesn't. The solid lumps above are images of a dead brain that has been preserved in a chemical called formaldehyde. Your real brain is very different. As you know, it is full of living neurons that are engaged in a lot of lively electrical and chemical activity. Underneath your hard skull, your brain is mushy, like custard or soft butter, and it requires oxygen and glucose (a form of sugar) to maintain its health. It is approximately 75-80% water. The average brain weighs about 3 pounds. It makes up 2% of your body weight but uses 25% of your calories. Information travels in your brain at speeds of 268 miles per hour.[7] If you make two fists and put them together, then you'll get a good idea about the size of your own brain.

Cerebral Cortex

The top layer of your thinking brain is the wrinkly part. It is called the cerebral cortex. Like the bark that covers a tree, the cerebral cortex covers your cerebrum. In fact, the word "cortex" comes from the Latin word for bark. This area is sometimes called your "gray matter" because it contains the cell bodies of neurons which look grayish. Beneath your gray matter is your "white matter". The term white matter comes from the white coloring of the myelin. The white matter area is the communications center of your brain where the axons of neurons are busy making connections across synapses. Making connections by sending signals is how brain cells "talk" with each other.

Two Hemispheres

As you can see in the previous image and in the image below, the brain looks something like a walnut. Like a walnut, your brain has two sides, called hemispheres. They are separated from each other by a groove called the medial longitudinal fissure which you can see. What you cannot see is the way they are connected to each other by the corpus callosum, a thick band of approximately 300 million axons of brain cells, which is located in the center of the brain beneath the cerebrum. The corpus callosum enables the two hemispheres to communicate with each other.[8]

Left-brainers and Right-brainers

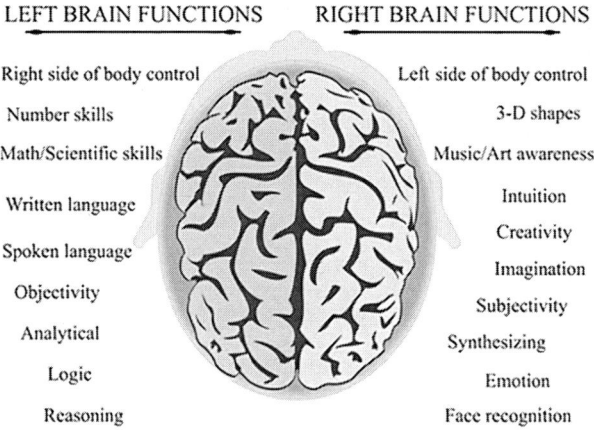

Each hemisphere has distinct responsibilities. Daniel Pink's book, <u>A Whole New Mind: Why Right-Brainers Will Rule the Future</u>, studied the recent findings in neuroscience to capture the differences between the hemispheres.[9] He describes four main differences: 1. The left hemisphere actually controls the right side of your body, and the right hemisphere controls the left side. 2. The left hemisphere is sequential and processes sounds and symbols in sequence, while the right side is simultaneous and can process several things at once and grasp their meaning. 3. The left hemisphere specializes in text; the right hemisphere specializes in context which includes emotional cues. 4. The left hemisphere focuses on details while the right hemisphere can synthesize the big picture. What causes the hemispheres to function differently? Part of the answer comes from the fact that each hemisphere has its own set of lobes, so in actuality you have two temporal lobes, two parietal lobes, etc. One set is on each side of the brain. Like twins, they have a lot in common, but they are also unique.

Many people have a tendency for one hemisphere or the other to dominate, so you may recognize the terms left-brainer and right-brainer. It is another over-simplification, but the general idea is that a person is a "left-brainer" if he specializes in textbook kinds of knowledge, is logical, sequential, and good at analyzing details. Left-brain thinkers are usually very successful in school situations because that type of thinking is emphasized and valued. The expression "right-brainer" usually describes a person who tends to be intuitive, creative, and artistic. Right-brain thinkers see the big picture and are empathetic. They are good at interpreting social and emotional clues. Traditionally, this type of thinking has not been emphasized and valued in most schools, but that is changing.

Pink refers to these differences as "L-Directed Thinking" for left-brain thinking that characterizes lawyers, accountants, computer programmers, and engineers, and "R-Directed Thinking" for right-brain thinking that characterizes inventors, entertainers, artists, caregivers, and counselors. Although there may be a preference for one side over the other, you use both sides of the brain, so you are a "whole brainer". The emphasis on the whole brain is one of the purposes of Pink's book. Successful people in the future will use both L-directed and R-directed thinking. He argues that R-directed thinking can no longer be an afterthought. In fact, he argues that the world is moving from the Information Age toward a Conceptual Age where right brainers, with their creativity, inventiveness, empathy, and big-picture thinking may rule the future. In the future, L-Directed Thinking, which used to be sufficient for human progress, is no longer enough. This is one of the reasons why Mega-Thinkers need to develop their R-directed thinking which includes creative thinking and systems thinking. As you develop R-directed thinking, you are preparing for success in the 21st century.

Cerebellum, the Little Brain

Cerebellum means "little cerebrum", so it is sometimes called the "little brain". It's about the size of a golf ball and is located at the back of your brain below the cerebrum. The names cerebrum and cerebellum can be confusing, and I told you names were not important. However, if you did want to remember the names and the differences, here is a little memory trick. Think about the letter "L". There are two "l"s in cerebellum and two "l"s in little, and the little brain is the cerebellum. Your cerebrum and your cerebellum communicate all the time, but their jobs are different. Your cerebellum controls all your motions and movements from blinking to walking. Once you master a skill, like riding a bike, your cerebellum remembers them automatically. You don't have to think about each step. This ability is called automaticity. It is similar to a car on "cruise control" or a plane on "auto pilot". You may be aware of what's going on, but you don't have to consciously think about it.

Brain Stem

Like a flower which has a stem, your brain also has a stem. Your brain stem is the first part of your brain to develop. This is the hindbrain, the R-complex, the oldest part of the brain, which is represented by the old eight-track cassette player mentioned in the quote at the beginning of this chapter. The brain stem comes down from the center of the cerebrum, and it is in front of your cerebellum. The stem is divided into three parts: the midbrain, the pons, and the medulla oblongata. These are the brain parts that keep you alive. They take care of the essentials of your life like breathing, digestion, blood pressure, body temperature, sleep cycle, etc. You are totally unconscious about these activities taking place within your body. Scientists call the brain stem a "high traffic area" because it serves as the entrance and exit ramp into and out of the brain. It connects your brain to your spinal cord, which connects your brain to the rest of your body. Together, your whole brain and your spinal cord make up your central nervous system.

Before leaving the brain stem, let's learn about a key part, the RAS, the reticular activating system. RAS acts as your personal bodyguard. It is sometimes called the "perpetual register" because it is always "on" and it never sleeps. It registers everything brought to your body by your senses. No sensory data gets past it. You were introduced to RAS in chapter one when you learned about perception. I described its activities but I did not name it. RAS is part of the reticular formation, which is the core of your brainstem.

Attention Center

It is here in the RAS that your attention is activated, and attention is at the core of thinking, learning, and remembering. If your RAS is not aware that something is occurring, if RAS does not pay attention to it, then you will never think about it, learn about it, or remember it. No matter how important the information or event is to your boss, your parents, your teachers, your spouse, or any other important person in your life, if RAS is not activated, you will never receive the information. It's like a light switch. It must be turned on to see the light. If it's off, you are in the dark. You are not aware of what's going on, so you don't pay attention. Attention is to the brain what the sun is to the solar system. It is the source of your brainpower, and it all starts with your RAS.

RAS is your brain's first filter or "delete button". RAS decides what information from your senses to let into your brain. Since it responds to data that signals danger in order to ensure your survival, and prefers data that is stimulating and pleasurable, RAS keeps out most sensory data. Remember, it is bombarded by millions of bits of sensory data every second but it admits only a small amount, perhaps 2,000 bits of data per second.[10] As a result, RAS prevents your brain from being overwhelmed and crashing from sensory overload. It is important to avoid sensory overload because when your brain is overwhelmed with data, the brain acts in one of three ways: 1. it makes no decision about what to think or do, 2. it makes a poor decision, or 3. it makes a decision that it later regrets.[11]

The Hidden Basics

I consider the parts described in the following section to be hidden basics, because they are snuggled inside the middle of your brain in your limbic system. Many people are not aware of them because they never learned about them, so they are unaware of their critical importance to the way you think and learn. These parts have major, MAJOR roles to play in your thinking processes.

Miss Amy G, the Queen Bee

I want you to meet Miss Amy G. Dala, the brain's drama queen. Miss Amy G is your amygdala, and the center of your limbic brain.[12] She may be the most important part of the brain for you to understand. That's why she's the queen. She is the seat of your passion and unconscious emotion, especially FEAR. She is your body's "panic button". She is also your brain's second filter, the second delete button. Remember, the first is the RAS. This little amygdala is a "big-deal-a", and you need to know about her, understand how she works, and learn strategies to tame her. Actually, she's a twin. You have two Amy Gs. Like your brain lobes, you have one in each side of your brain. Each is about the size of an almond. She has a lot of power for such a small package. With effort, you can learn to tame her; however, you will never control her.

Hippo Campus, the Memory Guide

Next, let's meet Miss Amy G's partner, Hippo Campus (aka hippocampus). I call them partners because they are located next to each other in the center of your brain. They are very important because they are both involved in memory and without memory, there is no learning. Miss Amy G is connected to emotional memory, naturally. Hippo is connected to temporary and long-term memory. Without a hippocampus, you will not have any memories at all. The hippocampus has been called the "Grand Central Station" of memory.[13] Just like Amy G, you have two Hippos, one in each hemisphere of your brain. Look at the location of these brain parts in the next image. You are looking at the center of the brain. Hippocampus is the Latin word for sea horse, because early scientists thought it looked like a seahorse. In this view, the amygdala sits beside it towards the inside of the brain.

Your Pleasure Center

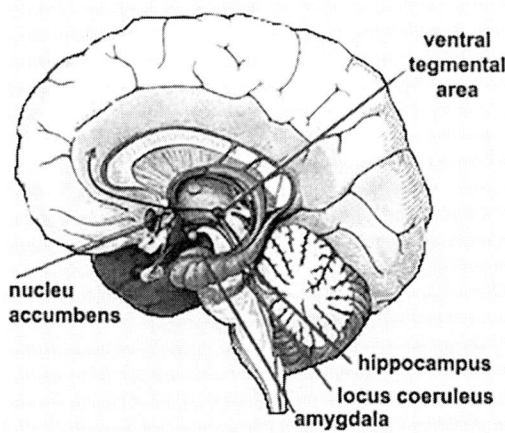

ventral
tegmental
area

nucleu
accumbens

hippocampus
locus coeruleus
amygdala

This image of the "pleasure center" is from an excellent resource, "The Brain from Top to Bottom". It is printed here with permission from McGill University [http://www.thebrain.mcgill.ca]. Besides showing the amygdala and hippocampus, two of the major parts of your brain, this brain image reveals other brain parts that work with Miss Amy G to make up its "pleasure center": the ventral tegmental area, also called the VTA and the Nucleus Accumbens (the NUC). The connection between these brain parts is called the "reward pathway". What travels along the pathway? A brain chemical called dopamine. Your body feels really good when it receives a blast of the neurotransmitter dopamine. Where does the dopamine come from? It is produced deep inside your brain in the VTA.[14]

Dopamine is the pleasure neurotransmitter. It is quite natural that people like to do things that give them pleasure and avoid things that give them pain or that punish them. When people engage in activities that make them feel good, they are unknowingly producing dopamine. When something happens that your brain likes, dopamine is automatically produced in the VTA; then it travels along the reward pathway to your Nucleus Accumbens, your NUC. Your NUC then releases the dopamine and POW! You feel great. You now know that when you do something that makes you feel a sense of pleasure, the brain chemical dopamine is involved.

What activities cause your body to have this feel-good reaction? It is purely personal. It depends upon what you as an individual like and enjoy. Your brain reacts to whatever your personal needs and wants are, because your brain is tuned in to you! Different people receive pleasure from different activities. It could be from playing or watching sports, shopping, listening to music, attending an opera, being romantic, eating sweets, acing a test, holding a baby, or getting to higher levels in a video game. That's the positive side of the neurotransmitter dopamine. Unfortunately, excessive pleasure seeking can lead to dopamine addiction. Whether it's playing video games, checking emails, gambling, or using alcohol and drugs, without realizing it, people are triggering brain chemicals, and they can become addicted.

Thalamus: Your Sensory Traffic Controller

You are now ready to meet your thalamus, which is located in the center of your brain. Its position makes it one of the most well-connected parts. Dr. John Medina, brain scientist and molecular biologist who wrote Brain Rules calls your thalamus "a control tower for your senses".[15] It processes the signals from the sensory neuron traffic, the information flow coming into your brain, and routes it to the different parts of your brain. How this happens is still a mystery. Nevertheless, some basic awareness of sensory traffic patterns will help you become a more skillful thinker.

Traffic Routes

This section is a gross oversimplification, but it is still valuable. Let's follow the journey that the sensory data traffic takes as it travels through your brain.[16] Remember, data enters through your senses and must make it past RAS, your bodyguard and the brain's first filter. Only then can it reach the thalamus. Your thalamus then controls the data traffic by choosing an information route for the sensory data to travel. It chooses one of two information routes: the regular route and the emergency route.

Regular Traffic Route: Acting as the traffic control tower, your thalamus directs information that is pleasant, non-threatening, emotionally calm, and connected to your areas of interest and personal needs to your CEO, your left prefrontal cortex. Your CEO has a personal assistant, the cingulate gyrus, which helps with controlling impulses.[17] Emotional situations that are not emergencies are handled by the cingulate gyrus assisting your PFC. Finally, the information moves along to your amygdala, your emotional center and your brain's second filter/delete button. Along the regular route, information from your senses, even some emotional information, is handled with reason and thoughtfulness.

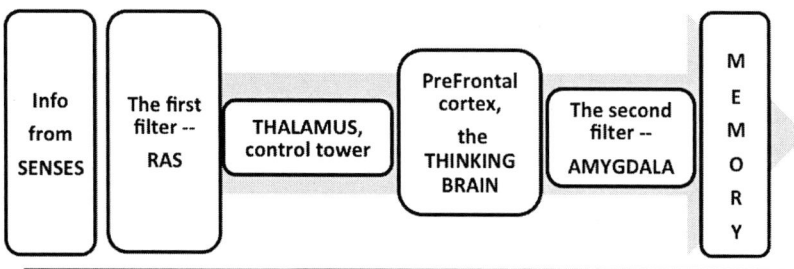

Figure 3.1: Regular Sensory Traffic Route

Emergency Traffic Route: The journey of sensory data **TO** the thalamus is the same, as you can see on the following chart. Information from your senses goes to RAS, and RAS then sends limited sensory data to your thalamus. The route changes once the thalamus receives the data. If the information from RAS makes your thalamus sense an emergency due to strong threat, fear, anxiety, stress, bullying, confusion, frustration, or anything of that nature, then, like a traffic controller at an airport, your thalamus goes into emergency mode. It immediately directs the sensory information traffic to the emergency route. You can clearly see the route in the following chart. Sensing an emergency, your thalamus sends the data directly to Miss Amy G, your Amygdala. **The information bypasses your "Thinking Brain"!**

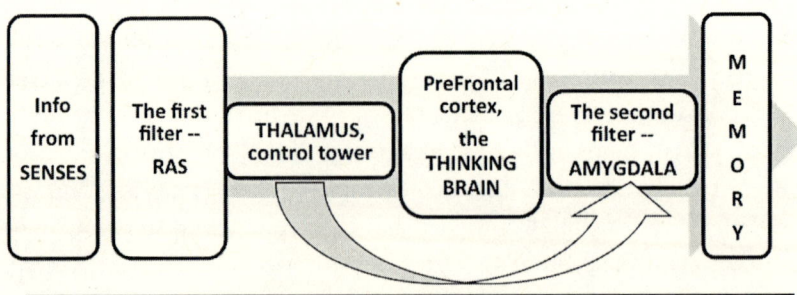

Figure 3.2: Emergency Traffic Route

This traffic pattern is VERY important and needs to be repeated. When your sensory data takes the emergency route, it bypasses your Thinking Brain! These two routes mean that the information entering your brain can be handled in one of two ways. The regular route involves conscious thinking on your part; the emergency route does not! In his book, Emotional Intelligence, Daniel Goleman calls this action "Emotional Hijacking". It occurs when the amygdala seizes control and triggers an action before the prefrontal cortex, the thinking brain, and its assistant know what is happening.

One of Goleman's key points is that "the workings of the amygdala and its interplay with the neo-cortex are at the heart of emotional intelligence."[18] Understanding the connection between the emotional amygdala and the rational prefrontal cortex is also at the heart of Mega-Thinking. You now know why your prefrontal cortex, your thinking brain, is not always involved in your thinking. The parts of your brain that are below your level of consciousness can allow sensory data to skip your thinking brain! That means that your survival instincts or your emotions are handling the information. Think about the impact this has on the quality of your thinking ability.

You have now learned about the most important brain parts that are involved in your becoming a Mega-Thinker. You may be curious why I am not only using visual images, but also using silly ones at times to depict brain parts. The fact is that your brain learns better with visual images, and your brain likes to have fun. It doesn't like to pay attention to boring things.[19] Basically, I'm trying to satisfy your brain, so it will pay attention.

Summary: It Takes a Village....

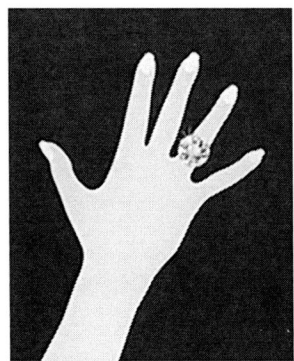

You have learned that your brain is a very busy place. As a summary for this chapter, I wanted to review some of the major brain parts that are responsible for your thinking, perception, emotions, memory, and learning. It is important to point out that these jobs are not limited to the brain part mentioned. There are abundant interconnections among the parts of the brain. The parts listed here are the major players mentioned in this chapter. You do not need to remember the brain parts, but if you did want to remember the first five, then here is a helpful mnemonic: a hand with a ring on it— for HAND-R (Hippo, Amy G, NUC, Dopa, and RAS).

- **H- Hippocampus** is the Memory Keeper and the Architect that combines received, processed, and stored memories into new designs. It directs them into either sensory/temporary, working, or long-term memory.
- **A- Amygdala**, Miss Amy G, is the drama Queen specializing in emotion, especially fear, so she always carries a "Panic Button". She also has one of the two "delete" buttons in the brain. In emergency situations, she receives information before it gets into your thinking brain. In many ways, she is your brain's boss.

- **N- Nucleus Accumbens** is explosive. It specializes in releasing dopamine which provides you with pleasure, motivation, and magical moments of feeling good.
- **D- Dopamine**, the Happy Chemical- the neurotransmitter that brings pleasurable feelings
- **R- Reticular Activating System** (RAS) in the brain stem is the Bodyguard. It keeps out unwanted information. It never sleeps and specializes in keeping things out of your brain by carrying the first "delete button".
- **Thalamus** is the control tower of your brain. Once RAS lets sensory information in, the thalamus routes the successful sensory data to their proper brain destinations using either a regular route or an emergency route.
- The **Prefrontal Cortex** is part of the **Frontal Lobe** of your cerebrum. It is the CEO, the Chief Executive Officer with intellect and judgment.
- **Parietal Lobe** is responsible for sensory information and movement.
- **Temporal Lobe** is responsible for language, hearing, and speaking.
- **Occipital Lobe** is responsible for vision.
- **Insula Lobe is the** "hidden lobe" and scientists are discovering new information about it. It may be responsible for perceptions and self-awareness as well as taste.
- **VTA (ventral tegmental area)** is a very primitive part of the brain that acts like a Chemist and produces dopamine.
- **Cerebellum** is the Personal Trainer that specializes in physical movement and coordination.

This chapter on brain basics has provided you with a lot of information about how your brain works, but it is not enough. To become a Mega-Thinker, especially in the dimension of "school-success" thinking, you need to know about memory. In the next chapter, you will learn how the activity of your brain parts turns the sensory data in your environment into memories. Memories matter because without memories, there is no learning.

Questions for Reflection

1. **HEAD**: What did you learn? Imagine that you belong to a Book Club that is reading this book. Summarize the key points that you want to highlight during discussion.
2. **HEART**: How do you feel about what you learned?
3. **ACTION STEP**: What are you going to do now? Suggestions: learn more about the topic; share what you learned, or practice what you learned.

CHAPTER 4

Memory Matters

We are who we are because of what we learn and what we remember.
— Eric Kandel

You are near the finish line now. This is the last part of your journey to learn how the brain works, and it is a major part—- memory. Memory really matters because, as the quote above states, it determines who you are. In addition, memory determines learning. If you cannot remember something, then you have not learned it. However, many people take memory for granted. Think about it. As you read the words on this page, do you realize that once upon a time you couldn't read? You learned and remembered how to decode words. As you take notes, do you think about your memory being involved? If you didn't remember the shape and sound of letters, then you could not write meaningful sentences. Think about everything you do on a daily basis including eating, showering, talking, and walking. You are on auto-pilot now with these activities. You are remembering what to do, but your memory is working at the unconscious level, so you are not aware of it.

Natural versus Trained Memory

Memory, like thinking, is natural. Unless you have a brain injury involving your hippocampus, you are born with the ability to remember. Memory is the ability to replay, in your mind today, events that took place in the past. You remember faces and places, your favorite foods, your favorite movies, and all sorts of things that enable you to live your life. You use your memory on a daily basis with little or no effort. It does not require training.

Mega-Thinking, however, is about more than natural memory. It includes the "art of memory", where you take specific steps to force yourself to remember things. By deliberately learning skills and strategies, as you will in part two of this book, you will develop a trained memory. In order to develop a trained memory, you need to learn about the biological processes that take place within your brain that enable you to remember. That foundation will help you understand the reasons you remember and the reasons you forget. The purpose of this chapter is to help you learn what is involved when your brain makes memories, so you will be a skillful memory-maker and a more successful learner and thinker.

Building Block of Memory

What part of your brain is the building block of your memory? Stop and think about it. In this chapter, I'll do my best to explain, with the information available today, how your brain works to enable you to remember. Let's go back to the question: What is the building block of your memory? The answer is the small but mighty neuron! You already know how neurons communicate, and the reason they communicate is to help you learn and remember.

Memory is complex. First and foremost, memory is biological. In his article, "Why We Remember, Why We Forget", Joshua Foer stated that "A memory is a stored pattern of connections between neurons in the brain."[1] Since you already read the chapter on neurons, you can grasp the meaning of that sentence. The connections among neurons enable you to perform the three key memory tasks: the ability to encode, store, and retrieve information.

As a result of these mental skills, you are able to demonstrate your memory by behaving in ways that show what you have learned and what you can recall. Your displayed memory is evidence that you have learned something, because you cannot say you learned something if you cannot remember it. Let's step back and find out how scientists learned about memory and what they learned.

Where is Memory Located?

Scientists first learned where memory is located from a man known as H.M. In 1933, when he was a seven year old boy, H.M. injured his head in a bad bicycle accident and started having seizures and blacking out. In 1953, by the time he was 27, his medical condition was so bad that his doctor decided that he needed surgery to stop the seizures. As a result, in 1953, he had surgery on his brain. His surgeon determined that his seizures started in his temporal lobes (remember, we have two, one on each side of our head), so he removed the inner surface of the temporal lobes as well as his hippocampus (again there are two), which is deep inside each temporal lobe.

The surgery was a success because H.M.'s seizures stopped; however, the surgery had an unintended consequence. H.M.'s memory was damaged. He was unable to remember new events in his life. His long-term memory was great for childhood experiences and events that happened well before his surgery in 1953, but he was unable to acquire any new long-term memories. On the other hand, his language, perception, and reasoning were not impaired and his short-term memory was good. In addition, he could learn new motor skills. This led to the realization that there are different memory systems located in different parts of the brain.

Principles of Memory

Some of the most important findings regarding HM's case were discovered by Dr. Brenda Milner, a neuropsychologist, who studied HM's memory for many years. She studied what he lost and what he retained. She was able to identify specific brain areas associated with different aspects of memory, and her findings became very valuable to other scientists who were studying memory formation and storage. Dr. Milner's research on H.M. identified three important principles about the biological basis of memory.

1. Memory is a distinct mental function, separate from other perceptual, motor, and cognitive abilities.
2. Short-term memory and long-term memory can be stored separately.
3. There are two forms of memory: a. conscious memory that is also called explicit and b. unconscious memory that is also called implicit. They are processed, stored, and retrieved in different places within the brain.[2]

In 2008, at the age of 82, H.M. died, and it was only then that his identity was finally revealed. Prior to his death, Henry Molaison's brain informed scientists where memory is located. After his death, his brain was donated to science, so there may be more revelations that H.M.'s brain contributes to the science of memory. You have now learned that the brain's inner secrets are revealed from three sources: 1. Experiments on animals in laboratories, like Aplysia, 2. Human patients, alive or dead, like Phineas Gage and Henry, and 3. Technology, especially brain imaging technology. Let's learn more about brain imaging, because this is a major source of dramatic breakthroughs today.

Learning from Brain Imaging

Brain imaging techniques have enabled doctors and neuroscientists to observe the activity of neurons in the human brain in real time with living subjects. Using brain imaging, researchers can actually see the brain areas at work, so they learn how brain parts are used for different functions. They can also see how information is stored and retrieved within the brain. Since the brain needs oxygen and glucose (sugar) to function properly, and it is blood that brings the oxygen and sugar to the brain, most of the tests show blood flow in the brain. Basically, the more active the brain, the more oxygen and sugar it needs, so blood flow increases. Let's briefly examine some of these tests.

1. CAT Scan, sometimes called CT scan: computerized axial tomography. It provides a structural, 3D image of the brain by combining the technology of an X-Ray machine with computer-imaging techniques. It produces cross-sectional images the brain. It can rotate to capture "slices" of brain images. When assembled together, they produce an image of the physical structure of the entire brain.
2. PET Scan: positron-emission tomography. This brain scanner measures the level of brain activity in specific parts of the brain at specific times, rather than measure physical structure like the CAT scan. In a PET scan, the brain is injected with radioactive glucose/sugar, so the scan can follow the glucose through the bloodstream until it shows up in the brain. It takes pictures of the brain as it is performing different mental or physical tasks like recalling facts or singing a song.
3. MRI (Magnetic resonance imaging). This test provides a 3D, structural image of the brain. Using a complex interaction of radio waves and magnetic fields, neurologists are able to study blood flow patterns in real time. It enables researchers to see and study brain activity as areas switch on and switch off as the subject is performing different tasks. However, the MRI is limited to still pictures.
4. fMRI (a functional MRI) is similar to an MRI, but it can take pictures so quickly that it can show a process, similar to a movie. It is flexible in that it can perform a variety of analyses, including classic structural scans, blood oxygen scans, diffusion-weighted scans that measure water flow in the brain, perfusion-weighted scans to measure capillary blood flow, and spectroscopy which detects levels of brain chemicals.

5. SPECT scan (single photon emission-computed tomography). Like a PET scan, it is a reliable measure of cerebral blood flow which shows patterns of brain activity. It costs less and is easier to use, but it provides less detail. Like the PET scan, it uses low levels of radiation.[3]

6. DTI (Diffusion Tensor Imaging). This is a neuroimaging technique that is based on MRI brain scanners, but it creates an image of the white matter. DTI works by studying water flow in the brain, not blood flow. The goal is to measure the direction and amount of water diffusion in the brain. It is looking for connections of the white matter with the gray matter-the cell bodies and dendrites of brain cells.[4]

7. qEEG: Quantitative Electroencephalogram. This tool is used in brain mapping. It measures electrical patterns on the surface of the scalp that reflect brain wave activity. It can determine the precise location and time of brain waves coming from specific parts of the brain engaged in an activity.[5]

Thanks to these imaging tests, scientists are seeing connections being made and learning taking place in real time. As a result, they are making fascinating discoveries about the human brain. These three sources of scientific information—experiments on animals, experiments on humans, and brain imaging technology— provide a window into memory processing.

Processing Memory

There is agreement among brain researchers that memory formation involves three processes: encoding, storing, and retrieving information. In addition, there is general agreement that there are several stages of memory: 1. Sensory/immediate, 2.Working, and 3. Long-term.[6] Perhaps you are wondering why short-term memory is not mentioned. Well, do you remember that Pluto used to be a planet? New information changes things. What used to be called short term memory has been divided into "sensory/immediate memory" and "working memory". They are both temporary memories. Within your brain, these temporary memory areas are located in your right prefrontal cortex, above your right eye and about one inch behind your forehead. Do you recall where your "executive function" area is? It is also in your forehead area. It is above and behind your left eye in your left prefrontal cortex.

Temporary Memory Areas

Sensory/immediate memories are processed on the right side of your prefrontal cortex. Since they are temporary memories, they are not stored. Encoding temporary memories begins with sensory/immediate memory, which is where RAS works. Your sensory memory is actually an extension of the RAS. It seems that RAS is making a decision in conjunction with your prefrontal cortex about handling the data. All of this is done at the subconscious level, so you are unaware of all the activity. For a sensory memory, the information can be held in a range of time from milliseconds to a few seconds before moving on or being deleted. Your brain uses your past experiences to see if the data is important. If the information moves on, immediate memory can hold the information in place for up to 30 seconds, while the brain is deciding what to do with it. Immediate memory works at both a subconscious and conscious level. Looking up a telephone number is a good example of a temporary, immediate memory. The numbers are remembered long enough to make the call. Sometimes not even that long; sometimes you have to look up the number several times! As soon as the call is made, the numbers disappear from your brain.[7]

In his research with Aplysia, Dr. Kandel discovered that a temporary memory requires the release of a neurotransmitter, glutamate. The release of a neurotransmitter requires lots of steps, and glutamate's release is a good example of this complexity. You don't need to know those details, but basically, the molecule "cyclic AMP" works with the protein "kinase A", and the neurotransmitter "serotonin" to release the glutamate. It's the presence of glutamate at the synapse that makes the information stick around in your brain for a short time. What a great word for something that sticks around; it sounds like GLUE. Just realize that complex changes occur in the strength of the connections between neurons at the synapse which increase the release of glutamate from the axon terminal into the synaptic gap. This enhanced glutamate leads to a functional change, not a structural change, and the change leads to a temporary memory.[8]

Working Memory

Like sensory/immediate memory, working memory is a temporary memory that is characterized by having a limited capacity and a limited timeframe, but it only takes place at the conscious level. When information is in working memory, you are paying attention to it. In working memory, the adult brain has approximately 10 to 20 minutes to manipulate the information to determine what to do with it. However, this is where attention and motivation kick in. Data may be able to last several hours or even days depending on the person's interest.[9]

The bottom line is that information is manipulated in working memory until your brain determines if the information should enter long-term memory or be deleted. As you know, any information that threatens survival or gets Amy G worked up with strong emotions will get in. What other kinds of information get in? Your brain will choose data that has meaning for you. If the information has personal meaning and it makes sense, then it is very likely that the information will be sent along to long term memory where it will be encoded and stored and ready for retrieval when you want it.

Long-Term Memories

How are temporary memories transformed into long-term memories? That's the job of your hippocampus. Remember, Hippo is the brain's architect, so it determines where the data fits into your brain's structure. The decision is based on several factors including 1.the connections the new information is making to old connections and patterns, and 2. the overall importance of the new information in meeting your needs and wants. As information was being processed in Aplysia's neurons, Dr. Kandel observed the activity taking place at the molecular level that put a memory into long-term storage. What did he see? He saw physical, **structural** changes taking place in the neuron.

He discovered that long-term memory (LTM) requires more that the stronger release of brain chemicals. LTM requires **structural, anatomical changes which cause neurons to grow new parts, new dendrites,** at the synapse as it make new connections. Glutamate is involved, but lots of other bio-chemical changes take place in the neuron during this process as well. If you want the scientific details, I recommend that you read Chapter 19, A Dialogue Between Genes and Synapses, in Dr. Kandel's book, In Search of Memory.

Here is a very oversimplified explanation, but it will enable you to get a very basic understanding, which is all you really need. For information to become a LTM, many things need to happen in order to create a new protein called CPEB (cytoplasmic polyadenylation element-binding protein). Did you notice the word "binding" in this protein's name? The newly created protein is called a "binding protein". It is involved in creating a new synaptic terminal which "binds" or perpetuates the memory for the long term. I find the word binding very helpful here. How do you keep a memory in place for a long time? You bind it with newly created parts.[10]

Long Term Memory Storage

Where is your long-term memory located? Is there one special place, a memory vault, where these long-term memories are housed? Of course not, your brain is far more complex that that! Dr. John Medina describes the interesting and messy process involved in memory storage in this way.

The moment of learning, of encoding, is so mysterious and complex that we have no metaphor to describe what happens to our brains in those first, fleeting seconds….The information is literally sliced into discrete pieces as it enters the brain and splattered all over the insides of our mind.

Stated formally, signals from different sensory sources are registered in separate brain areas. The information is fragmented and redistributed the instant the information is encountered. [11]

Yuck! What an image! Your memory is made up of sliced and splattered pieces of information. At this point, scientists believe that the pieces of long-term memories are stored where they were created. If what you remember has to do with sight, it is stored in the occipital lobe, the primary visual cortex. If it has to do with sound, it is stored in the temporal lobe, which is the primary auditory cortex. If it has to do with touch, it is stored in the parietal lobe, which is the primary somatosensory cortex. Many times a memory is encoded using multiple senses. What happens then? This is where the slicing comes in. The memory is broken into its different sensory parts and stored in the appropriate area. In addition, emotional memories are stored in your amygdala, and physical skills are stored in your cerebellum, if these are the areas where the memory was first created.

Memory Pathways

Thanks to brain-imaging technology, scientists are able to see neurons communicating and sections of the brain "light up" when thinking and learning are taking place and memories are being stored. As a result, brain scientists have learned that long-term memory is a unified whole memory system that consists of different "pathways" leading from encoding to storage.[12]

To date, there is general agreement that there are six memory pathways that neurons can take to put information into long-term memory (LTM) storage. Each pathway is for a different type of information. When you examine the pathways, you will see that you are consciously involved in making memories in only two out of the six of them. These two are called "declarative" pathways. There are three pathways that work only at the unconscious level. You make memories in these pathways with no conscious awareness of what you are doing. These three are called "nondeclarative" pathways. Finally, there is one pathway that sometimes works at the conscious, declarative level and sometimes at the unconscious, nondeclarative level. Can you guess who is involved in this pathway? Yes, it's Miss Amy G Dala, the queen bee herself. She will rule over your emotional pathway, if you let her.

Declarative versus Nondeclarative Pathways

There are two main divisions among memory pathways: declarative and non-declarative.

- **Declarative memories** are conscious memories that are explicit and voluntary. You actively participate in their formation. You declare and describe the memory with words. Therefore, if a long term memory is easy to explain or describe using words, it is declarative, like describing the plot of a favorite book. You can name and describe memories explicitly and with details, ex. "Let me tell you..." Declarative memories are divided into two types: semantic and episodic.
- **Nondeclarative memories** are the opposite: unconscious, implicit, and involuntary. Non-declarative memories cannot be expressed well with words, so they are expressed in other ways, ex. "Let me show you..." Therefore, if a memory is hard to explain with words, like describing how to ride a bike or a snowboard, it is nondeclarative. Nondeclarative memories are divided into three types: procedural, perceptual representation system, and automatic.
- **Emotional memories** can fall into both categories— declarative and non-declarative

In the following chart, each of the six pathways is described.

Long Term Memory Pathways

LONG-TERM MEMORY FILE CABINET – WITH SIX MEMORY PATHWAYS			
Pathway	Type of Information	Storage Location	Brain engagement
SEMANTIC — Declarative; Uses words to describe memories	Knowledge: dates; facts; names; school learning	Cerebrum and Hippocampus	Conscious and Voluntary
EPISODIC — Declarative; uses words	Personal Experiences; sense of time and place; natural memories	Cerebrum and Hippocampus	Conscious and Voluntary
EMOTIONAL — Can be Declarative or Non-Declarative	Feelings like Fear and love	Amygdala	Can be Conscious or Unconscious; Voluntary or not
PROCEDURAL — Non-Declarative; memory hard to explain with words; demonstrates	Physical procedures that involve muscles like bike-riding And swimming	Cerebellum	Unconscious And Involuntary
PERCEPTUAL REPRESENTATION — Non-Declarative; hard to explain with words; demonstrates	Structure and shape of words, letters, objects; Phonemic awareness	Cerebellum	Unconscious And Involuntary
AUTOMATIC	Compulsive, involuntary Response to a stimulus like a song or a smell	Cerebellum	Unconscious And Involuntary

- The **Semantic Pathway** is Conscious, Declarative, and Explicit, and it is stored in the Hippocampus and Cerebrum. Semantic memory includes things like names, dates, facts, and impersonal details that may not be easy to learn. These often require the trained memory you will learn about in chapter 10, School Success Thinking. There are some mental tricks that you can use to provide novelty to help your brain remember semantic information.

- The **Episodic Pathway** is also Conscious, Declarative, and Explicit, and it is also stored in the Hippocampus and Cerebrum. It contains personal experiences, events, and biographical details. These are formed using natural memory. They are easy-to-remember memories.
- The **Emotional Pathway** is the only one that can be both can be Conscious or Unconscious, Declarative or Non-Declarative, and Explicit or Implicit. It is stored in the Amygdala. It contains feelings like love and fear, and in an emergency it takes over conscious thought. You have some control only when System 2 is awake and you are paying attention. Otherwise, Miss Amy G takes over.
- The **Procedural Pathway** is Unconscious, Non-declarative, and Implicit. It is stored in the Cerebellum. It involves muscle movement and skills like bike-riding, swimming, and walking.
- The **Perceptual Representation System Pathway** is also Unconscious, Non-declarative, Implicit, and stored in the Cerebellum. It involves the structure, form, and sound of words.
- The **Automatic Pathway** is also Unconscious, Non-declarative, Implicit, and stored in the Cerebellum. It is also called "Conditional Response" and involves sensory experiences like sounds and smells that automatically trigger involuntary reactions.

Once your hippocampus selects a memory path, the neurons take the data and store it in the appropriate area. As you saw in the chart, your declarative, conscious memories are stored in the hippocampus— the memory keeper, and the lobes of the cerebrum where they were originally created. For example, visual images are stored in the occipital lobe.

Your non-declarative, unconscious memories are stored in the more primitive parts of the brain, the amygdala and the cerebellum. Finally, your emotional memories are stored in your amygdala with Miss Amy G. The final step in the long-term memory encoding process is—-Sleep! Research is showing that information is encoded into long-term memories during deep sleep. What happens next, when you want to retrieve a memory?

Retrieval

This is the really tricky part. How can a fragmented memory be retrieved? It seems that your mushy three pound brain is capable of extraordinary acts, so it can reunite the "splattered" pieces during retrieval to provide you with intact memories. How? According to Dr. Medina, researchers have organized the retrieval process into two models: 1. the library model, also called reproductive retrieval and 2. the crime scene model, also called reconstructive retrieval. Which is correct? It depends on what you are looking for and how much time has passed, so both are correct in different situations.

In the library model, think of memories being stored like books on shelves —intact, fully reproduced, and in a certain place. If the long term memory is retrieved within a relatively short period of time, minutes to days, then the library model will work. If a significant amount of time has passed, then the crime scene model may be more accurate.

In the crime scene model, a detective searches for clues and examines evidence to reconstruct the memory from fragmented data that is stored in many places. Although your brain uses the crime scene model to try to make sense of things for you, it can be inaccurate. Time gaps can be a huge problem when you are trying to access accurate memories, because unless the memory was encoded in a powerful manner using multiple senses, specific facts and detail weaken.[13] One of the most important messages of this chapter is that if you want to improve your memory, you must consciously focus on what you want to remember during the encoding stage in order to have an accurate memory of it during the retrieval stage.

Improving Memory

The good news is that memories can be improved. As Dr. Medina states, "The more elaborately we encode information at the moment of learning, the stronger the memory."[14] The more senses and strategies you use to encode a memory means there are more clues or memory cues to find the pathways to the stored information. Elaborate encoding makes it easier to reconstruct the memory during the retrieval process, and it helps to ensure a more accurate memory. If developing reliable, long-term memories is a goal for you, then Dr. Medina suggests you take the following steps:

The relationship between repetition and memory is clear. Deliberately re-expose yourself to the information if you want to retrieve it later. Deliberately re-expose yourself to the information more elaborately if you want the retrieval to be of higher quality. Deliberately re-expose yourself to the information more elaborately, and in fixed, spaced intervals, if you want the retrieval to be the most vivid it can be. Learning occurs best when new information is incorporated gradually into the memory store rather than when it is jammed in all at once. [15]

Notice the repeated use of the word "deliberately". It indicates effort on your part. It indicates the way you should behave, deliberately and effort fully. Use many senses; use many examples; look for similarities and differences with things you already know. Try to personalize the information. Remember, the brain likes to make patterns. If new learning can be associated with a pattern from previous learning, chances are it will be remembered easier.

Do you recall that in the introduction I recommended that you use color, change location, take breaks, and use graphic organizers when you read? Each of these strategies helps you to encode the information in your brain in a way to make it easier to retrieve. In order to engage in elaborate encoding, you must be paying attention.

Activate Attention

Attention is so important to strong memories that I want to define it here. In 1890, William James, an eminent American psychologist, wrote this classic definition:

Everyone knows what attention is. It is the taking possession by the mind, in clear and vivid form, of one out of what seem several simultaneously possible objects or trains of thought... It implies withdrawal from some things in order to deal effectively with others, and is a condition which has a real opposite in the confused, dazed, scatterbrained state which in French is called distraction... [16]

As the definition states, you need to select one thing from "several simultaneously possible objects". Attention is the action involved in focusing on the one thing you think is important and withdrawing from, or not being distracted by, things that are not. That sounds easy, but it is not. At every moment, there are many possible distractions surrounding you and everyone else, even in a classroom where a teacher is trying to focus your attention. The bottom line is that if you want to improve your memory then you need to pay attention and focus on what is important. Avoid distractions. Use strategies to encode the information and make it "memorable" using as many senses as possible. Also, try to use novelty to keep the memory clues interesting.

Summary

In this chapter, you explored one of the most important abilities of the brain—the ability to remember. You know that the answer to the question, "what is memory?" is complex. It can be answered in several ways including the following: 1. Memory is the connection among neurons. 2. Memory is the mental ability to encode, store, and retrieve information, and 3. Memory is evidence that you have learned something, because you cannot say you learned something if you cannot remember it.

In this chapter, you learned about sensory/immediate memories, working memories, and long-term memories. You learned about the three processes involved in memory formation: encoding, storing, and retrieving. You learned about the different kinds of memory and the multiple pathways for a long-term memory to travel. You learned that different kinds of memories are stored in different places within your brain. Most importantly, you learned that you can improve your memory if you do two things. First, pay attention! Second, powerfully and elaborately encode data that is important and you want to remember.

As the years go by, there will be much more scientific information about memory. According to Dr. Dean Buonomano in his book <u>Brain Bugs</u>, the quest to learn about memory storage in the brain is "one of the holy grails of neuroscience.[17] Use what you know now, and pay attention to future breakthroughs to keep making your memory sharper.

Questions for Reflection

1. **HEAD**: What did you learn? Imagine that you belong to a Book Club that is reading this book. Summarize the key points that you want to highlight during discussion.
2. **HEART**: How do you feel about what you learned?
3. **ACTION STEP**: What are you going to do now? Suggestions: learn more about the topic; share what you learned, or practice what you learned.

Part 1 is now complete. I am hopeful that you have a better understanding of how your brain works than when you started. This knowledge will help you as you acquire knowledge, skills, and dispositions for training your brain. Let's begin Part 2: Train Your Brain.

CHAPTER 5

Common-Sense Thinking

Thinking is the business of the brain.
— Frank Smith

Common-sense thinking is basic human thinking. It is how your brain works naturally. You are born with it; it's in your genes. Your brain is hard-wired with this skill. No training is needed. If you never learned to read or write, you would still think. Webster's dictionary defines common-sense as "sound practical judgment that is independent of specialized knowledge, training, or the like; normal native intelligence." It is so natural and intuitive that you aren't aware that you are thinking. It usually leads to accurate and appropriate decisions and actions. In the history of the world, man has survived and thrived using basic, everyday thinking—common-sense thinking. However, it is no longer enough.

There is growing evidence that common-sense thinking itself is prone to errors! Until the 1970s, social scientists accepted two assumptions about human nature: 1. People are basically rational and most decisions they make are sound, and 2. When people act irrationally, it is usually because of emotions like affection, fear, and hatred. Since the 1970's, the fields of behavioral, social, and cognitive psychology and of behavioral economics have challenged these assumptions. The evidence shows that because of natural, inborn cognitive biases, the human brain automatically and unconsciously makes predictable mental errors while making decisions.[1] As a result of these errors, your brain behaves illogically and irrationally, and you do not know it. This disturbing finding requires action!

If the errors are predictable and identifiable, then you can learn to recognize them. Once you know about brain biases and the traps that trick your brain, you can avoid them, or use an intervention that limits the damage that mental errors and bad decisions cause. That's the point of this chapter. It will help you learn to avoid the predictable errors that are made by common-sense thinkers. That will help to make you a more skillful thinker.

Brain Bugs

The flaws with common-sense thinking stem from two attributes of your brain: 1. its design and 2. its function. As you know, your brain's design, its physical structure, frequently gives control to Miss Amy G and your limbic system to ensure your survival. You also know that its function is to survey data to find patterns among the millions of bits of information it receives, so you can make sense of your world. In both matters of design and function, your brain works fast and often at an unconscious level. However, you probably didn't know until now that your brain makes predictable mistakes that can be avoided.

Two recently published books, <u>Brain Bugs</u> and <u>Thinking, Fast and Slow</u>, do a great job identifying the limitations of common-sense thinking. If you learn about the limitations, then you can take steps to avoid them. Dr. Dean Buonomano, a professor of neurobiology and psychology at UCLA, calls these flaws "brain bugs". In his book, Dr. Buonomano defines the "bugs" as the limitations, biases, and flaws of human thinking. He asks an important question:

... to what extent is the neural operating system established by evolution well-tuned for the digital, predator-free, sugar abundant, special-effects-filled, antibiotic-laden, media-saturated, densely populated world we have managed to build for ourselves?

The answer to that question is that the design of the human brain is not well tuned for the 21st century! It is built on the same platform used by cavemen. New parts are put on top of old parts, and although it has developed considerably, the operating instructions remain the same: start at the brain stem. As a result, you are often *"blissfully unaware of the arbitrary and irrational factors that govern our decisions and behaviors"*.[2] You cannot change the operating system, but you can upgrade it. You can improve the quality of your thinking by recognizing and controlling your brain bugs. Dr. Buonomano considers the effort to explore cognitive limitations and mental blind spots to be part of your quest for self-knowledge.

Thinking Fast and Thinking Slow

How do you control a brain bug? The answer is being revealed gradually. Nevertheless, the answers are coming. Dr. Daniel Kahneman is one of the leaders in this area. He specializes in the psychology of judgment and decision making. His work had a huge impact on the field of behavioral economics, which led to his winning the Nobel Prize in Economics in 2002. In his book, <u>Thinking, Fast and Slow</u> he explains what is happening within your brain as you make decisions. As the title of his books states, sometimes your brain works fast and sometimes it works slowly (relatively speaking).

Meet System 1 and System 2

Dr. Kahneman explains that these two brain systems are like separate characters which have distinctive personalities and thinking styles. They are like separate fictitious characters in a novel. He gave them names. He calls the fast system, System 1, and he calls the slow system, System 2. This idea is brilliant because it simplifies complex ideas. For that reason, I'll continue to use these terms, so you will continue to meet System 1 and System 2 in the rest of this book. Let's examine the following chart and compare them using some of his criteria for distinguishing them from each other.[3]

SYSTEM 1 THINKING: FAST	SYSTEM 2 THINKING: SLOW
Unconscious and Subconscious levels.	Conscious level only.
Involuntary; Automatic	Voluntary; Effortful
Always ON	Lazy: on when activated
Starting point: Most thinking originates here	Ending point; Takes over when things get hard.
Intuition guides decisions	Logic guides decisions
Emotional: Feelings; impulsive choices & judgments	Rational: deliberate choices & judgments made here
Impulsive	Self-control
Rushes to judgment	Slow to judgment
Main tasks: survival and self-protection	Main tasks: complex thinking
Errors are common	Error detection

Interestingly, the System 2 characteristics represent the view that most people have about their brain activity. They think that their conscious, rational self is playing the lead acting role in their lives. You now know that it is not true. System 1 is where Miss Amy G Dala resides. System 2 has a big role to play, but System 1 will always have the lead.

Common Sense Brain Errors

This chapter will cover three categories of common errors that result from the way your brain works: 1. Jumping to conclusions; 2. Taking shortcuts, and 3. Poor brain habits. Most of the examples that I use come from the books <u>Thinking Fast and Slow</u> and <u>Brain Bugs</u>. As you read the examples of common errors, ask yourself, "Have I made that error"? Write down the errors that you think you make, so you can do more research on those areas to help you correct yourself. You are on a quest for self-knowledge. You want to identify your weak points and try to improve them, so you can think more skillfully. This chapter also includes information about the dangers of another brain habit— overconfidence, and the dangers to decision-making that are inherent in a business tool— neuromarketing.

Jumping to Conclusions

System 1 loves to make leaps and jump to conclusions.[4] It uses fast thinking, intuition, and first impressions to make judgments, predictions, and decisions. It usually does this with limited information, because it is not really concerned with the quantity or quality of the information. It is actually easier for your brain to make a decision when information is scarce. That's because first impressions and the patterns that come to mind easily can create a consistent and easy-to-believe story. System 1 is not concerned with ambiguity or doubt. Your brain has a natural bias to believe and confirm what it is told. It is focused on finding patterns. The trigger for the jump to a conclusion can be as simple as how something is worded. The wording triggers the memory of an existing pattern and the brain leaps to make a connection to it. Let's examine two types of brain bugs that help you make decisions (not necessarily good ones) without effort: framing and priming.

Framing

The way something is worded or "framed" can impact the way you think about an issue. Like a work of art, the frame can make all the difference in how people respond emotionally to the work. With framing, decision-making is based on emotional responses.[5] Consider this. How would your decision be affected if you needed an operation and your doctor said, "The odds of surviving this surgery are 90%"? Compare it to how you would feel if she said, "The chances of dying from this surgery are 10%". Again, it's the same information, but it was framed differently. Would it affect how you would feel about having the operation? It might.

Based on your emotional reaction to the framing as stated in the second choice, you might jump to a conclusion and say, "I'm not having the surgery because it's too dangerous; 10% of the people who have it die." Rather than seeking additional information, you jumped to a conclusion on the basis of how the framing made you feel. It could be the wrong decision! Since the power of the "frame" can influence decisions, you need to be pay attention to the framing when a decision is important.

The Priming Effect

Answer the following question quickly. "What do cows drink?" What was your answer? If it was milk, then you join a large group of people who give that answer spontaneously and then laugh at its absurdity. Why is the answer frequently milk? The brain was primed! The two words, cows and drink, caused an automatic, unconscious, pattern-seeking activity in your brain that led to the word "milk" in your memory. Priming is an activity that triggers the powerful "association", pattern-making ability within your brain. Because making associations is such a core brain activity, it has been studied and measured extensively. Scientists have evidence that priming truly has an effect on your behavior. Unfortunately, they have also learned that it is responsible for many mental errors. There are many examples to show that priming works — for better or worse. I'll describe three: word fragments, question and answer, and experiments conducted specifically to prime behavior.[6]

1. Word Fragment.

Look at this word fragment. SO__P. Does one word come to mind immediately? It may or may not. However, if you see the word EAT before you see this word fragment, then you are more likely to fill in the blank with a U, so the word reads SOUP. If you see the word WASH first, you are more likely to fill in the blank with an A, so the word reads SOAP. That's priming.

2. Q & A: Read each of the following questions and answer them fast.

- On what continent is Kenya?
- What are the two opposing colors in the game of chess?
- Name an animal.

What animal did you think of? Did you think "zebra"? Many people do. Again, your brain is busy forming patterns and making associations. The questions themselves and the ordering of the questions primed your brain to associate the information in that way.

3. Experiment to prime behavior: The Florida Effect

The Florida Effect

The point of this experiment is to demonstrate that your actions and emotions can be primed in ways you would never imagine, and you have absolutely no awareness that it is happening. Dr. John Bargh, a psychologist, conducted the following experiment with college students at New York University. All of the students thought they were involved in a test of language skills. Each one received lists of scrambled words. There were five scrambled words in a group, and the students had to make sentences using four of the words. For example, if the five words were —finds, he, it, yellow, instantly—then the sentence might be: "He finds it instantly". For some student groups in this experiment, half of the lists of scrambled words contained language associated with the elderly like wrinkles, grey, Florida, forgetful, and bald. However, the word "old" was never used. For the control groups, there were no words associated with elderly people.

After participants finished the task of using the words to make sentences, they were told to go down the hall to participate in a second experiment. The students were completely unaware that the real point of the first experiment was to measure the time it took for them to walk from one end of the hall to the other. Since you know this experiment is about priming, what do you predict will happen?

The students who were given words that are associated with the elderly walked significantly more slowly than the other students. They really did! What happened here? First, as to be expected, the words primed thoughts and images of old age. Second, the thoughts primed a behavior—slower walking which is associated with old age! This classic study is named "The Florida Effect". After the experiment, the students were questioned, and none of them reported noticing the elderly theme. They had no idea that words created an idea that influenced an action. Psychologists call this the "ideomotor" effect.[7]

If simple exposure to words can produce thoughts that influence behavior, then Dr. Buonomano believes that lends some support to self-help books promoting positive thinking and positive attitudes. Priming is a very interesting area! On the negative side, these examples should frighten you. If your brain is in lazy mode and just wants to take the easy route to a decision, and if you are not paying attention, then you could be "framed" or "primed" to make decisions or take actions that may not beneficial to you. Does the idea that you can be influenced so easily make you uncomfortable? I hope so. That's the purpose of this book—to teach you about your brain, so you can think more skillfully.

Taking Shortcuts

System 1 likes shortcuts. Remember, it is always seeking patterns and trying to make sense of the world. It tries to simplify complex tasks, so you can make a decision. The shortcuts may be helpful, but they can lead to serious errors. Although most people use these shortcuts, they are not aware they are using them. In addition, they are not aware of the weaknesses attached to the shortcuts. Dr. Kahneman describes three major categories of shortcuts, or rules of thumb, that people use when they are making predictions: 1. Similarity, 2. Availability, and 3. Anchoring.

Similarity

When you need to make a decision, your brain frequently uses the similarity shortcut. As it seeks patterns, it finds resemblances to what you already know. As a result, it intuitively selects the first answer that comes to mind based on its similarity to the brain patterns you have already developed. Here is an example. Read the following description from Thinking Fast and Slow, and answer the question about it.

Steve is very shy and withdrawn, invariably helpful but with little interest in people or in the world of reality. A meek and tidy soul, he has a need for order and structure, and a passion for detail.

Is Steve more likely to be a librarian or a farmer? Based on the description of Steve, what do you think his occupation is? What does the data suggest? Most people quickly see resemblances between the description of Steve and the stereotype of a librarian. Some of the descriptive words become cues, or connections, that trigger System 1 to find patterns and leap to a decision. Therefore, using the similarity rule of thumb, many people would predict that it is more probable that Steve is a librarian than a farmer. Actually, there is a pretty good chance that this is incorrect. Why?

Think about statistics for a moment. In the general population, are there more male librarians or male farmers? You may not know it, but there are more than 20 male farmers to every male librarian. If you thought about numbers at all, you would probably figure out that there are more male farmers. Therefore, since Steve was selected from a representative group of all men, then it is more likely that Steve is a farmer. In taking the shortcut, people don't think about numbers; they use the cues in the data for resemblance and similarity. Dr. Kahneman calls this "base-rate neglect". In the end, when you take this similarity shortcut, your predictions are likely to be wrong.[8]

What could you do to prevent mistakes? Take a moment to activate System 2. Talk to yourself. Self-talk is valuable. Now that you know that similarity causes errors, you might say, "I see similarities, but am I leaping? Am I ignoring some basic facts here, especially numbers? What do I already know about men's occupations?" You might catch your error.

The Role of Availability in Predictions

"Availability" means how easily some ideas can be brought to mind. Let's start with an example from a study that asks the following question: Which is a more frequent cause of death: 1. Death by accidents or 2. Death by strokes? Which did you select? The majority of the people in the study selected accidents. Is the majority correct? No. Strokes kill twice as many people as all accidents combined. However, 80% of the people in the study picked accidents as the most frequent cause of death. Why were so many people incorrect? Basically, it comes down to where you get the information for your decision. Did you investigate before answering? If you did, then you would have answered strokes. However, research on decision-making finds that most people make predictions based on how easily examples came to their mind. That's the meaning of "availability" in this context.

Information comes easily to mind when you are informed about it over and over again. Remember, that's how mental models or perceptions are formed. The "availability" of information may come from your own experiences. If you thought the answer to the above question was accidents, then you may know several people who were killed in accidents and none who died from stroke. More than likely, your knowledge came from the most common sources of information for many people today— media in its many forms: television, radio, computers, and an assortment of hand-held technology devices. The media provides heavy coverage of accidents, but few stories about strokes unless a person who is very famous dies from a stroke. Remember, your brain likes novelty and excitement, and the media tries to provide it. However, it is not necessarily a fair representation of what is really happening. There is a danger in using availability in making predictions, and it is expressed well in the following statement by Dr. Kahneman:

The world in our heads is not a precise replica of reality; our expectations about the frequency of events are distorted by the prevalence and emotional intensity of the messages to which we are exposed. [9]

In taking the availability shortcut, people leap to a conclusion based on their perception of reality. Perceptions determine how readily information comes to mind, and you know that your perceptions are not always reliable. In the end, if you rely on "availability", then the predictions you make are likely to be wrong. What can you do to prevent mistakes? Pause. Wake up system 2 and ask yourself several questions: "Where does my information on this topic come from? Is it reliable? Do I have enough information? "Am I leaping?" Should I conduct some research before responding? You may catch your error.

The Role of Anchoring

An "anchor" is simply a random number that is used as a starting point to guide the thinking process. It is an uninformative number that may or may not be true; it may or may not be relevant, and it may or may not be helpful. In the first experiment, you will learn how anchors can effectively influence your thinking whether they make sense or not. In the second experiment, you will see how anchoring influenced how people spend money.[10]

Nonsense Numbers as Anchors

Two groups participated in the first experiment. Each group was asked the same two questions about redwood trees; however, the "anchor" was different in each group.

- Group 1 questions and anchor:

a. Is the height of the tallest redwood more or less than **1,200 feet**?

b. What is your best guess about the height of the tallest redwood tree?

• Group 2 questions and anchor.

a. Is the height of the tallest redwood more or less than **180 feet**?

b. What is your best guess about the height of the tallest redwood tree?

As you can see, the anchor for group one was 1,200 feet and for group two it was 180 feet. The difference between the two anchors is 1,020 feet (1,200 – 180). That is a huge difference. Is one of the anchors way off in its measurement? Of course it is. Do you have any idea which one? If you don't have any idea, then you would probably use the anchor you were given as a starting point. That's what most people do. They do it even if the anchor is absurd, as one of the numbers above is. An anchor does not have to make sense. I am sure that you don't want to believe that you could be influenced by an absurd anchor, but it is true. If you have no knowledge about a question, then your thinking is influenced by any random, uninformative anchor—- if you let it! Once you learn about anchors, it becomes more difficult to fool you.

Let's look at the results of this experiment. The participants who were given 1,200 feet as an anchor had an average estimate of 844 feet as the tallest redwood. The participants who were given 180 feet as an anchor had an average estimate of 282 feet. As you read these numbers, you can see the reliance on the anchor as a guide to making the prediction. Even though each group made adjustments to the anchor, the estimates stayed in the neighborhood of the anchor. As Dr. Kahneman states:

...one of the most reliable and robust results of experimental psychology: the estimates stay close to the number people considered—hence the image of an anchor.

What is the actual height of the tallest redwood tree? It's about 370 feet. That's almost 60 feet taller than the Statue of Liberty from the bottom of her foundation to the top of her torch. Can you now visualize the size of the tallest redwood? Knowing the facts, consider a 1,200 foot tree. That would be absurd. How about an 844 foot tree? It's also absurd. However, regardless of the absurdity, the anchor number was powerful in influencing the thinking of the participants.

Anchoring demonstrates how gullible people can be. Opportunities to take advantage of gullibility are everywhere. Is it ever appropriate for you to use an anchor to make a decision? If a question or issue is not important to you, then it is all right to use the anchor to guesstimate. However, if the issue is important to you, then beware of the anchor. What can you do to prevent mistakes? Be aware of the power that uninformative numbers have. Don't rush; slow down. Activate System 2 when you see an anchor so you can think rationally about the situation. You may need to do a little research.

Pocketbook Effect of Anchors

This example of anchoring demonstrates how it can affect your pocketbook. If you are involved in fundraising, you may be interested to know that anchoring may be a way to make people donate more money. An anchoring study in California focused on raising money for an environmental cause. The study prepared three different questions about making a donation to protect the environment. Visitors to an Exploratorium were randomly asked one of the three questions. The questions were similar to these three:

1. Would you be willing to donate $5 to save 50,000 off-shore Pacific Coast seabirds from small offshore oil spills, until ways are found to prevent spills or require tanker owners to pay for the operation? How much will you contribute?
2. Would you be willing to donate $400 to save 50,000 off-shore Pacific Coast seabirds from small offshore oil spills, until ways are found to prevent spills or require tanker owners to pay for the operation? How much will you contribute?
3. Would you be willing to donate to save 50,000 off-shore Pacific Coast seabirds from small offshore oil spills, until ways are found to prevent

spills or require tanker owners to pay for the operation? How much will you contribute?

The donation given by each visitor was expected to match the intensity of their feelings for the cause. However, the questions themselves actually influenced the amount donated. Questions one and two were anchoring questions with a pre-set, recommended number for a donation. Question three was open-ended with no anchor. The results provide valuable information for fundraisers. When question 1, with an anchor of $5, was asked, the average donation was $20. When question 2, with an anchor of $400, was asked, the average donation was $143. When question 3, with no anchor was asked, the average donation was $64. As you can see, a low anchor hindered the fundraising effort and a high anchor helped it. Anchors can have a powerful effect on your decision-making. What is the message here? Be skeptical when you see anchors. They are put there for a reason.

Poor Brain Habits

Becoming aware of poor brain habits is the first step in trying to break them. They include mental laziness, the inability to delay gratification, not paying attention to important things, and overconfidence. You now know that System 2, your thinking brain, prefers not to exert too much effort. Your brain often follows the "law of least effort"[11], so the first example involves mental laziness.

The Cognitive Reflection Test, created by Dr. Shane Frederick of MIT, provides a good example of the brain's basic laziness. The test itself consists of three questions. I'll only use the first to make this point. Read the following problem and then answer the question.

The Bat & Ball problem[12]

- A bat and ball cost $1.10.
- The bat costs one dollar more than the ball.

Question: How much does the ball cost?

This seems to be an easy problem. More than 50% of the students at Harvard, MIT and Princeton and more than 80% of students at less selective schools who participated in the test gave the same answer — $ .10. That's interesting, since the correct answer is $ .05. Don't be embarrassed if you answered incorrectly, because as you just read, you are in good company. Most students gave the intuitive, fast, and lazy answer, and they did not check their work.

Let's look at the problem. If the answer is 10 cents, as the majority thought, then it is assumed that the bat cost $1. However, look at the second sentence in the problem: "The bat costs one dollar more than the ball." Using that information complicates things, because if the bat costs $1 and the ball costs 10 cents, then the bat is only 90 cents more than the ball—not $1 more. Therefore, 10 cents cannot be correct. The answer is 5 cents. The ball is $ .05 and the bat is $1.05. The bat costs one dollar more than the ball: $1.05 - $.05 = $1.00.

In a follow-up, Dr. Frederick studied the characteristics of the people who took the test. People with low scores were more likely to be leapers. They didn't take the time to check their answers. They jumped to a conclusion. The characteristics of these people include the following: impulsive, impatient, and unable to delay gratification. They sound like System 1 thinkers and friends of Miss Amy G. As you can probably guess, the people with high scores were more deliberate, patient, and able to delay gratification. They sound more like System 2 thinkers.

Immediate Gratification

The ability to delay gratification is an important brain habit, but it's a challenge for most people. Why? Your brain does not like to delay gratification; it has a bias toward immediate gratification. Here is an example. If someone offered you a choice of $100 today or $120 one month from now, which would you choose? Receiving an additional $20 for waiting one month would be a wise economic decision. Would you be surprised to find out that most people in a study took the $100 immediately? This human bias for immediate gratification is called "temporal discounting". The value of a reward decreases with time. This trait is hardwired into human brains because thousands of years ago, food was scarce, survival was a challenge, and life was short. As a result, people did not have an innate tendency to plan for the future.

What would happen if the offer above was tweaked a little? The choice now becomes receiving $100 in 12 months or $120 in 13 months. The majority of the people in the study are now willing to wait the extra month! When the reward is not immediate, people can become more patient. Immediate rewards are exciting and pleasurable, so people do not want to wait. One person could display the trait of patience and another of impulsivity in their regular behavior, but when faced with an immediate reward, both brains are rigged to seek immediate gratification.[13] This brain bug can impede your ability to make intelligent long-term decisions. The focus on long-term planning needs to be developed through culture and education.

Not Paying Attention to Important Things

You know how important it is to pay attention. However, did you realize that you could pay too much attention to one thing and miss something important altogether? When a person is focused intensely on an activity or job, he can become effectively blind to things going on around him to which he would normally pay attention. Just think about someone playing a video game. That person is frequently zoned out to everything else in his environment. However, even knowing that this happens, I was surprised by the results of the following experiment.

The Gorilla Study

Two researchers made a short film about two teams passing basketballs back-and-forth across a court. One team wore white shirts and one team wore black shirts. Participants in the experiment simply observed the action. They were told to count the number of passes that the team wearing white shirts made and to ignore the team wearing black shirts. Each participant had to focus intently, since the action was fast. Here's the fun part. In the middle of the video, a woman appears wearing a gorilla suit. She crosses the court and for nine seconds, she thumps her chest, acting like a gorilla. When the experiment ended, about half of the participants said that they never saw a gorilla!

In fact, some insisted that they needed to see the film, because they could not believe a chest-thumping gorilla was really there. They were shocked when they saw the film. What happened? What made the gorilla invisible? The instruction to ignore the black shirted team and to focus on the passes made by the white-shirted team caused a form of "mental blindness". No one who watches the film without the instructions misses the gorilla. What does this experiment show? As Dr. Kahneman states:

The gorilla study illustrates two important facts about our minds: we can be blind to the obvious, and we are also blind to our blindness. [14]

Think about this. It is a very important point. With your human perception, something can be right in front of your eyes, and you can miss it. What is the point? To avoid errors in judgment or decision making, you need to be aware of the kinds of issues swirling around you, and pay attention to the important ones. You don't want to make errors because you were so busy focused on something that was relatively unimportant that you missed something important.

Overconfidence

The final category of errors stems from your brain's excessive confidence in what it thinks it knows. Using the processes of your brain, you developed perceptions of the world that you believe are true. According to Dr. Kahneman, humans beings believe they know more than they know, and they have difficulty acknowledging how ignorant and uncertain they are about the world.[15]

One of the signs of wisdom is admitting you do not have all the answers. A wise person has a tolerance for ambiguity and an appreciation for uncertainty. However, many people find it hard to deal with ambiguity and uncertainty. It is especially difficult for people who are considered experts in their field. One of the major problems with overconfidence is that it can seriously interfere with further learning.

In 1991, Dr. Chris Argyris wrote the article, "Teaching Smart People How to Learn", which focused on the inability of many experts to deal with failure.[16] Argyris explained that people who are professionals live with the assumption that "I am an expert. I do not make mistakes; therefore, I cannot fail". These people are stuck on side A of the following chart.

LEARNING TO LEARN: AVOIDING EMOTIONAL TRAPS	
Side A: EMOTION Inhibits learning	Side B: LOGIC Facilitates learning
Thinks Win/Lose; Thinks "Us versus Them"	Thinks Win/Win; Thinks "We"
Resists Change	Facilitates Change
Unwilling to suspend assumptions	Willing to suspend assumptions
Seeks solution that fits own worldview	Seeks best solution
Seldom fails; Cannot deal with failure; Learning does not take place	Accepts failure; Admits mistakes; Learning takes place
Defensive; places blame	Recognizes that he/she may be part of the problem.

Since smart people are usually successful, they have not developed brain pathways for dealing with lack of success. They think they are always right, so they cling to old assumptions, and they remain stuck in old ways of thinking. Rather than admit mistakes, they engage in "defensive reasoning". They look for blame outside of themselves. As a result, they live in an emotional trap and they don't know it. Since awareness is the first step in any change effort, "experts" need to become aware that they may have a problem. Experts need to realize that when they automatically avoid personal criticism and blame outside factors for failure, their unconscious, automatic, emotional brain is making decisions. Once they become aware of this, they need to learn how to learn again. They can reflect on the factors in side A that inhibit learning, and they can take action to change their behaviors to the factors on side B which promote learning.

Before leaving the topic of common brain errors, I want you to be aware of an emerging field of study, neuromarketing. Without your awareness, it is influencing you and affecting your pocketbook and maybe your vote.

Power of Neuromarketing

On the positive side, brain science is making it easier for many fields of study to act on scientific findings rather than guesswork or intuition. Neuromarketing, a field of study that links neuroscience and marketing, is benefiting greatly. On the negative side, neuromarketing uses knowledge about the associative architecture of the human brain to make it easier for advertisers to target you.[17] Using brain imaging and brain scanning technologies like fMRI (functional magnetic resonance imaging) and EEG (electroencephalography), neuromarketing researchers can identify which part of a consumer's brain is reacting to ads, brands, products, and even political candidates. What they are seeing is a brain at work making associations and searching for patterns that make sense, make it happy, or even entertain it. Remember, the brain loves novelty.

Neuromarketing researchers also use devices to measure physical changes in a body like respiration, heart rate, and sweating which can record both conscious and unconscious responses of consumers. This helps the researchers learn why people think, act, vote, and buy as they do. Neuromarketers are then able to identify what people want and predict what they will buy or for whom they will vote. As a result, marketing messages can be targeted to specific groups. If you fit the group they are targeting, then you are susceptible to their advertising messages. Their objective is to persuade you to take action—the action they want you to take. This sounds a bit sinister, but it is nothing new.

Vance Packard wrote a book in 1957, <u>The Hidden Persuaders</u>. In the 1950's, there were no technology tools to study the human brain and its preferences, so information was gathered by talking with people and observing them. Nevertheless, the research was able to reveal subconscious yearnings and cravings that marketing research people identified as "hidden needs". Marketing though advertising, commercials, and slogans then targeted these "needs". Packard wrote:

This book is an attempt to explore a strange and rather exotic new area of American life. It is about the large-scale efforts being made, often with impressive success, to channel our unthinking habits, our purchasing decisions, and our thought processes....Typically these efforts take place beneath our level of awareness; so that the appeals which move us are often, in a sense, "hidden". The result is that many of us are being influenced and manipulated far more than we realize, in the patterns of our everyday lives. [18]

Imagine, this powerful statement was written more than fifty years ago. If strategies in the 1950s were effective in figuring out how to manipulate people's thinking, then what will the tools of the 21st century be able to do? You need to know that there are modern hidden persuaders who aim to influence your thoughts and your behavior. After reading this chapter, you now know how easy it is for them to succeed. Can you guess which part of your brain neuromarketing tries to target? Of course you know it by now. It's your emotional center and your fear center—Miss Amy G, your amygdala. The good news is that by learning how your brain works and what its limitations are, you are preparing a very strong defense. You are ready to prevent outside influences from hijacking your thinking brain. You are educating yourself to be a strong and skillful thinker.

Brain Bugs Beware

As you have been learning about the limitations of common sense thinking, your brain has been rewiring and forming new connections. It is learning about brain shortcuts and biases. It is forming patterns that can recognize some of the signals that announce when brain bugs are nearby. It is on alert to the hidden power of organizational and marketing manipulation. However your brain needs one more thing. It needs you at your conscious best. Make sure that when a decision counts, when something important is happening, that your System 2, you conscious thinking brain is awake. Pay attention to important things! Just as you use self-knowledge about your body to recognize when you have the symptoms of the common cold and take action to cure it (more rest, more liquids, more hand washing, chicken soup, etc.), you can now use self- knowledge about your brain to recognize brain bugs and avoid them. Use the following checklist.

Three Part Checklist for Recognizing Brain Flaws and Cognitive Biases

The following checklist will help you block errors that originate in System 1.

Part 1. Actively look for the signs that you are in a "cognitive minefield".
Do you see signs for:

A. Jumping to Conclusions:

- Framing: using and arranging words deliberately for a purpose; words used to "frame" an issue to trigger a planned response or behavior.
- Priming: deliberately linking two or more words to make an association that triggers a planned response or behavior.

B. Taking Shortcuts

- Similarity: using something familiar as representative of something else.
- Availability: how fast an idea comes to mind.
- Anchoring: using uninformative numbers as a starting point.

C. Poor brain habits

- Mental Laziness
- Inability to delay gratification

- Impulsivity
- Easily distracted; not paying attention to important things
- Overconfidence

D. Neuromarketing

- Persuasive advertising in media and on products targeting your emotions and fears

If you see any of these signs, take mental action! Wake up System 2.

Part 2. Conduct a self-assessment. How do you feel?

A. Do you experience Cognitive Ease? Ask yourself the following questions:

- Am I too comfortable with the information?
- Does it feel familiar, true, good, or effortless?
- Am I biased in its favor?
- Am I being too casual or superficial in my thinking?

B. Do you experience Cognitive Strain?

- Do you feel suspicious?
- Do you feel uncomfortable?

If the answer is yes to any of these questions, then take action! Wake up System 2.

Part 3. ROUTINE MENTAL ACTION

- Slow down!
- Ask for reinforcement from System 2. Wake up your conscious brain!
- Delay immediate gratification.
- Do not be easily distracted.
- Pay attention to important things.
- Exercise humility and recognize that you can make mistakes.
- **Follow a 5-step routine:**

1. Clarify the problem to be solved.
2. Collect the relevant information.

3. Reflect.
4. Review.
5. Decide what to believe or do.

Power of the Unconscious Mind

You have learned that your unconscious brain uses shortcuts that can be valuable as well as problematic. It is like a secret partner that you didn't know you had. You couldn't live without this partner, but like most partnerships, there are strengths and weaknesses. I have been pointing out weaknesses, and now that you are aware of them, you can be alert to spot them. With your conscious effort, you can avoid these weaknesses and improve the power of your thinking.

However, before leaving this chapter, I want to emphasize an important point: no one could survive without the power of the human brain working at an unconscious level. Although I am pointing out limitations of the unconscious brain as you engage in common-sense thinking, I do not want to diminish the importance of unconscious thinking. Your intuitive System 1 is more influential in your judgments and decisions than most people realize.

In his book Brainwork, Dr. Sousa explains the value of delaying important decisions in order to allow the information you gather to "percolate" in your unconscious.[19] Remember, your brain has a powerful memory system and much of it is retained at the unconscious level. If you provide the time, your unconscious brain will explore your memory system for experiences related to the issue at hand. According to Dr. Sousa, some studies found that by engaging both your conscious and unconscious thought processes, you increase your chances of reaching the best decisions.

Summary

In this chapter you learned that your everyday thinking system, common sense thinking, develops naturally and is remarkable. However, it has limitations that impact the quality of your judgment. You learned that there are distinctive patterns in the mental errors that people make. Therefore, you can learn to identify them and make conscious interventions to improve your decisions and judgments. You learned about three categories of limitations: 1. Jumping to conclusions with limited information based on the wording used when "framing" and "priming" a problem; 2. Taking shortcuts while making predictions when you experience the cues used in "similarity", "availability", and "anchoring" 3. Poor brain habits characterized by mental laziness; the inability to delay gratification, not paying enough information to important things, and overconfidence. You also learned how your brain can be manipulated through neuromarketing. When you combine this knowledge about your brain's limitations with your knowledge about how your brain works, you have with a very strong foundation for Mega-Thinking.

In the following chapters in this section, "Train Your Brain", you will learn some mental tools that will help you to specialize your thinking. There are no mysteries in the rest of this book. All the skills and strategies presented are conscious mental tools that you can choose to use—or not. Basically, I have selected a handful of tools in each thinking category. You may choose to delve more deeply into an individual category of thinking skills to deepen your understanding and to acquire additional thinking tools for that category. The only "unconscious" factors you face for the rest of this book are your personal will, drive, determination, and effort to learn some skills and become a Mega-Thinker.

Questions for Reflection

1. **HEAD**: What did you learn? Imagine that you belong to a Book Club that is reading this book. Summarize the key points that you want to highlight during discussion.
2. **HEART**: How do you feel about what you learned?
3. **ACTION STEP**: What are you going to do now? Suggestions: learn more about the topic; share what you learned, or practice what you learned.

CHAPTER 6

Critical Thinking

Critical Thinking is reasonable and reflective thinking that is focused upon deciding what to believe or do.
— Dr. Robert H. Ennis

Are you stumped by the question, "What is critical thinking?". A lot of people are. The quote above is a widely respected and widely used definition that helps to clarify what it is. According to this definition, critical thinking is "reasonable" and it is "reflective". Most importantly, the purpose of critical thinking is to help you decide "what to believe or do". That's why it is essential for you to become a critical thinker. At its core, critical thinking is about ACTION—your personal action.

Don't forget that the action you take is based upon the parts of the brain that you are using. To be a critical thinker, you need to be using your cerebrum. You need to be consciously aware of what you are deciding. System 2 must be awake. Look at the following images to help develop your understanding of critical thinking. These images suggest core aspects of this mental skill.

Components of Critical Thinking

This image represents justice and the courts, where people are expected to suspend their judgment, to remain skeptical, and to be open-minded in their search for truth.

This image represents a detective who is searching for clues, for facts, and evidence. He has an inquiring mind, so he asks many questions including follow-up questions.

This image suggests a jury that will take action and make a decision, but only after the facts and evidence are presented and evaluated. Each of these images represent a brain activity that is required before deciding to take action. Overall, the critical thinking process follows a three-part formula:

Critical Thinking =

Suspended Judgment + Extended Questioning + Evaluation

Getting Started

If the end result of the process of critical thinking is action, then where does the process start? It starts by developing a trained mind, a disciplined mind that supports critical thinking. A disciplined mind uses the critical thinking formula. That means you need to be willing to suspend your judgment and not jump to conclusions. Critical thinking is "reasonable". That means you need to ask lots of questions so your thinking process is using solid facts, reasons, and evidence. Critical thinking is "reflective". That means you need to evaluate all the data and think about the implications and consequences before you decide what to believe or do.

Training Your Brain

Critical Thinking requires you to train your brain to engage in slow thinking. Critical thinking needs conscious and effortful System 2 thinking. In order to be a critical thinker, you need to control Miss Amy G.

You cannot allow the feeling and emotional parts of your brain to control your thinking and your actions. You must get your thinking brain involved and that requires effort. A trained brain needs to learn and to use a set of thinking dispositions and skills in order to examine information in a reasonable, reflective, and focused manner. These dispositions and skills provide "an effective mental attack"[1], so you can make wise and informed decisions for yourself about what to think and do. That's what this chapter is all about—getting you armed with some critical thinking dispositions and skills, some effective weapons, so you can make intelligent decisions about your beliefs and actions. That's what will make you a critical thinker.

Societal Need

Society needs critical thinkers. I believe that one of the problems with attempts to develop critical thinking on a wide societal basis is that there is too much information about it. There are so many books, websites, conferences, and experts on the topic that a person can become overwhelmed trying to figure out the best approach to follow. Another problem is that critical thinking skills have been dissected and fragmented into so many separate pieces that it is hard to know where to start. Therefore, my goal is to simplify a complex topic, so you can start being a critical thinker today. My plan is to provide you with a manageable foundation in critical thinking. That's important, because if you can't manage something, you'll never use it.

Concept Formation

Let's use concept formation to help you develop a manageable foundation. It is a tool that can be used in any discipline to help develop understanding by comparing what something "is" with what it "is not". The following chart should help you wrap your head around the concept of critical thinking and its opposite—uncritical thinking.[2]

Critical thinking is not "critical" in the sense of being negative, finding fault, or expressing disapproval. It is "critical" in the sense of critiquing and carefully evaluating or judging the value or truth of something before you take action on it. It might be easier to explain if it was called "Evaluative Thinking". In order to be able to think and behave like a critical thinker, you need to have a clear picture of the characteristics of critical thinking.

Critical versus Non-Critical Thinking

CRITICAL THINKING	UNCRITICAL THINKING
CONSCIOUS: System 2 Is Awake	UNCONSCIOUS: System 1 Dominates
DISCIPLINED Impulse Control Suspends Judgment Delays Gratification	UNDISCIPLINED Impulsive Jumps To Conclusions Seeks Immediate Gratification
FLEXIBLE	INFLEXIBLE
OBJECTIVE Unbiased	UNOBJECTIVE Biased
CURIOUS	INCURIOUS
REASONABLE	UNREASONABLE
EVALUATIVE	NON-EVALUATIVE
CHALLENGES ASSUMPTIONS	ACCEPTS ASSUMPTIONS
REFLECTIVE	UNREFLECTIVE
FOCUSED	UNFOCUSED
PERSISTENT	NONPERSISTENT
SKILLFUL	UNSKILLFUL
CLEAR	UNCLEAR

Figure 6.1: Concept Formation for Critical Thinking

As you examine the chart, ask yourself if you behave more like a critical thinker or an uncritical thinker. Your goal is to learn to think and behave like a critical thinker. You can see, as you look at the chart, that a critical thinker is a conscious thinker who is disciplined. He manages impulsivity and suspends judgment before deciding what to believe or do. He is flexible, objective, and unbiased. He seeks differing points of view and is willing to examine evidence that conflicts with his world view. He is curious and has a questioning attitude. He seeks evidence for his beliefs, and he evaluates the reasons for his beliefs and actions. He is a reasonable person who looks for and uses reasons in his thinking. He challenges assumptions. He is reflective, thoughtful, and he is not in a rush to judgment. He takes time to think. He is focused and persistent and directs his attention to the issue at hand. He has a trained mind and engages in clear, precise, and logical thinking. The rest of this chapter focuses on five "tools" you can use to reach the goal of becoming a critical thinker.

Critical Thinking Tools

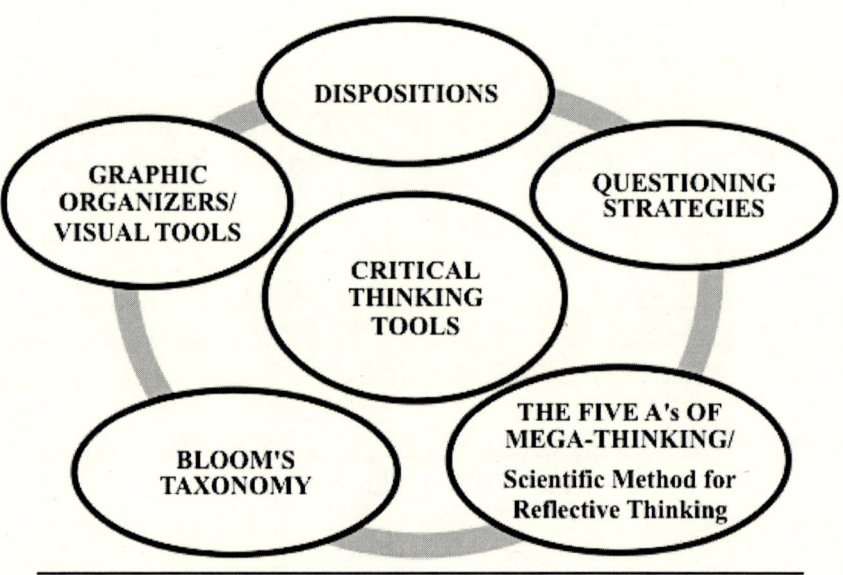

Figure 6.2: Tools for Critical Thinking

As you can see, these are not mysterious tools. You will find that you are familiar with some, if not all, of the tools that I'll review. They fall into five categories: 1. Dispositions; 2. Questioning; 3. The Scientific Method for Reflective Thinking; 4. Bloom's Taxonomy; and 5. Graphic Organizers.

Tool #1. Dispositions

A disposition is a habit, mood, or inclination that describes a person's nature, his temperamental makeup. It's the tendency of a person to act in a certain way. Dispositions are sometimes called "habits of mind". Discovering and Exploring Habits of Mind is the title of a book written by Art Costa and Bena Kallick.[3] In their book, they identify sixteen dispositions that describe intelligent behavior. These are the habits that intelligent people use when they are confronted with problems that do not have easy solutions. Four of these 16 dispositions are essential for critical thinkers: 1. Persisting; 2. Managing Impulsivity; 3. Thinking Flexibly, and 4. Questioning and Problem Posing. Let's examine each of them.

- **Persisting**: keeping at a challenge in spite of obstacles or setbacks; not quitting; sticking to it; staying focused; demonstrating perseverance.
- **Managing Impulsivity**: the ability to delay gratification; think before you act; control Miss Amy G; goal-directed; no leaping allowed.
- **Thinking Flexibly**: consider other opinions, assumptions, and perceptions; generate alternatives; change perspective; be open-minded.
- **Questioning and Problem Posing**: the ability to carry on organized and in-depth inquiry; the ability to ask a range of questions; the courage to ask tough questions and then ask follow-up questions; ability to formulate problem statements.

Dr. John Dewey identified another disposition that is essential for developing critical thinking. He stated, "Knowledge of the methods alone will not suffice; there must be the desire, the will, to employ them".[4] If you value critical thinking, then your WILL and DESIRE will compel you to employ the methods and the skills of a critical thinker. If you do not value the process, then the skills are worthless, because they won't be used. The fact that you reading this book demonstrates that you value skillful thinking in general, and you have the desire and will to improve your critical thinking ability. So far, I described five dispositions which are essential for critical thinkers to possess. If you do not possess these dispositions right now, what can you do to develop them? Engage in self-talk.

Simple Slogans

Many years ago, I read a research study that made me realize that developing critical thinking dispositions does not need to be difficult. In an effort to promote skillful thinking in a classroom with special education students, the researchers in this study focused on the following three negative dispositions that were prevalent in the classroom: non-persistence, impulsiveness, and inflexibility. Since these dispositions impeded skillful thinking in general, teachers needed to change them. They needed to turn these negative dispositions into positive ones—persistence, managing impulsivity, and flexibility. How did they do it? The solution was effective and so simple. The researchers had the teachers use simple sound bites to promote the desired behavior.

- For non-persistence, the sound bite was "Keep at it".
- For impulsiveness, the sound bite was "Take time to think".
- For inflexibility, the sound bite was "Consider Alternatives".

These simple slogans, consistently applied, were effective and made a positive difference in the quality of thinking that went on in the classroom.[5] This study shows that changing negative dispositions into positive ones does not have to be difficult or complicated. If you want to improve your dispositions, then use these slogans, or make up some for yourself, and engage in "self-talk" using simple sound-bites. Remember that your brain likes novelty and likes to have fun, so you can be silly in your slogan choice. It doesn't matter what words you use, as long as you use them to control your negative dispositions.

You could also use mental images. How about a green traffic light when you feel like quitting to remind yourself to keep going and be persistent? What about a red traffic light, or a simple stop sign, to remind yourself to stop being impulsive and to stop and think. Imagine a detour sign when you feel compelled to stay with your opinion. The image may help you to consider alternatives, because your way is probably not the only way in any situation.

Use slogans, images, or self-discipline itself to develop the dispositions essential for critical thinking. What is happening within your brain when you practice using these slogans and images? Your brain is being retrained. You are letting your brain know what is important to you now. As a result, as your brain processes the sensory information, System 2 will be more involved. The connections your neurons make will begin to change as you reshape your brain to meet your new goals. You will be deleting old brain pathways and establishing new pathways. Since dispositions are so important for critical thinking, you should stop here and conduct a self-assessment. Examine the following chart. Ask yourself; to what degree do I possess these dispositions?

Positive Dispositions	YOU										Negative Dispositions
Values Critical Thinking	10	9	8	7	6	5	4	3	2	1	Does not value Critical Thinking
Persistence	10	9	8	7	6	5	4	3	2	1	Non-persistence
Impulse Control	10	9	8	7	6	5	4	3	2	1	Impulsiveness
Flexible Thinking	10	9	8	7	6	5	4	3	2	1	Inflexibility; rigid
Questioning and Problem Posing	10	9	8	7	6	5	4	3	2	1	Limited Range of Questions; Weak Problem Statements

Figure 6.3: Self-assessment Chart for Critical Thinking Dispositions

As you examine the chart, think about how you behave. If you are impulsive, then you leap into action without thinking of consequences. If you lack persistence, then you get tired of examining options or seeking more information, so you may make a quick choice rather than the best choice. If you are inflexible, then your beliefs and actions may be stuck in familiar patterns, and you do not even see options or alternatives. As you can see, if you do not train your brain to develop positive dispositions, then it acts as it wants. A lazy brain is more likely to be impulsive, lack persistence, and be inflexible. When you engage in these negative behaviors you will be thinking; however, it will not be "critical thinking".

Based on your responses, you'll know where you need to put in some effort. If you are closer to the positive side, preferably a seven or higher, then relax, because it will be easier for you to engage in critical thinking. If you are closer to the negative side, then you need to make an effort to change your dispositions. Start simply and use self-talk or mental imaging consistently.

In summary, developing dispositions for critical thinking is the essential first step in becoming a critical thinker. Without them, you cannot function as a critical thinker, because you would not be inclined to suspend judgment, ask questions, and evaluate information. Let's move on to tool number 2— Questioning.

Tool # 2. Questioning Strategies

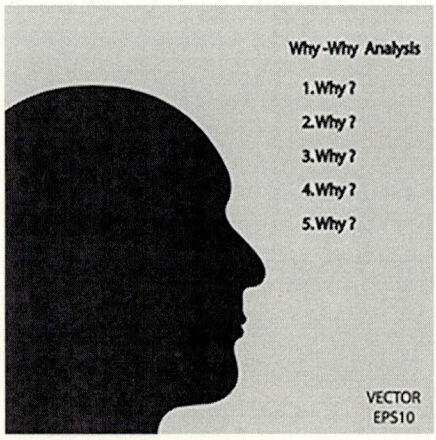

Questioning is not only a disposition but it is also a skill. It is an essential tool for a critical thinker. You need to release your inner inquisitive child when you are seeking information about what to believe or do. You need to be skeptical and critically examine and question the statements made by different people before adopting the ideas of others into your own belief system. Just like a child, you need to start by asking the question, "Why?". What could be simpler? Why start with such a simple question, "Why"? First, it's natural to ask questions. It's a sign of your basic curiosity. Second, simple questions demonstrate that critical thinking does not have to be complicated.

There is actually a questioning strategy named "The 5 Whys".[6] Using this strategy trains you to dig for information and clarification. One "why" usually leads to identifying one obvious event or person as the cause of a problem or as a reason for action. You need to realize that a simple answer to one question is seldom enough for decision making, so do not limit yourself to one "why". Keep asking "why". You are seeking to find the main, root causes for a situation. Five whys is usually sufficient to get the facts you need.

The questions are easy; the hard part is having the guts to ask a question and to keep asking. Follow-up questions are important. You need to dig deep and find the strength to ask questions when you are determining what you should believe and do. You need to act like a detective.

The 5 Ws & the H

There are many sources of questions. Besides "why" alone, another easy source comes from the field of journalism. It is the 5Ws & the H strategy that is pictured above. In an effort to get to the facts and the truth of a story, reporters and detectives ask a series of questions: Who? What? Where? When? Why? and How? In some cases these basic questions may be all you need.

Since you are continually bombarded with opinions like—Vote for this candidate! Buy this car! Eat this food! See this movie! Stop this war!—you can ask questions. *Who* said so? *What* are his credentials? *What* evidence do you have that what he is saying is true? *What* are the facts? *What* are your reasons for believing him? *When* did you hear this? *When* did this happen? *Where* did it happen? *Where* is the evidence? *Why* do you believe it? *Why* is he considered an authority? *How* do you know for sure? *How* can you prove it? The questions do not have to be difficult. They simply need to be asked in order to help you find reasons for believing or for not believing what someone tells you. After questioning, you can then decide whether to believe or do something. However, if you are not satisfied with the answers, then keep searching for additional information before you take any action.

Critical Thinking Questions

There are a variety of sources for questions that specifically develop critical thinking. You can simply Google "questions for critical thinking" and you will find a lot of information. One excellent source for critical thinking questions is Dr. Richard Paul's book, <u>Critical Thinking: What Every Person Needs to Survive in a Rapidly Changing World.</u>[7] Remember, the questions are important, but more important is developing the attitude that you cannot always believe what others tell you. You need to learn to be an independent thinker, and that's not easy to do. Keep at it!

Dr. Paul believes that learning begins when people ask questions, because thinking is the result of questions, not answers. As a result, he developed a useful, six-level taxonomy of Socratic Questions that people can adopt to become more skillful critical thinkers. The taxonomy includes the following six categories of questions: Questions about Clarification; Questions that Probe Assumptions; Questions that Probe Reasons and Evidence; Questions about Viewpoints or Perspectives; Questions that Probe Implications and Consequences, and Questions about the Question. Here are a few examples of each category of questions.

- **Questions of Clarification**
  What do you mean by that? Could you give me an example? Could you put it another way? Let me see if I understand you; do you mean…?
- **Questions That Probe Assumptions**

What are you assuming? You seem to be assuming ____ (name the assumption). Do I understand you correctly?

- **Questions That Probe Reasons and Evidence**
  What are your reasons for saying that? Could you explain your reasons to us? How can we find out if that is true? Do you have any evidence for that?

- **Questions about Viewpoints or Perspectives**
  You seem to be approaching this from a (fill in a term) perspective. What might someone who believed differently think? Can anyone see this another way?

- **Questions That Probe Implications and Consequences**
  What are you implying by that? But if that happened, what else would happen as a result? What effect would that have? What are the consequences?

- **Questions about the Question**
  Why is this question important? Can we break this question down at all? Is the question clear? Do we all understand it?

Using Socratic questioning helps a person to discover the truth about an issue versus what he has simply believed until now. One of the major characteristics of Socratic questioning is the follow-up question. One answer is not sufficient to get at the truth. You need to dig for it. The questions become your shovel. You don't find valuable material goods like gold, diamonds, and oil sitting on the surface of the Earth waiting for you to find them. You must dig. For the gold, diamonds, and oil of your thinking, to avoid errors and find the truth, you must also dig. Dare to dig by developing skillful questioning strategies.

Tool #3. The Scientific Method for Reflective Thinking

In chapter one, The Power of Perception, you learned that the futurists Heidi and Alvin Toffler consider the Scientific Method to be a "gift to humanity" because it provides a strategy to help people find the truth. Finding the truth is one reason why the scientific method is a good tool and a good fit for critical thinking. Let's briefly examine this powerful tool.

The Scientific Method is a five-step process by which scientists work to create an accurate and reliable understanding of the world and everything in it. They seek the truth by minimizing bias and prejudice during experiments. The scientific method follows a series of steps in a systematic way to get truthful answers to scientists' questions.

Steps:

1. State the problem. Ask a question.
2. Collect and analyze data. Research the problem.
3. Form Hypothesis
4. Test hypothesis; Experiment
5. Draw conclusions. Accept or reject the hypothesis.

Using the Scientific Method by itself is an excellent tool for a critical thinker. In fact, its framework for getting at the truth had such a huge impact on Dr. John Dewey, a twentieth century philosopher and educational reformer, that he modified it to become his Theory of Reflective Thinking. He believed that a trained mind also needs to follow a series of steps to reach a decision, so he developed steps that became his most specific "tool" for developing thinking. Let's briefly examine his strategy.

Theory of Reflective Thinking

Like the Scientific Method, John Dewey's Theory of Reflective Thinking is a five-step process for transforming the natural act of thinking into a more skillful process. In this process, people seek an accurate and reliable understanding of the world and everything in it. They seek the truth by minimizing bias and prejudice as they decide what to believe and do by suspending judgment and engaging in protracted inquiry.

Steps:

1. An awareness, a felt difficulty; a problem. State the problem.
2. Clarify the problem, Determine its nature, its location and definition, so it is clear. Restate the problem. (According to Dewey, the first two steps may fuse into one if the problem is clear.)

3. Form hypothesis; a suggestion of possible solution(s).
4. Test hypothesis—Explore the bearings of the suggestion. Engage in extended questioning and reasoning to gather facts; consider implications and consequences.
5. Draw conclusions. Further observation and experiment leading to the hypothesis' acceptance or rejection. Reach a state of belief or disbelief.[8]

Dewey likens the process of reflective thinking to a doctor diagnosing a patient. If the patient states his problem and the doctor accepts it immediately, then the doctor's scientific thinking is cut short and he could be making a serious error. A skilled doctor listens but does not accept the first suggestion for a cause of the problem. Before he reaches a conclusion, a doctor fully explores the nature of the problem to clarify it. He considers possible solutions and their consequences before completing his diagnosis. The same steps are used by scientists with the scientific method. Skillful thinkers, especially critical thinkers, need to approach all serious problems in the manner of doctors and scientists. Do not accept the first suggestion for solving problems or making decisions. Explore many possible alternatives.

As you compare these two strategies, the Scientific Method and the Theory of Reflective Thinking, I hope you are able to see that they have a great deal in common including dispositions. Both methods value and promote the dispositions of mental discipline, respect for evidence, curiosity, persistence, flexibility, suspending judgment, managing impulsivity, and valuing reason.

Both tools are valuable to have in your mental toolbox. In fact, I used these two tools as the foundation for another five-step process: **The Five A's of Mega-Thinking**. I wanted to help make the hard work of skillful thinking as simple as possible, and this tool may help. Primarily, I just modified the language of the Scientific Method and Dewey's Theory of Reflective Thinking to make it easier to remember the steps. I think this adapted strategy remains clearly linked to them.

The Five A's of Mega-Thinking

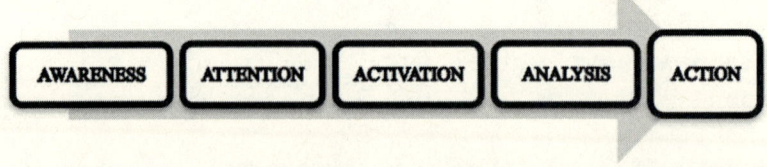

Figure 6.4: The 5 A's of Mega-Thinking

1. **Awareness** of a problem. State the problem.
2. **Attention.** Suspend judgment. Clarify the true nature of the problem. Restate it.
3. **Activation**. Form a hypothesis. Predict possible solutions.
4. **Analysis**. Test the hypothesis and/or predicted solutions: engage in questioning and gathering facts. Consider implications and consequences.
5. **Action**. a. Draw conclusions; b. Accept or reject the hypothesis/predicted possible solutions, and c. Decide what to do or believe.

The Five A's for Mega-Thinking could also be called The Scientific Method for Reflective Thinking, but that's not easy to remember. Simply remember the "Five A's" and you have a simple structure that you can use to organize your thinking.

Tool #4. Bloom's Taxonomy

For many people, teachers in particular, Bloom's Taxonomy is a tool that is used to develop critical thinking.[9] Let's step back a moment to describe the taxonomy in case you do not know what it is. In 1956, Dr. Benjamin Bloom, an educational psychologist, and his associates developed the "Taxonomy of Educational Objectives". It was intended to help educators design and assess learning by creating systematic categories of learning behavior. It has three parts: 1. Cognitive, 2. Affective, and 3. Psychomotor, which can translate to 1. Intellectual, 2. Emotional, and 3. Physical or 1. Knowledge, 2. Dispositions, and 3. Skills.

I made three separate charts to depict the three categories. Figure 6.5 depicts the "cognitive" taxonomy, the one that is widely used by teachers to develop critical thinking. You will notice that there are two columns for the cognitive domain. The first column lists the words used by Bloom in his original taxonomy in 1956. Today it is considered the "old" version. The second column is the "new" revised 1990s version by Lorin Anderson, a student of Bloom.[10] I include them both because some people reading this book, who have used Bloom for years, may not be aware of the change. Note the changes. Both versions have six levels, but the old version uses nouns and the new version uses verbs to describe the learning behaviors. In addition, as you can see, the new version uses a new word,"creativity", to replace "synthesis". Finally, creativity is considered a higher-level cognitive behavior than evaluation so it is at the top of the chart now.

Components of Bloom's Taxonomy

BLOOM'S COGNITIVE DOMAIN	
COGNITIVE (KNOWLEDGE: INTELLECTUAL) OLD version by Bloom & Associates (1956)	COGNITIVE (KNOWLEDGE; INTELLECTUAL) NEW version by Anderson & Associates (2001)
EVALUATION	CREATE
SYNTHESIS	EVALUATE
ANALYSIS	ANALYZE
APPLICATION	APPLY
COMPREHENSION	UNDERSTAND
KNOWLEDGE	REMEMBER

Figure 6.5: Bloom's Cognitive Domain

From now on, I'll focus on the NEW version of the cognitive chart. As you can see in the following charts, the cognitive taxonomy is often divided into two levels: 1. the "lower-order" thinking skills of remembering, understanding, and applying and 2. the "higher-order" thinking skills (sometimes referred to as HOTS) of analyzing, evaluating, and creating.

In an effort to promote higher-level, critical thinking in their classrooms, teachers frequently create assignments that use verbs connected to the higher-order level. Compare the two verb lists in figures 6.6 and 6.7. As you examine them, you become aware of the power of words, specifically verbs, to promote different levels of thinking. To obtain additional lists of verbs, you can Google "Bloom's Taxonomy Verbs".

Using "higher order" verbs as an approach to developing thinking ability is relatively easy to do and it can be useful, so it belongs in your toolbox. However, use of these verbs alone does not promote true critical thinking.

LOWER ORDER VERBS FOR THINKING		
REMEMBERING	**UNDERSTANDING**	**APPLYING**
Memorize	Understand	Apply
Define	Classify	Choose
List	Categorize	Demonstrate
Recite	Describe	Illustrate
Select	Explain	Prepare
Name	Summarize	Produce
Match	Show	Sketch
State	Elaborate	Solve
Label	Select	Use
Describe	Paraphrase	Interpret

Figure 6.6: Verb List for Lower Order Thinking Skills

HIGHER ORDER VERBS FOR THINKING		
ANALYZING	**EVALUATING**	**CREATING**
Analyze	Evaluate	Create
Compare	Appraise	Construct
Contrast	Defend	Design
Differentiate	Judge	Develop
Distinguish	Justify	Formulate
Debate	Criticize	Produce
Examine	Measure	Compose
Justify	Prioritize	Invent
Survey	Determine	Write
Infer	Conclude	Devise

Figure 6.7: Verb List for Higher Order Thinking Skills

Since Bloom's Taxonomy is commonly used with a focus on the cognitive domain, it is not used to its maximum benefit. When attention is directed at the cognitive taxonomy alone, you miss the opportunity to develop real critical thinking which is, at its most basic level, a mindset, not a set of micro or macro thinking skills. As a result, using the cognitive domain by itself ignores how the brain actually works.

In addition, the hierarchical structure that is used to identify Bloom's cognitive domain can be a problem too. It is a static image even though thinking is an active process. A graphic that depicts action is preferable, and Kathy Schrock, an educational technologist, designed one using gears. It is printed here with permission.

The Cognitive Process

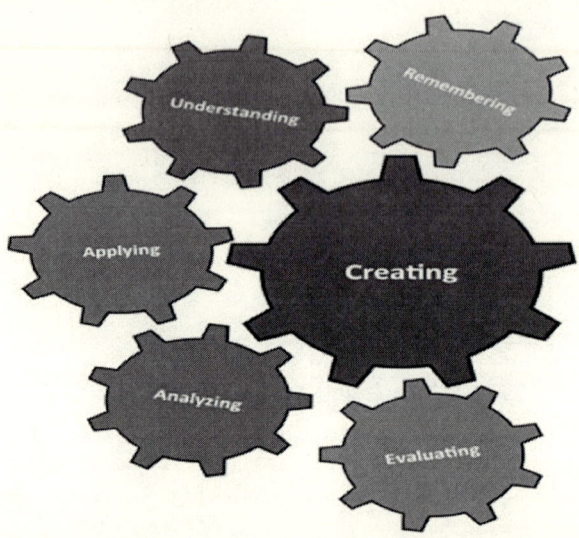

THE COGS OF THE COGNITIVE PROCESSES
BLOOM'S REVISED TAXONOMY
c2012. KATHY SCHROCK. ALL RIGHTS RESERVED.

As you can see, Schrock used the revised version of the cognitive taxonomy. In describing the image, she writes: "As one encounters new content, the ability to move among the cognitive levels as needed is important to the acquisition of knowledge. The cognitive process involves aspects of all levels".[11] This graphic shows that creating, while it may be the highest cognitive category, works with all the other levels in the continuous movement towards deciding what to believe and do. Get more information about it   by visiting "Kathy Schrock's Guide to Everything [http://www.schrockguide.com]".

Keep the gears image in mind when you consider Bloom's Taxonomy as a whole. Just as the components of the cognitive level work together in continuous motion, so do the other categories. The psychomotor, affective, and cognitive domains work together as "gears" too. They are not separate components of learning. If you want to use Bloom's Taxonomy as a tool to promote critical thinking, then use it in its entirety. The complete Bloom's

Taxonomy helps to explain how thinking in general really takes place. Since I believe that the entire taxonomy needs to be used because it aligns well with how your brain actually works, let's look at the domains that are seldom used. I'll start with the psychomotor (the physical) domain, which shows that perception matters.

BLOOM'S PSYCHOMOTOR DOMAIN
(PHYSICAL; SENSORY SIGNALS; SKILLS)
PERCEPTION: AWARENESS use sensory clues to guide activity
SET- readiness to act mentally, physically, & emotionally
GUIDED RESPONSE- early skill development
MECHANISM- Intermediate stage; Basic proficiency
COMPLEX OVERT RESPONSE- skillful: expert (automatic now)
ADAPTATION- Ability to modify skill
ORIGINATION-creates new movement

Figure 6.8: Bloom's Psychomotor Domain

Remember that within your brain, RAS, the reticular activating system, is paying attention to what matters to you. Awareness and attention do not occur at the cognitive level. Think back to the model of the triune brain. Your brain begins to perceive that something important is happening at the survival level, the psychomotor (physical) level, when RAS is receiving sensory signals from the environment. That's when your unconscious thinking process begins and your perceptions begin to form. Your brain only pays attention to the sensory input that has meaning for you. If it's not paying attention to something, then you will not learn about it, so you cannot think about it. Next, let's examine the affective (the emotional) domain, which shows that attention matters.

BLOOM'S AFFECTIVE DOMAIN
(EMOTIONAL; ATTITUDE)
Receiving Phenomena; Awareness triggers selected ATTENTION
RESPONDING to Phenomena; paying ATTENTION
VALUING; setting beliefs about what is valued
ORGANIZATION; Assembling ideas to clarify beliefs and valued
INTERNALIZING VALUES; belief system developed; impacts behavior

Figure 6.9: Bloom's Affective Domain

More focused attention kicks in at the affective (emotional) level when Miss Amy G or your PFC receive and respond emotionally to the perceptions. This is where you begin to value sensory signals and develop your will to focus on them. Only now, after being processed in the psychomotor and affective domains, will your brain become engaged at the cognitive domain level.

This following image, Figure 6.10, displays Bloom's Taxonomy with the whole brain in mind. It depicts the need to include the complete sequence of Bloom's categories in order to really impact the cognitive level. Notice that perception, the awareness level comes first. It is followed by the "will" area, and it finishes with the "skill" area.

The image itself denotes action. That's how your brain works. It is constantly active. It scans sensory data in the environment and forms perceptions; it pays attention to some things and not to others. Only when the "will" area is engaged can the "skill" area become involved in meaningful ways for critical thinking to take place.

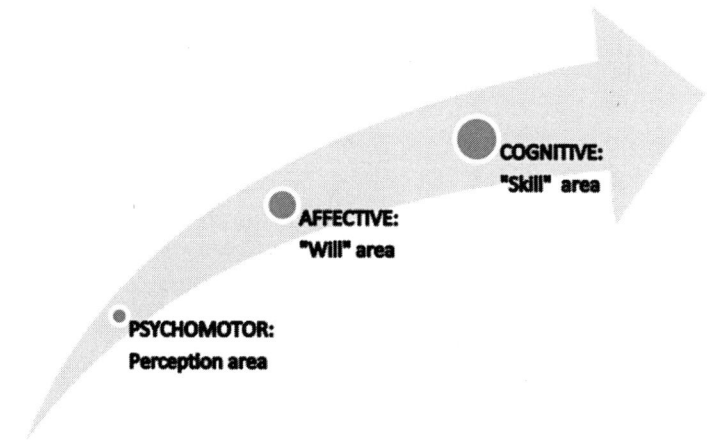

Figure 6.10: Developing Critical Thinking using Bloom's Complete Taxonomy

The bottom line is that Bloom's Taxonomy is a useful tool to have in your mental toolbox. However, you will not become a critical thinker simply by mastering the verbs in the cognitive domain. By jumping to the cognitive domain and skipping over the psychomotor and affective domains, many people, teachers in particular, jump over the basic facts about how the brain works and how people learn.

If you want to be a critical thinker, your heart has to be in it as well as your head. Bloom's Taxonomy is a helpful tool to remind you of this fact. You will develop your critical thinking skills by keeping the whole taxonomy in mind—perception, attention, will, and skill. Making this point does not have to be difficult. Simply recall or display the image above to remind yourself that skillful thinking, critical thinking, requires more than higher order verbs. A critical thinker engages the whole brain in deciding what to believe and do.

Tool #5. Graphic Organizers and Visual Tools

Graphic organizers are visual tools to help you organize information into a picture, a structured graphic, that is easy to read and understand. An image containing many examples of graphic organizers was included in this book's Introduction. In the process of collecting and analyzing the data that you put into a graphic organizer, you are examining relationships, increasing understanding, making connections, and generating ideas. For these reasons, graphic organizers are often used in schools and in businesses to help people think clearly.

One of the main values of a graphic organizer or any visual tool, especially in problem solving situations, is that it helps you avoid impulsive decisions. Graphic organizers force you to slow down. They help ensure that Miss Amy G is not in control of your brain!

Research scientists have known for a long time that the more visual information is used during the storage phase of memory, the easier it is to recall during the retrieval phase. They named it the "pictorial superiority effect or PSE".[12] That's the reason I use a number of graphic organizers and images throughout this book to clarify some ideas. Visual images will help you remember.

There are many graphic organizers for the micro-skills involved in critical thinking including comparing and contrasting, classification, sequencing, uncovering assumptions, reliability of sources, and prediction as well as the macro-skills of decision making and problem solving. There are also many graphic organizers for thinking skills in general. There are hundreds of books and resources on the topic. You can Google "graphic organizers" and obtain some excellent examples. In this section, I will present you with four graphic organizers to help you become a more skillful critical thinker. I'll start with a worksheet that expands on the visual image of the 5 A's of Mega-Thinking that you learned about earlier. It is a helpful tool that can be used as you engage in the process of problem solving and decision making.

The Five A's of Mega-Thinking

THE FIVE A'S OF MEGA-THINKING	
Lifelong Goal: **Skillful Thinker; Mega-Thinker** *Academic Goal:* **Scientific & Reflective Inquiry Skills**	
Step 1. AWARENESS Describe the difficulty you are feeling. What is happening? Why is it happening? State the problem.	**Step 2. ATTENTION** [Focus; avoid distractions; suspend judgment] Clarify the problem. Collect data. What is the true nature of the problem? What are the most important factors to consider? Why is a decision or solution needed? Restate the problem.
Step 3: ACTIVATION Form a hypothesis or state possible solutions: Identify tools to use for analysis.	
Step 4: ANALYSIS List criteria for evaluation:	Check-list for testing validity of hypothesis/solutions: Meets criteria? Yes or No Implications if solution is implemented? What will it look like if implemented? What are the consequences (intended and unintended)? How important are the consequences?
Step 5: ACTION • Draw conclusions. Accept or reject the hypothesis/solution(s). • What is the best choice based on analysis? State your decision. • Implement choice.	

Figure 6.11: Worksheet for the 5 A's of Mega-Thinking

Next, you will read about three relatively simple yet very powerful visual tools that will help you become a skillful critical thinker: 1. The Creative Tension Tool; 2. The Six Thinking Hats, and 3. The Ladder of Inference.

Visual Tools

For the remainder of this chapter, I want to focus on three visual tools that you may not be familiar with, but I think you will find them very helpful in your effort to become a critical thinker. They are simple, useful, and powerful. These visual tools will help you to develop probing questions, and that is a central feature of critical thinking. You will be able to remember these tools by thinking of their graphic design clue.

1. "Creative Tension Tool". Imagine an elastic band.
2. "Six Thinking Hats". Imagine a hat rack.
3. "Ladder of Inference". Imagine a ladder.

Creative Tension Tool

Every once in a while, you may have an awareness, a feeling, that something is wrong, but you can't pinpoint the problem. That's a good time to stop and assess your journey in life. The "Creative Tension Tool" is useful at times like that, because this simple tool triggers some important questions. In his book, The Fifth Discipline, Dr. Peter Senge uses it to help people achieve personal mastery—becoming the best they can be, as well to help organizations achieve their vision of being the best they can be.[13] An image that is frequently used to depict **creative tension** is of two hands pulling an **elastic band** apart. To get a real sense of the tension, it may be useful if you actually hold an elastic band and pull the ends apart.

Can you feel the tension that is created as you pull the ends apart? It is a physical feeling; it is not imaginary. With the creative tension tool, one end represents you and your current reality or an organization and its current reality. The other end represents your vision of yourself in a future state or an organization's view of itself in a future state. In between there is a gap — the real, physical tension that represents the difference.

It would be great to let go and snap right into your future desired state, but that is not real life. The concept of creative tension helps you to realize that you are on a journey and you should have a destination in mind. You know where you want to end up, so you need a plan to get there. You need to become physically and mentally engaged in achieving your personal vision.

As you know, even the best-laid plans need to change sometimes because change is inevitable and change can be messy. You can expect that your journey may take twists and turns, but creative tension helps you understand that to reach a goal, you need to set a direction for action. As a thinking tool, it can help you formulate probing questions. This tool starts with questions about events. You identify where you are and where you want to be, or you identify where a system is and where it wants to be. The important part is to notice the gap and create a strategy to overcome it, so you can reach the future state someday.

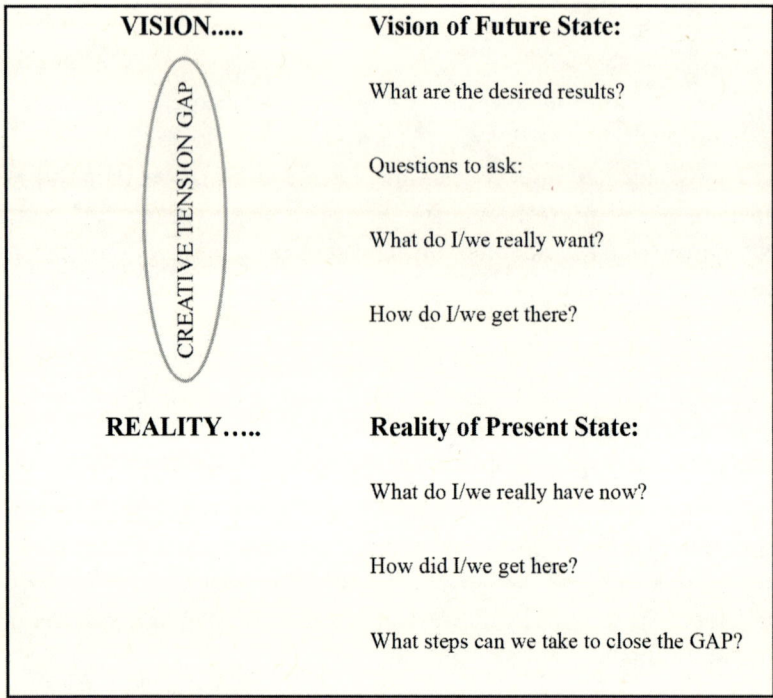

Figure 6.12: Creative Tension Tool

Noticing the gap between your current reality and your vision of the future helps you to define your problems. It helps you to figure out what events led to the current situation and what steps you need to take to get closer to your vision. Focus on the facts. Resist the urge to come to a quick conclusion. Too often, people identify problems in the "events" level of their present reality and use that limited information to seek quick solutions.

Unfortunately, when they focus on events, people are responding to the symptoms of a problem, because they did not look deeply enough to find the root cause of the problem. As a critical thinker, you know that you need to resist the symptomatic solution and dig deeper. Use the Creative Tension Tool to help you engage in deeper questioning into your current situation so you can wisely reflect on your vision. These actions will help you be better informed about what you want to believe or do.

Six Thinking Hats

The next visual tool, The "Six Thinking Hats", is a thinking tool that provides an easy, effective, and safe structure for questioning and for dialogue. [14] It can be used in all dimensions of thinking, but I thought it made the most sense to introduce it in critical thinking where the most difficult questions may be asked. It was created by Dr. Edward deBono. Dr. deBono advises people not to be alarmed, confused, or tricked by the simplicity of the Six Hats' strategy. It is intentional. He believes that simple tools, those that can be used with ease, are more valuable than complicated methods.

With this tool, six different kinds of thinking are described as "hats", and everyone has the opportunity to engage in the six different types of thinking. To remember this strategy, imagine that you have a **hat rack** in your home for six colored hats: white, green, yellow, red, black, and blue. The "Six Thinking Hats" is a technique for "parallel thinking", and it can be used in many situations. Parallel thinking is another term introduced by deBono. With parallel thinking, each of the six types of thinking is equally valuable; however, only one type of thinking is used at a time. This is an essential point. The focus on one line of reasoning at a time helps to prevent arguments and conflicts.

In a typical meeting, whether it involves businessmen, lawyers, politicians, teachers, student council members, or many other groups, good ideas sometimes do not get off the ground because negative comments stop the thinking process. Such thinking falls into the "black hat" category. However, black hat thinking is not negative thinking. It is true critical thinking. It is concerned with evaluation and judgment. It can be very valuable, but when used too soon, it can be harmful to the creation of new ideas. There is no set order to using the hats, although starting with the white hat for information and waiting to use the black hat makes sense. The following chart summarizes the different kinds of thinking hats, their purposes, and the types of questions used with that type of thinking.

Dr. Edward deBono's SIX THINKING HATS	
COLOR **&** **TYPE OF THINKING**	KEY QUESTIONS
WHITE INFORMATION	What information do we have? What information do we need?
RED FEELINGS	What do I feel about this? What do you feel about this?
BLACK WEAKNESSES	What is wrong with this? What are the weaknesses?
YELLOW STRENGTHS	What are the good points? What are the benefits?
GREEN NEW IDEAS	What is possible? What ideas do we have?
BLUE THINKING ABOUT THINKING	What thinking is needed? What's the next step?

Figure 6.13: deBono's Six Thinking Hats

As you can see as you examine the chart, each hat triggers core questions. In addition, you can use the hats in four ways:[15]

1. **Put the hat on.** A good way to start a meeting would be to say, "What are the facts? Let's have some white hat thinking. What do we know about this problem?" After information is gathered, you might say, "We appear to be stuck. Let's put the green hat on to generate some new ideas."

2. **Take the hat off.** If the discussion has gone on long enough, you could say, "We have some new ideas. That's good green hat thinking. Let's take off the green hat now." It is also useful in redirecting a group or individual that is bogged down in one type of thinking, you could say, "We've had some extensive red hat (or black hat) thinking. Let's take it off for now."

3. **Switch hats.** Using the hat tool, you can request an instant change in the type of thinking being used. You could say, "With the yellow hat, we learned the benefits of this approach. Let's switch to black hats now. What could go wrong if we try to do it?"

4. **Signal your thinking.** When you begin to speak, you can signal the kind of thinking you intend to use. You could say, Putting my red hat on, I do not like the last suggestion. I prefer the first one and this is why..."

Benefits of the Six Hats

As you examine the benefits of this thinking tool, be aware that you are engaged in "yellow hat" thinking, because you are considering its strengths. According to deBono, the benefits of the Six Hats technique include the following:

- Addresses a problem from a variety of viewpoints
- Deliberately focuses on one type of thinking at a time
- Provides directed role-playing
- Encourages participation & collaboration; input from all
- Simple to use
  - The colors are directions for thinking, not labels
  - Parallel thinking is made easy
- Describes the thinking, not the thinker
- Group Thinking becomes transparent—all dimensions are identified
- Discussion becomes relatively safe (Personal note: "relatively" is the key word here. You know best when it is safe to display red hat or black hat thinking.)

The "Ladder of Inference" is another useful visual tool that helps you to understand and explain the thinking process. It is particularly good at helping you identify assumptions. Let's examine that tool now.

The Ladder of Inference

The Ladder of Inference was developed in 1990 by Dr. Chris Argyris when he was a professor at Harvard Business School.[16] According to Dr. Argyris, everyone unknowingly carries around an invisible, personal "Ladder of Inference". It's very obvious that the mental image for this tool is a ladder! It provides a concrete structure for describing the steps your brain takes in the process of forming your assumptions and your beliefs. Do you recall from chapter one that your assumptions are sometimes wrong? They reflect your personal view of the world, not the real world. This ladder helps to make visible the mental pathway that often leads to these incorrect or misguided assumptions and beliefs. Once you are aware of the problems with the pathway, then you can take steps to correct it. Without the ladder as a tool, you might never become aware of your errors.

What is an INFERENCE?

Let's start using the tool by understanding its name. What is the meaning of the word "inference". Dr. John Dewey describes inference as "The exercise of thought...; by it one thing *carries us over* to the idea of, and belief in, another thing".[17] Does that definition give you a hint as to why the ladder might lead to misguided beliefs? As your brain is forming patterns, the associative architecture of your brain is hard at work carrying you over from the idea of one thing to another thing. It is making inferences! This happens even though there may not be evidence for it. Remember, when in doubt, your brain makes guesses so it can make sense of your world for you. When you receive a piece of information and make an inference from it, your mind is engaged in a complex yet rapid process to make connections and find meaning for you.

As a result, you do not climb the ladder slowly. You LEAP up the ladder! You leap up the "Ladder" so fast that you are unaware of your brain's activity. This leaping action interferes with critical thinking. The main benefit of the Ladder of Inference is that it makes visible how your brain works. It makes you think about your reasoning process, and it makes you aware of how you reached a conclusion or formed a judgment. With that knowledge, your thinking becomes more skillful. Let's look at Figure 6.13 to see the steps on the ladder.

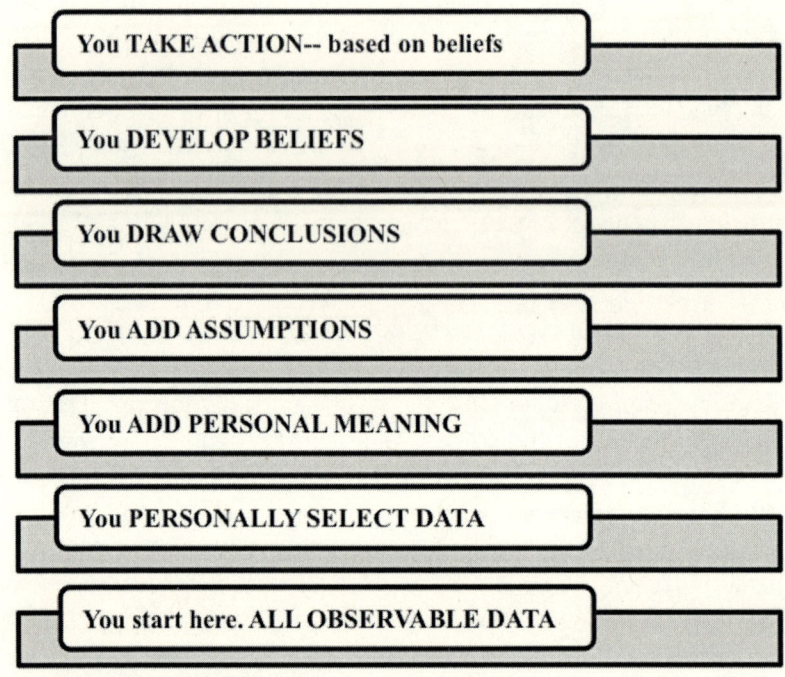

Figure 6.14: The Ladder of Inference

Naturally, you start at the bottom. You begin your climb on the first rung with all the observable "data and experiences" in the your environment at the time. A movie camera might be able to capture all of the data at that moment. You however, cannot. Your brain cannot process all the data that bombards you, so as you climb the ladder you select only some of the "data" from what you observe and experience. You believe that what you select is true. You continue to climb and add "meaning" based on your individual experiences in your personal world. You then add your personal "assumptions" and draw "conclusions" which assist you in adopting your "beliefs". Once you reach the top, you decide whether or not to take action based on your beliefs.

Except for the first step where you are surrounded by all observable real data, all of the activity involved in climbing the ladder is taking place within your brain. Your brain is using information from your "personal world", not the "real" world, as you climb the ladder. Your personal world is helping to form your beliefs. **Your beliefs then determine what data you will select the next time.**

You have created a "reflexive loop", since your assumptions and beliefs determine the data you choose in the future. This reflexive loop keeps you stuck in the personal world of mental models that you have already created. This is a complex and rapid process, and it is mostly invisible. I'll repeat an important point. Except for the first step, all observable data, and the final step, the action you take, nothing about this climb is visible to anyone else. The other steps take place in your brain, and like most people, your brain is probably STUCK. The new information is therefore evaluated by a biased brain. Unless you are willing to be open-minded and consider alternatives, the "new" data that you admit either fits, therefore reinforcing your beliefs, or it doesn't fit with your worldview, so it is rejected.

The benefit of the Ladder of Inference is that it helps to make this process of selecting and evaluating data VISIBLE. As a result, the mental image of the "Ladder of Inference" can be an excellent tool to promote critical thinking. If you catch yourself in the act of leaping, say to yourself, "I think I'm leaping up the ladder of inference; I want to slow down and ask questions." Then move back down the ladder, and start climbing back up slowly and deliberately and ask questions at each rung.

If a decision is important enough, then you must activate lazy system 2, your slow, conscious, effortful thinking. Before you make a decision about what to believe or do, ask yourself if you are examining the data in an open-minded manner. What's the data here? What's missing? How did I get from that data to these assumptions? What am I assuming and taking for granted? Is the assumption I am making justified? How can I find out if it is true? Ask yourself, "What did I actually see and hear that led me to these conclusions? What reasons, what evidence do I have for this conclusion?" If you focus on avoiding errors and seeking the truth, the questions won't be hard to verbalize.

The Ladder of Inference was actually designed to be a group tool for organizational development. In that capacity, it is very valuable because it enables the group members to "see" the links they are making in their thinking. Within the group, assumptions are often made visible. Productive dialogue and thinking can then take place. If you are in a group where the other members are aware of the Ladder of Inference tool, you can use it as a strategy to change the conversation in a safe way. You can say, "I can tell that I'm moving up the Ladder of Inference. Maybe we all are. Let's slow down and ask a few questions.

Overall, the "Ladder of Inference" is a useful tool for reminding you how your brain works. A major benefit of using the Ladder is that it helps you to engage in self-reflection. You are better able to see yourself as you engage in thinking activities. It can help you to control your impulsivity and curb your desire to leap. The Ladder of Inference is also a valuable tool to improve communication. It can be used in several ways:[18]

1. Reflection: It makes you more aware of your own thinking.
2. Advocacy: It makes your thinking and reasoning more visible to others.
3. Inquiry: It provides a safe way to inquire into the thinking and reasoning of others.

Summary

The purpose of critical thinking is to help you decide what to believe or do. At its core, the center of the bulls-eye, critical thinking is about the personal action you take after you deliberately and consciously use your brain to make judgments and decisions. You have now learned about five valuable critical thinking tools to help you engage in critical thinking.

My hope is that after reading this chapter, some of the "mystery" surrounding critical thinking is gone, and you have confidence that you can become a critical thinker. The real mystery is why more people are not critical thinkers, but I think you know the answer now. Unknowingly, people allow leaping System 1, the unconscious brain, to do most of the work. You need active, effortful System 2 brain activity when you are involved with skills involving questioning, analyzing, and evaluating.

However, you also know that critical thinking involves more than these important "outside skills". A critical thinker has "inside skills" that start with a critical attitude and a set of critical dispositions. The importance of the total package is expressed powerfully in the following excerpt from the Chancellor's message delivered by Sheikh Nahayan Mabarak Al Nahayan, the Minister of Higher Education and Scientific Research for the United Arab Emirates, at the second Festival of Thinkers[19]. The "Festival of Thinkers [http://www.festivalofthinkers.com]" started in 2005 and it is held every two years in Abu Dhabi, the capital of the United Arab Emirates. People from all around the world, including many Nobel Prize winners, attend this conference.

I consider his message to be a wake-up call to the world about the importance of developing skillful thinkers. It is also an excellent introduction to the next chapter on creative thinking.

A Wake-up Call

Our world – the people of this planet, and every living being, as well as the environment – depends for its existence and welfare on the thoughts and thinking power of so many.

To think is to realize, to draw in diverse elements of information, to seek to understand and review perspectives. In a world that is advancing at a pace never before imaginable, we need urgently to revisit our views on thinking, to rekindle the spirit of thought....

The secret for success lies in learning better how to think and how to use our power of thought so that we are not only a part of the future – we are designers of the future, creative thinkers who can imagine how things can be, and show the way.

Questions for Reflection

1. **HEAD**: What did you learn? Imagine that you belong to a Book Club that is reading this book. Summarize the key points that you want to highlight during discussion.
2. **HEART**: How do you feel about what you learned?
3. **ACTION STEP**: What are you going to do now? Suggestions: learn more about the topic; share what you learned, or practice what you learned.

CHAPTER 7

Creative Thinking

There is nothing more marvelous than thinking of a new idea.
There is nothing more magnificent that seeing a new idea working.
There is nothing more useful than a new idea that serves your purpose.
— Dr. Edward deBono

Are you ready to have some fun? Albert Einstein said that, "Creativity is intelligence having fun". Combine his quote with the quote above and you should feel a sense of joy. Learning how to be a creative thinker is going to involve mental playfulness. You are about to learn some creative thinking skills that will help you to be creative. It doesn't seem to make sense that you learn a set of "skills" to be "creative", but you can. This is <u>Serious Crea-</u>

tivity, as stated in the title of one of Dr. Edward deBono's many books on creative thinking. It may seem illogical, but you will learn about some powerful, yet relatively simple, creative thinking tools that will help you to mentally play and get creative!

Did you think that creative thinking only belonged to naturally artistic geniuses like Michelangelo, Shakespeare, and Beethoven? Absolutely not, because if it did, then why would you bother reading this chapter? However, you need to know that this chapter is positively not about the kind of creative thinking that belongs to artistic geniuses like the ones I mentioned. Their talents may be imitated but not taught. This chapter is about the kind of "creative" thinking that everybody can learn and apply. It's creative-thinking-on-demand, so you can use it when it's needed.

Breaking Patterns

What magic do these tools possess that they can fill you with creative thoughts? There's no magic involved, just an understanding about how your brain works. Let's review a basic fact. Your brain is not designed to be creative; it is designed to keep you alive. Remember, your brain's most important job is to recognize patterns and take action on them, so that you can survive. Pattern finding and pattern making are not creative; they are predictable. In fact, your creativity is actually limited by your brain's basic activity— finding patterns in data. In order to be creative, you don't want things to make sense and fit within your established mental patterns. Therefore, in order to be creative, you need some tools to help you breakout of your established mental pathways or, in some cases, your very deep mental ruts.

You already know how important creative thinking will be in the future. You know that jobs in the 21st century will be driven by people who are designers and innovators who use their creativity and intuition. This world needs more creative thinkers, so let's begin to make you one. The first step is to make sure that you understand the differences between trained creative thinking and uncreative thinking. They are compared in the following chart.[1]

"Trained" Creative Thinking versus Uncreative Thinking

TRAINED CREATIVE THINKING	UNCREATIVE THINKING
ORIGINAL	UNORIGINAL
PATTERN-BREAKING	PATTERN-MAINTAINING
SKILLFUL	UNSKILLFUL
CHANGE AGENT	CHANGE PHOBIC
CONCEPTUAL BLENDING	ISOLATED CONCEPTS
SOLUTION DRIVEN	SOLUTION FINDER
NON-JUDGMENTAL	JUDGMENTAL
FAILURE IS A FRIEND	FAILURE IS AN ENEMY
BRAIN FIREWORKS	BRAIN RUT

As you can see, the differences between trained creative thinking and uncreative thinking involve more that skills. The qualities that describe trained creative thinking involve attitudes. A trained creative thinker believes there are possibilities ahead and wants to know how to find them, while an uncreative thinker only sees "what is" and accepts the limits. In order to become a creative thinker, you not only need to develop skills, but also a creative thinking attitude.

Creative Thinking All Stars

The importance of a creative thinking attitude is shared by some creative thinking All Stars. There are a number of people who write about and teach creative thinking, but in this chapter, I'll focus on the ideas and strategies of three giants in the field: Dr. Edward deBono, Michael Michalko, and Alex Osborn. They agree on the importance of the creative thinking attitude.

Creative Thinking Attitude

According to Dr. DeBono, it is not enough to learn the techniques. He writes, "There still has to be the motivation to practice them and the will to use them."[2] Does this sound familiar? It sounds just like Dr. Dewey and his thoughts about the importance of "will" in critical thinking. In everything you do, you will find that your will, your motivation, your effort, and your determination are critical to your success.

According to Michael Michalko, a creative thinker embodies the following three traits: "First, you must have the intention and desire to be creative; second, you must consciously cultivate positive speaking and thinking patterns; and last, you must act like a creative thinker and go through the motions of being creative every day."[3]

You already possess the first trait, because you are reading this chapter. You will most likely try to do the last one when you finish the chapter. You need to learn more about the middle one, consciously cultivate positive speaking and thinking patterns. Michalko is very helpful here. In his book, Creative Thinkering, he provides some strategies for developing a critical thinking attitude: "Change the way you look at things, and the things you look at change", and "Change the way you speak, and you change the way you think". Now you will be developing your ccreative thinking attitude as you learn some creative thinking tools.

Change Your Perception

First, let's consider, "change the way you look at things, and the things you look at change".[4] This advice focuses on perception. You know that perception is an active process that your brain engages in all of the time without your conscious awareness of it. Your perception influences how you see the real world. You know that your perception creates your personal world view, not a view of the real world. Your perception can blind you, so you see only what you expect to see. However, as you train yourself to become a creative thinker, you will learn some tools to help you climb out of your established mental pathways. Once you see the world in new ways, then your view of the world can change. This changed viewpoint can stimulate your creativity.

False Faces

Michalko provides a strategy to help you change your perceptions, which you know also means assumptions and mental models. It's called "False Faces". He states that "an assumption presents a false face that we mistake for something immutable; a truth that cannot be challenged." This tool teaches you to challenge assumptions by reversing them.[5]

This tool fits into a category of strategies that is called a "reversal" which is also a strategy presented by Dr. deBono. It is simple yet powerful tool. Do you recall the image of a man trapped in a cage? That image represents a person who is trapped in his perceptions and assumptions, but he doesn't know it. He definitely needs to learn how to change the way he looks at things. The blueprint for "False Faces" shows you how to do it.

First, let's consider when you will use this tool. Suppose you have a problem, a challenge of some type that you are trying to solve. As you start thinking of ways to solve it, you will probably base some solutions on your existing assumptions, because that's what you know and believe at this point. However, what if your assumptions are wrong? What if they are "false faces" and you don't know it. In that case, your solution won't work. This strategy will help you to question your assumptions. Remember, it is basically a simple reversal, so it is not difficult to use. The challenge is to use it!

Blueprint to Reverse a Challenge or Problem

1. State your challenge or problem.
2. List your assumptions.
3. Challenge your fundamental assumptions.
4. Reverse each assumption. Write down the opposite of each one.
5. Record differing viewpoints that might prove useful to you.
6. Ask yourself how to accomplish each reversal. List as many useful viewpoints and ideas as you can.

The following are a few examples of "reversals".

- Question: When is the best time to reward employees? Assumption: Give employees a bonus after the busy time of year. Now challenge this assumption. Reversal: Give employees a bonus before the busy time of year. Real Result: In one company, productivity rose 50%.
- Problem: How can medical personnel collect accurate data on patients? Assumption: People must be stationary and connected to machines to have vital signs monitored. Reversal: People do not need to be stationary and connected to machines to monitor vital signs. Real Result: Navy doctors develop a "Smart Shirt" with sensors woven in. Vital signs are collected remotely while a person is engaged in activity
- Problem: How can a city improve the car parking situation? Assumption: Drivers control the parking time of their cars. Reversal: Cars control the parking time. Idea Triggered: Cars can park anywhere as long as the driver leaves the lights on.
- How can a chef get on the "farm to table" bandwagon for healthier eating? Assumption: Restaurants have menus. Reversal: Restaurants have no menus. Idea triggered: Chef communicates with patron about available main ingredients and patron selects items. Chef creates a unique meal for a specific customer.

After taking these steps to reverse assumptions, you should have a new perspective on your challenge or problem, and you may find a better way to solve it. Keep in mind that you are not looking for one right answer. You are looking for new ways of looking at things. Think about the phrase, "Make the familiar strange and the strange familiar". In a sense, that is what you are trying to do.

Change Your Language

Now let's examine this advice: "Change the way you speak, and you change the way you think."[6] Michalko believes that if you listen carefully to how other people talk, you will often hear the language of exclusion and deficiency. It seems that many people have developed speech patterns that focus on the negative, using words like no, never, not, and don't. For example, you might ask someone how they are feeling, and you will receive responses like "not bad" or "no complaints." Perhaps you suggest an idea, and the response is "It won't hurt" or "It can't be any worse than what we've got now". What about the frequent question, "Why don't we get together for...?" He believes that the word 'No' is unconsciously part of many statements. He argues that creative thinkers think "yes". Yes is part of the language of possibility. This focus on language is valuable, because people have more conscious control over what they say compared to what they think and feel.

Michalko puts word patterns into five categories according to what they suggest for outcomes: impossibility, desire, possibility, necessity, and certainty. He uses the following seven sentences to make this point. Read each out loud, as if each one were true about you.

- *I can't be creative.*
- *I want to be creative.*
- *I can be creative.*
- *I'm able to be creative.*
- *I should be creative.*
- *I need to be creative.*
- *I will be creative.*

Do you notice the subtle differences in how they make you feel and think? Each sentence carries a message about your ability to become creative. Now read them again, with the words and pattern categories emphasized.

- *I **can't** be creative. (impossibility = "world of negativity, helplessness, and hopelessness")*
- *I **want** to be creative. (desire = "but not necessarily any level of action")*
- *I **can** be creative. (possibility = "world that allows human will, intention, and choice")*
- *I'm **able to** be creative. (possibility = "world that allows human will, intention, and choice")*
- *I **should** be creative. (necessity = "world of force, pressure, and obligation")*
- *I **need** to be creative. (necessity = "world of force, pressure, and obligation")*

- *I **will** be creative. (certainty = "implies action and active involvement")*

Without your realizing it, these words are priming the way you think. You learned about "priming" in chapter 5, common-sense thinking. You know that your brain can be influenced and sometimes manipulated to automatically and unconsciously seek patterns and make associations based on the words presented to it. Michalko suggests that creativity is enhanced when negative word patterns are replaced by the word patterns of possibility, including can, will, able to, want to, and love to. Speak about "what is" and "what can be" versus "what is not" and "what will never be". Change "yes, but" into "yes, and". Positive words help to produce a positive attitude, and positive attitudes are needed to see a world of possibilities.

Types of Creative Thinking Tools

Michalko divides creative thinking tools, which he calls "Thinker-toys", into two groups: 1. Linear and 2. Intuitive. Linear thinkertoys provide conscious, specific steps for you to take to manipulate, divide, or combine information that is already known into new ways. "False Faces" was a linear tool. Most of the tools that I describe will be linear.

Intuitive thinkertoys tap into your unconsciousness to find ideas that may be there but you didn't know it. Your unconscious, intuitive brain is a powerful storehouse of information. Sometimes the answers to problems can be found there. You simply need some strategies to help you look for them.[7]

Although tapping into your unconscious brain is not mentioned in linear tools, you know that your unconscious brain never shuts off. It will always be playing a part in your thinking. When you use these linear and intuitive tools, you can unleash some creative powers that you never knew you had. The next tool you will learn about may be a familiar one. It's brainstorming.

Brainstorming

Brainstorming is a commonly used creative thinking tool. It is a group method for "thinking up" ideas. It is attributed to Alex Osborn who wrote a little 38 page book in 1942 to help average Americans think up new ideas during the World War II years. His book, <u>How to Think Up</u>, worked. Many creative ideas were produced as a result of his technique. He believed that people can think up ideas better if they work in a group. However, many people are self-conscious about expressing their ideas, so they don't want to work in groups. One of the reasons is that they fear being criticized. Since it's also easy for most people to be a critic or a judge, Osborn recommended setting three ground-rules before beginning any effort to "think up" creative ideas:[8]

1. Judgment is ruled out. No criticism is allowed until all ideas are in.
2. Wildness in thinking up ideas is wanted. The crazier the ideas, the better they are. It's easier to tone down an idea then to "think up" a good one.
3. Keep ideas simple, because the best ideas are simple. Some complex ideas are actually simple ideas that are put together. The best ideas are synthesized. Don't worry if you cannot come up with an original idea. Think how to turn someone else's idea into a better one.

Although Osborn believed that it is difficult to develop a formula for creative thinking, he suggests that the following six steps for brainstorming provide a useful technique:

1. AIM: Identify your target. What do you hope to create or improve?
2. FIRE: Generate wild, crazy, and silly ideas. No judgment of ideas at this point.
3. REVIEW: Clear-headily and coldly, examine your ideas. Pick three or so to "brood over". Let the thoughts percolate in your brain.
4. RELAX: Forget about the ideas. Do something you enjoy. Relax or even sleep. Your unconscious brain will be examining your ideas. The best idea may pop-up now. It may seem like it came out of the blue, but you prepared your brain to work on it. (Are you noticing the overlap here between linear/conscious thinking and intuitive/unconscious thinking tools?)

5. CONFER: If you still don't have a creative idea that you like, then talk about your goal. What is the purpose for the new idea? You will be making your creative thinking more clear to your brain when you examine it like this.
6. RELOAD: If you still don't have a creative idea, then reload and start again ———- aim, fire, review, relax, confer, reload![9]

In many situations, the first three steps are most frequently used— aim, fire, and review. Since you know how your brain works, you can understand the real value in Step 4 which incorporates your intuitive, unconscious thinking.

This is the basic brainstorming procedure, but if you feel more comfortable with specific suggestions for carrying out brainstorming, then the SCAMPER technique is a good one.

SCAMPER

SCAMPER is a linear, creative thinking and brainstorming tool that helps you generate new ideas about a problem, a product, a challenge, or a subject by asking a series of questions.[18] It has been widely used as a creativity tool for many years. The questions stimulate your thinking about how to make changes or how to create alternatives to things that currently exist.

The questions were created by Alex Osborn, the originator of the brainstorming technique. Bob Eberle, an educator, used Osborn's questions as the foundation of the method. He rearranged the questions to fit the mnemonic "SCAMPER" that is an acronym for a checklist of verbs to stimulate your thinking. The word itself suggests movement. If you find yourself stuck in a brain rut, you can use each verb to make up questions to jumpstart your thinking.

This is the original SCAMPER format.

- **S = Substitute something**
- **C = Combine it with something else**
- **A = Adapt something to it**

- **M = Modify or Magnify it**
- **P = Put it to some other use**
- **E= Eliminate something**
- **R = Reverse or Rearrange it.**

Originally, there was one M and one R in SCAMPER. However, M stood for both modify and magnify; R stood for both reverse and rearrange. You may see some more recent versions that are spelled SCAMMPERR. The name sounds the same but the spelling is different. The process of using the tool remains the same.

Michalko includes the SCAMPER technique in his book, Thinkertoys, as a linear tool to manipulate and transform existing ideas into newer, better ideas.

Michalko's Blueprint for SCAMPER

Michalko expands on this technique by using nine separate categories of questions. His blueprint for SCAMPER includes the following two steps:

Step 1. *Isolate the topic, subject, or challenge you want to think about.*

Step 2. *Ask SCAMPER questions about each step of the topic, subject, or challenge and see what new ideas emerge.*

What follows is a sampling of the questions that Michalko suggests. You can also create your own questions using each verb as a starting point.

- **S = Substitute:** Who or what can be substituted? What else? What place, scenario, ingredient, approach, format, etc.?
- **C = Combine:** What can you combine, mix, or integrate your subject with? What materials, ideas, purposes, products, resources, people, etc.?
- **A = Adapt:** What can you adapt or change? Can you adapt something to your subject? What idea, process, context, behaviors, materials, etc.?
- **M = Modify:** What can you modify? Can you change it or alter it in some way? What changes: purpose, form, packaging, attitudes, marketing, etc.?

- **M = Magnify**: What can you magnify? What features can be added? What can be exaggerated? What functions can be added?
- **P = Put to other uses:** What other ways can you use this? Are there new ways? What else can you make from this? What other fields can use it? Can it be modified for other uses?
- **E= Eliminate:** What can you eliminate from it? Can you reduce or simplify it? What can be streamlined, minimized, divided, made smaller, etc.?
- **R = Rearrange:** What can be rearranged or interchanged: components, schedule, pace, pattern, layout, sequence, etc.?
- **R = Reverse:** What can be reversed? What is the opposite? What is it like backwards, upside down, down side up, etc. Can services, schedules, or processes be reversed? What can you add that would be unexpected?

Michalko provides some interesting examples of real business challenges that were helped by using the SCAMPER tool. I thought the paper clip example was very interesting, so I am including it here. A paper clip manufacturer who wants to improve his product could ask the following questions:

- What can be *substituted* in the paper clip?
- What can I *combine* the clip with to make something else?
- What can I *adapt* to the clip?
- How can I *modify* the clip?
- What can I *magnify* or add to the clip?
- What *other uses* can I find for the clip?
- What can be *eliminated* from the clip?
- What is the *reverse* of clipping?
- What *rearrangement* of the clip might be better?

He describes one paper clip manufacturer who *substituted* plastic for metal and *added* color. It produced plastic clips in various colors, so color-coding could be used to organize papers. As a result, the company created *another use* for paper clips.

As you can see, SCAMPER provides a simple way to manipulate an item or idea into a new way of looking at it. You may or may not solve your problem or create a better product, but using it is a tried and true thinking tool to jump-start your creative thinking juices.

Lateral Thinking Tools

The following tools were created by Dr. Edward deBono. He invented the term "lateral thinking" in 1967 to make the differences clear between creative thinking that leads to artistic expression by talented and creative people, and creative thinking on demand that enables people to escape from locked-in patterns and perceptions. As a result, "lateral thinking" is another name for the kind of trained creative thinking that you are learning about in this book. Since it has become a commonly used term, I thought you needed to know about it, so you are not confused if you hear the term used. It is not a new type of thinking.

Basically, lateral thinking has to do with change. Something, like a provocation, is deliberately introduced into a thinking situation that causes you to change the way you think, so your mind moves in a new direction. The term itself, "lateral", suggests movement, and with the tools of lateral thinking (or trained creative thinking) you learn how to escape from your usual brain patterns. Lateral thinking is the opposite of vertical (up and down), or logical thinking, which is the way our minds usually work. When you apply the tools of lateral thinking, you are moving sideways — "cutting across patterns in a self-organizing information system." The unusual sideways movement deliberately forces you out of your preconceived patterns, your established perceptions, your mental models. It enables you to look at things in new, unique, and hopefully improved ways.[10]

To help remember this sideways action, this cutting across activity, you can make up a silly sentence using the word "lateral" like this one: *To win the game you need to create change, so you throw a lateral pass at your neurons, and they change patterns!* Now let's examine two simple yet powerful lateral thinking tools, the "escape method" and the "random input method". Both creative thinking tools deliberately use a provocation, a "po", to stimulate your thinking.

The "Po" technique

Dr. deBono believes that the very nature of "self-organizing pattern-making and pattern-using information systems", like your brain, requires provocative operations to get them to change. "Po" stands for the phrase "provocative operation". Dr. deBono invented the term "po" to indicate a deliberately provocative statement that is made to disturb your normal thinking patterns and force the forward movement of ideas. It is derived from words like hy**po**thesis, sup**po**se, and **po**ssible which also indicate forward thinking.[11] The idea behind this technique is that if you are mentally provoked, then you will be stimulated to think in new ways. Remember that the goal is to create ideas you never had before, not to reaffirm ideas you already have.

Using the "po" Technique

The word "po" sends the signal that you are going to use a provocation to get people to break out of their established brain patterns and think creatively. There are basically three steps for using this technique:[12]

1. **Choose the focus area for the creative thinking.**
2. **Set up the provocation**. There is no trick involved; it is a simple, mechanical procedure. The goal is to escape from your current reality, where you use your established thinking pattern, and discover the benefits of looking at things you take for granted in new ways. You are taking something familiar and making it strange. You are challenging conventional wisdom as you know it. You are unlearning what you have learned.
3. **Use the provocation.**

Two relatively simple tools that use the "po" technique will be described here: the escape method and the random input method. They are among deBono's many lateral thinking strategies.

1. The Escape Method

Use this tool when you want to change or improve something that you take for granted. The Escape method is useful for looking at things that are working well like established methods and procedures for doing things at home, at work, or at play. You may want to improve the methods, but you do not know where to begin because your brain is fixed in a pattern. You want to escape from your established mental pattern, upset the regular procedures, and force yourself to think about something in new ways. How? You negate, deny, remove, or cancel the thing you take for granted. You escape! You turn a positive statement into a negative one. Then you think about it. Using the "escape" tool, you may find a creative way to change.[13]

Here are three of Dr. deBono's examples of things that are taken for granted:

1. We take for granted that classrooms have teachers.

Now escape from this idea. Po, classrooms have no teachers. Now use this idea!

2. We take for granted that doors have handles.

Now escape from this idea. Po, doors have no handles. Now use this idea!

3. We take for granted that taxi drivers know their way around the area.

Now escape. Po, taxi drivers do not know their way around the area. Use it.

Are you getting the idea? Here is a specific example from Dr. deBono's book, Serious Creativity to demonstrate the use of the "Escape Method".

Step 1. Choose focus area. Focus area = Restaurants. We take for granted that restaurants have food.

Step 2. Set-up the provocation. Since we take for granted that "Restaurants have food", ask yourself, "Is that the only way to run a restaurant?" Could there be a better way or a different way? To become creative, escape from the idea that you take for granted. Make the statement negative and therefore, provocative.

Po, Restaurants do not have food.

3. Use it. Start thinking. How can a restaurant without food succeed? To answer that question, you need to move from your normal way of thinking into a new mode.

You are provoked to think in new and different ways now. Many wild and crazy ideas emerge. Here is one idea that Dr. deBono suggests as a new way of looking at restaurants.

Dr. deBono's idea has people returning to the restaurant bringing their own food. Why? The restaurant is elegant and the atmosphere makes people feel special. Because of the wonderful environment, people are willing to return with their own food, but they must pay a service charge to the restaurant's owner for use of the facility. In this way, people can entertain guests in special surroundings, and the owner does not have to cook, but he makes a living. He doesn't charge for food but he charges for use of the space. This example should help you get the idea for how the "Escape Method" works. Try it yourself with something you take for granted and see if it works for you.

2. The Random Input Method

The "random input method" is the easiest method to use to stimulate creative thinking. If you wanted just one strategy to help you become more creative, this is it. deBono says that use of the random input method, also called the random stimulation method, is widespread and used by many different kinds of organizations around the world including major advertising agencies, new product groups, and rock groups. The key to its success is the random component. You absolutely cannot choose the item that is used to get the creative juices flowing. The random item is the provocation (po). It provides a completely new entry point for thinking about a situation. You do not need to do anything special except find a random item to get you going. It could be anything including a word, person, picture, or magazine. The method seems illogical, but experience has shown that it works.[14]

For convenience sake, people often choose to use a **word** when using this technique. There are many simple ways to find a random word. You can use Google, and type in "random words". You will be directed to random word generator sites. You could use a book that has a list of random words, like Michael Michalko's Creative Thinkering[15] which lists over 1,000 random words. This list is particularly useful because the words are nouns which are familiar, simple, visual, and connection rich. You could also use a dictionary. First, find out approximately how many entries are on a page. Use that as your number range and randomly select a number. Second, open the dictionary to any page, then use your random number to count down the list of the words on the page. Let's say you picked the number seventeen. Start at the top of the randomly selected page and count down until you come to the seventeenth word. If it is not a noun, continue looking at the following words until you come to a noun. That's your random word.

You could also use a newspaper or magazine. Open to any page, close your eyes and touch your finger to a spot. Use the noun nearest to your finger. That's your random word. Basically, you can use any strategy you want to find a random word, except one. You cannot select it yourself. It absolutely needs to be random. Let's look at the steps.

- First, you have an issue or problem that you are focused on.
- Second, you select a random stimulus (oftentimes a word)
- Third, you write a "po" sentence that links the random stimulus and the focus area.
- Fourth, you unleash your creative juices as you have fun making connections.

You now make a list of your crazy creative ideas in the hope of finding a useful one. As strange as it may seem, this mental tool usually works, because your amazing brain is so good at making connections. No matter how random the stimulus is, eventually your brain will connect it with the focus area, and during the process of making the connections, creative ideas will flow. The goal is for something to provoke you into new ways of thinking. The provocation helps to trigger new ideas. Let's use one of deBono's examples to help clarify the random input technique.

Step 1. Attention is focused on the office copier. Could it be made better?

Step 2. Random word selected is "nose".

Step 3. Write a po sentence linking focus area and random stimulus: *Office copier "po" nose.*

Step 4. Make connections.

Your trained creative thinking should be activated now. What ideas come to mind? List them. At first, it may just seem weird. Logical thinking would never link office copiers with nose. However, eventually you will appreciate the value of this simple tool. For this example, the sentence "Office copiers po nose" led Dr. deBono to "nose and smell". Since nose is what random input gave him, he thinks about copiers and smell to get the creative juices flowing. What if a cartridge could be invented that gave off distinctive smells when something was about to go wrong with the copier? For example, if you smell lavender, then the copier needs more paper. If you smell orange, then the ink cartridge needs to be replaced. Chances are that without that random word, this new line of thought would not have been imagined. It did not result from a logical thought process, but it did result in creative thinking. That's the start. How to implement the connection between copier problems and smells is another issue, but the creative process has started.

Does this technique always work? No, but it often does when it is done right. However, sometimes people modify this already simple process by looking for a "better" random word, and that is a pitfall to its success. Even if you do not like the random word, you need to work with it. If you select a word that you think works better, then you are connecting it to preconceived ideas, and you will not be provoked into new ways of thinking.

BRUTETHINK

Random input is an effective technique, and it goes by other names as well. For example, Michael Michalko has a random stimulation technique called BRUTETHINK. The names may change, but the basic process is the same. In all random input or random stimulation models, you pair two things that have nothing in common and see what creative ideas emerge.

I wanted you to see both the similarity and differences between these two techniques. The goal is the same, and the steps to the goal vary only a little. The message I want you to receive is that thinking tools are not set in stone. Do not be fearful about following the exact steps of someone's formula. Once you understand what the tool is trying to do to influence your brain's activity, then it becomes easier to remember. Whether you use deBono's Random Input model with a "po", or Michalko's BRUTE-THINK, or anyone else's, it does not matter. It is the basic process that counts. Finding a random stimulus and linking it with a problem you are having can lead to imaginative solutions. No matter how different two objects may be, if you concentrate on both of them, your amazing brain will eventually find some connections between them.

Let's examine the basic steps for BRUTETHINK.

Purpose: If you are looking for a fresh approach to a challenge, bring in a random word.

1. Name the Challenge: ex. How can I increase sales this month?
2. Select a random word: example, bottle
3. Think about things that are associated with the random word: What does it look like? What does it do? What do you do with it? Identify some characteristics.
4. Force connections—similarities, associations, etc.
5. List your ideas as they occur

The BRUTETHINK model: Challenge statement + random word.

Example: How do I increase sales this month? + bottle

Here are a few examples of creative ideas, provided by Michalko, that resulted from this random stimulation example.

- Bottles can be packaged in six-packs. Can you repackage your own product in a new and novel way?

- Bottles can be filled up. Perhaps you are not listening to customers. Should you devise a program that lets customers fill you up with their real needs and desires
- Bottles break. If a bottle slips from your hands, it breaks. How can you prevent the factory from slipping up on orders and causing lost sales?[17]

These examples provide evidence of the possibilities for new ways of thinking by simply using a random word. This is one powerful technique for a "trained" creative thinker to use.

The Creative Green Hat

You learned about Dr. deBono's thinking skills' strategy, The "Six Thinking Hats", in chapter six. As a whole, it is not a creative thinking strategy, However, he chose his hat colors carefully, and the green hat makes space for creative thinking. The color green makes us think of creativity in nature with vegetation and growth. Nature is full of possibilities and the "green hat" specifically asks questions requesting possibilities, creativity, and new ideas. Although none of the Hats provides step-by-step instruction, each hat is valuable for providing the opportunity to think about each category of thinking. As a result, when creative thinking is needed, the Six Hats can be used as a creative tool. In that case, deBono suggests the following sequence of hats:

- *White Hat: the information base. What do we know?*
- *Green Hat: alternatives, suggestions, and new ideas*
- *Yellow Hat: feasibility, benefits, and valued of the ideas*
- *Black Hat: difficulties, dangers, problems, and points of caution*
- *Red Hat: intuition and feelings about the ideas*
- *Blue Hat: conclusion*

Since it safely enables people to consider possibilities, the green hat ensures that creative thinking is addressed.[16]

An Intuitive Tool

As I mentioned earlier, Michalko divided creative thinking tools into two categories: linear and intuitive. I'd like to introduce you to one of his intuitive tools now — "The Three B's".[19] With intuitive tools, you tap into the power of your unconscious brain and your intuition. The Three B's is an effective tool that may even seem familiar to you. Do you ever try to remember something, but you can't? You might have struggled to think of a person's name, or the title of a book, or the name of a movie. Frustrated, you say, "Well, I'll just sleep on it, and it might come to me" or "It will come to me tomorrow when I don't need it". When you do this, you are recognizing that your mind keeps looking for the answer, even when you stop. It's just the way your brain works. Even though you were not consciously thinking about the problem any longer, your brain was still actively processing it—especially if it was important to you. Usually, hours or days later, the answer pops into your mind when you don't expect it! The Three B's is a creative thinking tool that uses your unconscious brain and your intuition in a planned way.

The Three B's

The Three B's refer to bus, bed, and bath, since many successful people report that their best ideas occur when they are relaxing or at least not thinking about the problem. Michalko designed a blueprint to take advantage of your brain's natural behavior. The Three B's is the blueprint for you to follow to make it more likely that your intuitive brain will find answers for you when you allow it incubation time. When you use the "Three B's" tool, you are consciously putting your unconscious brain to work for you!

Blueprint for the Three B's

Step 1. Identify the problem or challenge.

Step 2. Prepare your brain for action by gathering lots of information about the challenge.

Step 3. Instruct your brain to find a solution. You are letting your brain know that this challenge is important to you. Mentally say, "I'll check back in three days" or "Let me know as soon as you find an answer."

Step 4. Incubate. Let go of the problem. Forget about it. Incubation needs to take place.

Step 5. Eureka! It may be hours, days, weeks, or months later, but insight will occur.

This simple technique puts your unconscious, intuitive brain to work for you. Michalko wrote that Einstein took a nap when he was troubled by a problem, so you are in good company if you use this tool. When an idea or solution eventually pops into your head, you may be examining it from a different perspective, because you let it go for a while.

Do you recall that "Relax" was also a step in Osborn's brainstorming technique? People who understand how the brain works know that relaxing and letting ideas simmer slowly can bring about very intuitive and creative ideas. Don't be afraid to go to sleep when you are being pressed for new ideas. It may be the solution! Keep a pen and paper nearby you during the night in case you do wake up with a brainstorm!

Natural Creative Thinking: Conceptual Blending

You have been learning about some specific tools that you can use to help your brain break out of established patterns and perceptions. However, in the history of the world, there were not always tools to promote creative thinking. There are times when your brain naturally engages in creative thinking. Conceptual Blending is an excellent example.

In Conceptual Blending, a person takes two dissimilar objects and makes connections between them. Conceptual blending can be forced as it is in the random stimulation model. However, many times it comes naturally without any thinking tools involved. Here are two interesting examples of "conceptual blending" that occurred naturally.[20]

1. A pine-cone and reading

When he was nine, Louis Braille became blind by accident while he was helping his father make horse harnesses. As a result, he couldn't read or write. Years later, a friend gave him a pine-cone. As he was moving the pine-cone around with his fingers, he noticed tiny differences between the individual scales/leafs/part of the pine-cone. His imagination combined the feel of the pine-cone with his desire to read, and he created the Braille system for reading—using raised dots on paper to enable blind people to read.

2. A shower-head and the Hubble telescope

When the Hubble was first launched, scientists were not able to focus it. Scientists figured out that they could refocus it by inserting very small mirrors behind the main mirror. However, it was orbiting the earth, so the new problem became one of delivery and installation. The solution came to James Crocker, an electrical engineer for the Hubble, while he was taking a shower in Germany. As he was manipulating the shower-head that used adjustable rods, he imagined the mirrors on the shower head. As a result, scientists created an instrument that was a success in establishing the focus.

Summary

You have learned that the main purpose of "trained" creative thinking is to generate new ideas in order to find creative and hopefully better ways of doing things and making things. Trained creative thinking involves mental playfulness, but it is serious business. You must learn how to break away from established mental patterns. These patterns have become your perceptions, your assumptions. To successfully break away, you need a creative thinking attitude as well as creative thinking tools. With that combination, you will be joining with other international "thinkers" who are committed to progress and change through creative thinking in order to make our "real world" a better place. Let's view some remarks made by Sheikh

Nahayan Mabarak Al Nahayan in the Chancellor's message at the 5th Festival of Thinkers:

As with past Festivals of Thinkers, the 2013 edition will be a strong platform for great experiences, impressive knowledge, superior intellect, and a commitment to global progress. It will reflect the philosophy that thinkers, together with students from around the world, have the capacity and the responsibility to effect necessary progress and change.

Such sentiments resonate strongly with the words of the late Nobel Peace Prize recipient Wangari Maathai, who said at the 2007 Festival of Thinkers conference: "I hope that by the time we finish this conference we shall be inspired by each other and sometimes we never know where that inspiration will lead. Just allow yourself to think freely and let your mind create."

The unpredictability of thinking freely and with vision and creativity is worth the risk if it can possibly lead to such wondrous results. This conference will encourage attendees to think outside the box; to think laterally and creatively when considering how to approach and solve some of the pressing issues that face society today, or as Ralph Waldo Emerson once said: "Do not go where the path may lead, go instead where there is no path and leave a trail."

In this chapter, you learned a few simple yet powerful tools that you can put to work immediately to help you become a more creative thinker. In the next chapter, you will learn the basics of systems thinking, which is "big picture" thinking.

Questions for Reflection

1. **HEAD**: What did you learn? Imagine that you belong to a Book Club that is reading this book. Summarize the key points that you want to highlight during discussion.
2. **HEART**: How do you feel about what you learned?

3. **ACTION STEP**: What are you going to do now? Suggestions: learn more about the topic; share what you learned, or practice what you learned.

CHAPTER 8

Systems Thinking

The unleashed power of the atom has changed everything save our modes of thinking,   and we thus drift toward unparalleled catastrophe.
— Albert Einstein

A New Way of Thinking

Einstein's quote is a terrifying warning that mankind has to change its way of thinking to avoid catastrophe. Are you surprised to read his warning? I hope not. You know that mankind cannot rely on basic common-sense thinking to solve complex 21st century problems like terrorism, climate change, drug addiction, pollution, and national defense issues to name a few. You have already learned some critical and creative thinking skills that are changing how you think. In this chapter, you will learn about "Systems Thinking", which may be closest to the new way of thinking that Einstein believes mankind needs.

Dr. Barry Richmond (1947-2002), a giant in the field of systems thinking, systems dynamics, and computer simulation software, agreed with Einstein about our outmoded modes of thinking. He stated that

... the way we think, act, and communicate is outdated. As a result, the way we act creates problems. And then, we're ill-equipped to address them because of the way we've been taught to think, learn, and communicate....However, it is the premise of systems thinking that it is possible to evolve our thinking, learning, and communicating capacities.[1]

This statement makes it clear that although Richmond saw that human thinking was outdated, he didn't plan to drift towards catastrophe. He planned for action, for change. He believed that people become over-whelmed with the complexity of problems in the modern world; therefore, they need to take deliberate steps to learn a new way of thinking, called Systems Thinking, so they can solve the problems.

During his life, Richmond worked hard to make systems thinking accessible to all including students in K-12 schools. He believed in "big tent" systems thinking where everyone could practice it at some level. His hope was that everyone should try to become systems thinkers because wide-spread systems thinking would make the world a better place.[2]

The purpose of this chapter is to provide an introduction and overview of systems thinking. It will assist you in becoming a systems thinker by providing a short and gentle approach to a complex topic. It will provide you with the basics. If you think back to the change model in the introduction, I'll get you past the "awareness" phase and into the "initiation" phase.

As I mentioned earlier, I am not an expert. Although I have attended conferences and workshops and have read widely in the field, my understanding of systems thinking is limited to a beginner's level. The experts come from graduate programs at places like MIT, Dartmouth, and Worcester Polytechnic Institute. I am hopeful that this chapter serves as a significant starting point for you. I am hopeful that it provides you with the desire to learn more, much more!

Remember, even if this new way of thinking is the break-away strategy that helps people break out of old ways of thinking, no change will occur unless an individual has the WILL to change. You have heard this before. You need the will to develop the skill. By reading this book, you are demonstrating that you have the will, so let's get started by taking the first step, which is recognizing the major obstacle to systems thinking.

First Step

How do you become a systems thinker? The first step is to recognize that your mental models are a major barrier to systems thinking, so you need to be prepared to change them. The power of your perception, another name for your mental models, has been an ongoing theme in this book. Since chapter one I have been emphasizing that an obstacle to skillful thinking in general is being stuck in one's own perceptions and clinging to one's personal mental models. I want to repeat Dr. deBono's quote about perceptions: *Outside highly technical matter, perception is by far the most important part of thinking. Perception is how we look at the world, what things we take into account, how we structure the world.*

Your mental models control how you think about everything. Remember, they are not true depictions of the "real world". They are true depictions of your "perceived world". They exist as reality only within your head. They may be right or they may be wrong. You must take a hard look at them and critically examine them to determine if they are true. Only then can you make wise decisions about what to believe or do.

The power of mental models is captured in Barry Richnond's definitions of thinking and learning. Thinking consists "of two activities: constructing mental models and then simulating them in order to draw conclusions and make decisions".[3] Learning takes place when "mental models change".[4]

Peter Senge, another giant in the field of systems thinking, supports Richmond's position. He explains that "...our organizations work the way they work, ultimately, because of *how we think* and *how we interact*." He informs us that to become systems thinkers, so we can solve systems problems, we must do three things: 1. change how we think; 2. change how we interact, and 3. redesign our mental models because "We do not 'have' mental models. We 'are' our mental models".[5]

That is a powerful statement, but it should not come as a surprise to you. You know that some people choose to live their lives as if their mental models, their personal worldviews, are reality. They refuse to examine their own perceptions, and they refuse to acknowledge different worldviews. They are unaware of, or uninterested in, the fact that there may be new and better ways to think about and solve problems. They resist making any changes to their way of thinking. In a changing world, they do not want to change. One of the most important messages of this book is that a Mega-Thinker needs to be aware of his perceptions, his mental models, and be able to examine them critically. Based on his conclusions, he needs to be willing to change. People who refuse to do that cannot become systems thinkers. They are stuck in mental pathways. They are trapped. They cannot become Mega-Thinkers.

Becoming a Systems Thinker

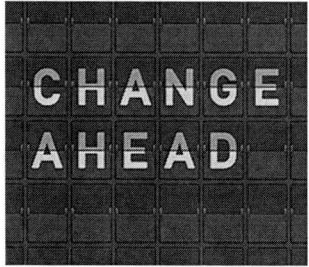

Systems thinkers are aware of the need to change. Change is real, and the concept of change is not new. About 2,500 years ago, the ancient Greek philosopher Heraclitus stated, "The only thing constant is change." Like it or not, change is everywhere and as you have learned, some people don't like it. You know that even "experts" become stuck and forget that they need to continue to learn and change. However, complex problems, systems problems, will not be solved if the majority of humanity continues to resist change.

People need to take their blinders off and recognize that change is all around them. In order to overcome the major obstacle to systems thinking, people need to examine their perceptions, their mental models, in the light of real and continuous change. That's what needs to happen to avoid the catastrophe that Einstein warned the world about. As an individual, you may or may not be able to change the world, but as your own CEO, you can change yourself and be a role model as a systems thinker. That's how change starts.

Hard Work Ahead

Yes, there is hard work ahead as you learn about systems thinking, but you are already on your way. You have already learned some strategies that will help you examine your mental models. You learned how to reverse your assumptions and "change your perceptions" using "False Faces". You learned how to "change the way you speak" which influences how you think. You learned how to ask wide-ranging, deep, and probing questions using Socratic Questioning, The Ladder of Inference, and The Six Thinking Hats. These tools will help you to critically examine your mental models.

Another thing you can do is to use the Scientific Method. Donella Meadows, a pioneer in the field of systems thinking, wrote about the need to "Expose your mental models to the light of day". She said the process of exposing them to scrutiny and testing them against evidence to see if they are supported is no more than the scientific method.[6] The Scientific Method, Dewey's Theory of Reflective Thnking, and the Five A's for Mega-Thinking are also in your toolbox. You already have a set of tools to get you started thinking like a systems thinker. Now let's get specific and focus on the components of systems thinking.

What is Systems Thinking?

Systems thinking is a multi-dimensional thinking process. It attempts to help people understand how complex and dynamic systems work, so the challenging issues these systems face can be improved or the problems they face can be solved. The multi-dimensional characteristic is captured in Barry Richmond's definition:

*We can use the phrase (**systems thinking**) to refer to a **set of tools** – such as causal loop diagrams, stock and flow diagrams and simulation models – that help us map and explore dynamic complexity. We can also use it to mean a **unique perspective on reality** – a perspective that sharpens our awareness of whole and of how the parts within those wholes interrelate. Finally, systems thinking can refer to a **special vocabulary** with which we express our understanding of dynamic complexity. For example, systems thinkers often describe the world in terms of reinforcing and balancing processes, limits, delays, patterns of behavior over time, and so forth.[7]*

What is systems thinking? It is a powerful problem-solving strategy that includes these three dimensions: 1. visualization tools; 2. a unique mindset, and 3. specialized vocabulary.

Why is Systems Thinking Needed?

According to Steve Peterson, a leader in the fields of systems thinking and system dynamics, systems thinking is needed to solve challenging systems problems, which have the following four characteristics.[8]

1. Dynamic. This simply means that systems change over time. They are not static. When you consider a systems problem, you need to consider how the system got to where it is now and how it might change in the future. A common error in problem solving is to treat a dynamic problem as a static one.

2. Multiple players with diverse interests. Systems problems are made more difficult to solve because they often involve many stakeholders with different interests and mental models. Communication is inhibited as individuals or sub-groups promote their perspectives at the expense of a "big-picture" common view.

3. Interdependencies. The parts of a system create a whole as a result of the interdependencies and interconnections among the parts. These interdependencies drive the dynamics in systems. As the world increasingly becomes interconnected and interdependent, the interdependencies in systems problems sometimes move across borders and disciplines. That makes them even harder to see.

4. Hard to communicate. Words alone make it very difficult to explain systems problems which are characterized by dynamic, multiple players with diverse interests, and interdependencies! If you cannot communicate clearly about systems problems, then you cannot solve the problem.

As a result of these four factors that characterize systems problems: dynamic, multiple players with diverse views, interdependencies, and being hard to communicate, a new way of thinking about problems was needed— systems thinking. As you face problems to solve, ask yourself if the problem fits these characteristics of a systems problem.

If it **does not have** these characteristics, then you have a static, non-changing, and linear problem. It can be solved using tried and true traditional tools and problem solving strategies. There are a number of thinking skills books that provide templates for organizing thinking to solve problems using linear tools like graphic organizers.

However, if it **does have** these characteristics, then you have a dynamic, nonlinear problem on your hands, and you cannot solve it with traditional methods. You need a new language, a new mindset, and a new set of tools. You need the new way of thinking—systems thinking. Let's begin to get into details with the first component of systems thinking —- the specialized vocabulary.

Specialized Vocabulary and Concepts of Systems Thinking

If you are going to visit a foreign country, it is helpful to know a few phrases in the language of that country. In order to make your trip into the world of system thinking more meaningful, you need to understand its language. Actually, the language used in the systems zone is made up of two major parts: systems thinking and system dynamics. "Systems Thinking" does not exist as a stand-alone discipline. It is built upon the foundation of "System Dynamics", a field of study that was founded in the 1950s by Dr. Jay W. Forrester, Professor Emeritus at MIT's Sloan School of Management.

System dynamics is a specialized field that designs and uses a special language and a variety of tools including sophisticated computer simulation models to analyze and understand how dynamic systems behave. Although you may not realize it now, there is magic in this language! It can actually change the way you think. By the time you finish this chapter, you will understand what I mean. Let's begin our language lesson with the following vocabulary words from systems thinking: systemic structure, leverage, mental models, linear and nonlinear thinking, and these words from system dynamics: stock, flow, feedback, feedback loops, balancing feedback, and reinforcing feedback.

What is a System?

You cannot understand systems thinking unless you understand the concept of a "system". Basically, a system has the following components:[9]

1. A system has many elements, so it is **complex.**
2. The elements within the system are **interconnected**, so each part influences every other part either directly or indirectly. The parts work together to form one whole thing.
3. A system has a **structure**. It is made up of all the interconnected parts.
4. A system is **dynamic**, and it changes over time.
5. A system has a **purpose**. It has a reason for its existence.

Your Brain as a System

To help you understand what a system is, think about your brain as a "System". It has a **purpose**. It keeps you alive and enables you to think. It is **complex** with many **interconnected** parts. You know all about neurons, Miss Amy G, Hippo, and the whole cast of characters and how they interact with each other and influence each other either directly or indirectly. Your brain has a **structure**. You know how the structure of your brain, with its new parts on top of old parts, is interconnected and influences your behavior. It is **dynamic**. Your brain is continuously changing. Through the processes of neuroplasticity and neurogenesis your brain is growing and changing right now.

You also know how difficult it is to "see" the whole structure. Neuroscientists are still learning about the mysterious human brain! They believe the 21st century will see amazing progress in revealing the brain's structure and figuring out how it influences human behavior.

As you study any system, it is also changing—- we could consider it to be systems-plasticity! Let's look at a few systems. There are living and non-living systems. A car is a non-living system, and your body is a living system. You could take a car apart and examine its engine, battery, tires, and even the windshield wipers. Each part is important, but the parts must work together to make up the whole mechanical system of a car. The separate parts are not a means of transportation which is the purpose of a car.

You could take a human body apart and examine the heart, lungs, legs, or even the eyelids, but the separate parts do not give the body life. Every part needs to work together with every other part to make a complete human body system which is needed to make a live human being. Your body is a good example of a complex system that has systems within a system. The bottom line is that everything affects everything else within a system, and everything keeps changing. You now know that a system is more than the sum of its parts. If you break a system into all of its parts, it loses its purpose and reason for being. If you only focus on the parts of a system, then you will not understand how it works. You need to understand how the parts are interconnected.

It can be fairly easy to identify the parts in a system, but it is more difficult to identify the interconnections. Often, the most difficult part to see within a system is its purpose. However, it can be the most important part to identify, because the purpose often determines the system's behavior. It is also important to be aware that the real purpose may not be what is explicitly stated or written down as a goal, although it could be. The best way to discover the real purpose of a system is to examine how it behaves.[10] Overall, a system is a structure with a purpose and when it's working well, its parts work together to achieve that purpose. Systems thinking will make more sense now that you have a basic understanding about what a system is.

Systemic Structure

Let's start with the definition of a structure. A structure is something that is built, and it is made up of multiple parts that are put together in a particular way. A building, an organizational chart, and a skeleton are examples of structures. Systemic structure is similar, but it has an interesting twist. Many of its parts are often invisible!

Systemic structure is the underlying pattern of interrelationships among the key elements in a system. In a system, these elements can include the decision making process, the mental models of the participants, and formal and informal communication channels. These elements are often invisible until someone points them out. That's the value of systems thinking. It provides a problem-solving strategy that enables people to identify visible and invisible parts of the systemic structure.

The whole structure needs to be identified and understood because **the structure**, the pattern of interrelationships, **influences the behavior of the system over time.** In fact, Senge believes that the very first principle of systems thinking is that within a system, **structure influences behavior.**[11]

To help you understand systemic structure, think back to the structure of your brain. The brain stem, limbic system, and cerebrum are the three key visible parts of its structure. However, what you see is not a true picture of its systemic structure which explains how your brain operates. Only when you understand the invisible interrelationships among the parts, for example between the thalamus and Miss Amy G, and among the neurons within the brain can you really begin to understand why you behave the way you do. That's why you needed to know how your brain works. Remember, the main job, the purpose of your brain is to enable you to survive. Your brain's systemic structure influences your behavior.

"Systemic structure" is not easy to identify, because the underlying structure of a system can be complex, dynamic, and yes, sometimes invisible! Systems thinkers need to find all parts of the structure including the invisible ones. You probably sense that there is a problem here. If some of the parts of the "systemic structure" are invisible, then how are they identified? They are identified by using the tools of systems thinking and system dynamics.

People as Part of the Structure

One more major point needs to be made before leaving the topic of systemic structure. In human systems, the "structure" is not outside of people. People themselves are part of the structure, but many people are unaware of that fact. That means that the human element of the system is often invisible. If a system is having problems, people frequently look for something or someone "outside" the system on which to blame its poor performance. They seek an identifiable cause to explain the way the system is behaving, but they do not look within the system.

Systems thinkers, however, know that the cause of a systems problem is seldom "out there". Using systems thinking, the cause of a systems problem is usually found "inside" the system itself—in the interrelationships among the components that form its structure. People are one component of the structure. The good news is that since people are part of the structure of human systems, they have the power to change it from within. [12] This is a major point in systems thinking. It also leads to the next vocabulary word — leverage.

Leverage

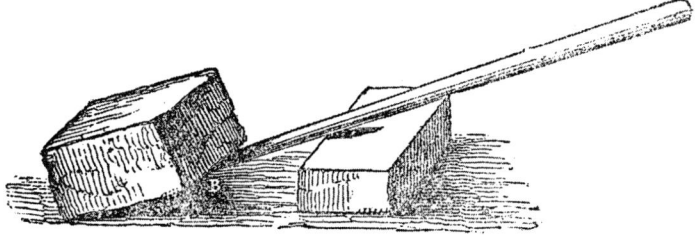

Once you have identified the systemic structure, you then try to find the point within the system where a relatively small change can lead to huge improvements within it. That's the leverage point, and that's where the power lies. That's the gold mine in systems thinking.

Knowledge about the power of leverage is not new. Almost 2,300 years ago, Archimedes, the Greek scientist and mathematician, wrote about the power of leverage when he said, "Give me a lever long enough and a ful-crum on which to place it and I shall move the world." In modern times, Senge states that leverage is "… seeing where actions and changes in struc-tures can lead to significant, enduring improvements."[13] However, it's not easy to find the leverage point, because it is seldom obvious. It is often not found close in either time or space to the symptoms of the systems problem. Sometimes it is completely counter-intuitive, so you would never find it using traditional thinking alone.[14] That's why the tools of systems thinking are needed. It is worth the effort to find where the leverage is, because it is a point of real power.

There is a major barrier to finding the leverage in systems. Do you have any idea what it might be? What seems to be the obstacle to everything? You'll find the answer in the next vocabulary phrase.

Mental Models

Did you know the answer? Mental models are a huge barrier to finding the leverage point and solving systems problems. As you know, they are often unstated, which means they are invisible. Everything within a system including its beliefs, purpose, and goals stems from its mental models. The concept of mental models is a key part of systems thinking, and they are important elements of systemic structure. Everything flows out of mental models:

MENTAL MODELS to BELIEFS/GOALS/PURPOSE to STRUCTURE to BEHAVIOR.

Mental models form the beliefs, goals, and sense of purpose that shape the structure of a system which influences its behavior. You already know that mental models are often difficult to identify, but now you also know how essential it is to identify them. Systems thinkers use a strategy to find them. When they study systems problems, they reverse the way the process flows. In order to identify the mental models, they watch the system's behavior. Remember, the behavior helps to identify the structure, and the structure helps to identify the system's purpose—its real purpose, as seen from its behavior, not simply the stated purpose. From there, they back up into understanding the mental models that are driving the system. Once mental models are identified, they can be examined.

Although it is extremely hard to change mental models, this is the location within a system where leverage will be most effective. Change efforts that help people examine their mental models and change them can trigger structural change that can transform systems.[15]

Linear and Non-Linear Thinking

A traditional thinker thinks about the world from a linear, cause and effect, point of view. **A causes B.** Traditional thinkers expect predictable behavior from the variables they are studying. They do not anticipate surprises. The problem with this is that the real world is full of surprises. Unfortunately, that means that it is not predictable, so linear thinking is not enough to solve systemic problems.

A systems thinker thinks about the world from a nonlinear point of view. He "sees" **looped interconnections** everywhere. He knows that he cannot totally understand, control, or predict what will happen as he tries to solve a systems problem. As a result, and this is a key point, systems thinkers know that systems problems are unpredictable, not controllable, and only understandable in a general way. I'll repeat Dr. Kahneman's quote from chapter 1, The Power of Perception, "An unbiased appreciation of uncertainty is a cornerstone of rationality". Systems thinkers understand the value of uncertainty.

The following example about growing crops helps to explain the difference between linear and non-linear thinking.[16] It starts with a linear relationship. If you add fertilizer to the soil, then you increase the production of crops.

- Put 10 pounds of fertilizer on a field and the crop yield increases by 2 bushels.
- Put 20 pounds of fertilizer on a field and the crop yield increases by 4 bushels.
- Put 30 pounds of fertilizer on a field and the crop yield goes up by 6 bushels.

The predictable conclusion is that more fertilizer leads to more crops. A causes B. That's a linear relationship, and so far it makes sense— common sense. If you were a farmer, then you may want to continue this practice. However, as you increase the fertilizer, you will eventually see your predictions change.

- Put 100 pounds of fertilizer on field and crop yield goes up by 10 bushels.
- Put 200 pounds of fertilizer on field and crop yield does not go up at all.
- Put 300 pounds of fertilizer on field and crop yield goes down.

If a little fertilizer produced good results, then the expectation is that a lot of fertilizer will produce even better results. That's not what happened here. The results are not what the farmer expected. It does not make common sense based on the earlier crop output. What happened? Instead of growing more plentiful crops, the soil was damaged by too much of a good thing. The results are unexpected and surprising, and they interfere with normal, linear thinking expectations of cause and effect. That's what nonlinearity does.

The important lesson here is that reasonable expectations lead to classic mistakes in a nonlinear world. Systems thinkers recognize that the real world is nonlinear; therefore it is unpredictable, uncontrollable, and full of surprises, so they should expect them and learn from them. The chances of your understanding how systems operate in the real world are greatly increased if you use nonlinear thinking instead of linear thinking.

Stock, Flow, and Feedback

You are now going to learn some specialized vocabulary that will enable you to understand the way systems function. These terms are used to describe processes that make systems visible so systems problems can be solved: stock, flow, and feedback.

A "**Stock**" is the foundation of a system.[17] It is an accumulation of an element within the system that has built up over time. Stocks are things you can count, see, feel, or measure, and they are identified using nouns. A stock could be population, water, money, minerals like oil, or even emotions like anger. A stock will change over time as a result of "flows".

Flow represents rates of change within a system as quantities of an element (population, water, money, oil, anger, etc.) flow into or out of the stock. Flows represent action, so they are identified using verbs. Stocks and flows are linked together. Stocks change over time based on the action of the flows.

If you can understand the dynamic activity of stocks and flows, then you can develop a good understanding of the behavior of complex systems.[18] To help you solidify the meaning of stocks and flows, let's consider a very simple example of a system — a bathtub system. It has one stock — water; it has one inflow — the faucet, and one outflow — the drain.

Imagine that the drain (outflow) is closed and the faucet (inflow) is open. Over time, water will accumulate in the tub. When the tub is half full, close the faucet; stop the inflow. Except for a little evaporation, you now have a static system with no change. Now let's get the flows moving to make a dynamic system. Imagine that you open the faucet at full blast (inflow) and also open the drain (outflow). What happens? Most likely the water cannot drain from the tub as fast as more water enters the tub. If the outflow is slower than the inflow, then the water will continue to rise. This is a basic systems principle: "As long as the sum of all **inflows** exceeds the sum of all outflows, the level of stock will rise".

Imagine that the tub is half full again. Open the drain, but this time open the faucet just a little bit so the water trickles in. What happens? Most likely the water will drain from the tub faster than more water enters it, so the water level will fall. This is another basic systems principle: "As long as the sum of all **outflows** exceeds the sum of all inflows, the level of stock will fall".

Finally, imagine the tub is half full again. Do not turn on the faucet. Now pull the plug and let the water drain out until the tub is a quarter full. At this point, turn on the faucet and match the rate of the water's inflow to the rate of the drain's outflow. What happens? The water level does not change, because the rate of inflow and outflow are identical. This is a balanced state which leads to another basic principle of systems thinking: "If the sum of all outflows equals the sum of all inflows, the stock level will not change; it will be held in dynamic equilibrium at whatever level it happened to be when the two sets of flows became equal".[19]

Systems thinkers pay close attention to stocks and flows. Learning about them provides you with a good foundation in systems thinking. Think about the bathtub example as you read this next systems thinking principle. Within a system, the stock "allows inflows and outflows to be independent of each other and temporarily out of balance with each other".[20] As a result of this independence, the inflows and outflows do not cause each other, but they can influence each other. This principle leads right into the next topic — feedback.

Feedback. A basic and important fact about systems is this — systems are dynamic because they change in response to feedback. Feedback is the term used to describe what happens when one element within a system influences another and that element "feeds back" information to influence the first. It is the aspect of systems thinking that strikes at the heart of traditional, linear, cause and effect thinking. With systems thinking, there is an awareness that cause and effect does not always happen. In many cases, one element does not cause another, but one element can influence another in the feedback process. Senge defines feedback as "any reciprocal flow of influence…. every influence is both *cause* and *effect*. Nothing is ever influenced in just one direction."[21]

Systems thinkers know that the elements in a system do not move in a straight line, they loop back on one another in a circular fashion. As a result, systems thinkers see "loops" instead of straight lines. Understanding "feedback" is what separates systems thinkers from traditional thinkers.

Feedback Loops: the Building Blocks of Systems Thinking

In part 1, Know Your Brain, you learned that neurons were the building blocks of the brain. Now you will learn that feedback processes or "feedback loops" are the building blocks of systems thinking.[22] A feedback loop is formed when changes in a stock influence the flows going into or out of a stock. Systems thinkers work hard at identifying the feedback loops within systems. They analyze a problem by focusing on how the elements continually influence each other through the feedback process. In fact, systems thinkers see the world around them as a collection of "feedback processes".[23] At some point, once you really grasp the concept of feedback loops, and it takes time, you will begin to see looped interconnections everywhere. You won't be able to read a news report without seeing them. Although systems can be complicated, there are only two types of feedback loops—balancing and reinforcing.

Balancing and Reinforcing Feedback Loops

Balancing Feedback Loop: The balancing loop, which is also called a stabilizing loop and a negative loop, is about stability, equilibrium, and making adjustments to either fix or prevent problems. It is a self-correcting process that keeps the performance of a system close to its desired state or within its normal operating range. It attempts to limit change and maintain the status quo.

Balancing feedback loops are found whenever goal-directed behavior is expected. For example, the human body and its process of homeostasis is a good example of a system in a balancing loop. One of your body's targets is to keep your temperature around 98.6 degrees Fahrenheit, which is considered normal. If you get too hot, you sweat to help your body cool down. If you get too cold, you shiver to warm your body up. Your body is programmed with a temperature balancing process to maintain internal stability. If the balance is disturbed, then your body takes action to get the system back in balance. Balancing feedback loops like to remain stable and do not like change.[24]

Reinforcing Feedback Loop: The reinforcing loop, which is also called an amplifying loop and a positive loop, is all about change. Frequently, reinforcing feedback loops represent "engines of growth" according to Senge. When you are in a system that is growing, you can be sure that you are experiencing reinforcing feedback. A reinforcing feedback loop seeks to run away from the status quo. It generates change in only one direction— bigger. However, the change will either generate bigger growth or generate bigger collapse. If the reinforcing loop generates growth, it is known as a **virtuous cycle**. For example, if you put money in the bank every month, the compound interest will generate growth, and that's a virtuous and good result. However, a reinforcing loop can also generate collapse, and in that case, it is known as a **vicious cycle**. For example, the stock market sometimes receives bad news and stock prices start to drop. This can cause some people to panic, so they take their money out and the collapse gets worse. This vicious cycle can lead to devastating results for the economy and individual investors.[25]

With this vocabulary, you have acquired the basics of a new language that will help you develop a more precise understanding of systems thinking and of systemic structure. The vocabulary will help you to understand systems stories and to tell them as well. With this new vocabulary as a foundation, you are in a better position to understand the mental habits of a systems thinker. Let's explore the 13 habits.

The Unique Mental Habits of Systems Thinkers

The following chart, "Habits of a Systems Thinker" (HOST), is an excellent tool that visually depicts the unique mental habits of a systems thinker. It is reprinted here with the permission of the Waters Foundation [http://www.watersfoundation.org].

Seeks to understand the big picture

Observes how elements within systems change over time, generating patterns and trends

Recognizes that a system's structure generates its behavior

Identifies the circular nature of complex cause and effect relationships

Habits of a Systems Thinker

Changes perspectives to increase understanding

Surfaces and tests assumptions

Considers an issue fully and resists the urge to come to a quick conclusion

Considers how mental models affect current reality and the future

Uses understanding of system structure to identify possible leverage actions

Considers both short and long-term consequences of actions

Finds where unintended consequences emerge

Recognizes the impact of time delays when exploring cause and effect relationships

Checks results and changes actions if needed: "successive approximation"

The Mental Habits of Systems Thinkers

The Waters Foundation is an outstanding resource that exists to bring systems thinking into K-12 schools. As you read through the habits, think about the dispositions that you need to be a systems thinker. Is there any overlap with other categories of thinking?

The following information explains more fully each of the 13 mental habits. The quoted information is located on the Waters Foundation website. The text in bold print is very similar to the caption accompanying each image.

1. Engages in Holistic, "Big Picture" thinking. This girl looks into the distance and **seeks to understand the big picture**. She sees the forest rather than the details of a single tree. "A systems thinker 'steps back' to examine the dynamics of a system and the interrelationships among its parts."

2. Awareness of the Inevitability of Change. This boy is working with an hourglass and **observes how elements within systems change over time, generating patterns and trends**. "Dynamic systems are made up of interdependent elements, the values of which change over time. A systems thinker may use a tool such as a behavior-over-time graph to record and observe the patterns and trends these changes generate."

3. Inside Focus Avoids Placing Blame. These young people **recognize that a system's structure generates its behavior.** They don't try to blame each other for the break. "A systems thinker understands that blame is not an effective practice to bring about lasting change to a complex system….to effect change within a system, s/he must use knowledge of the system's structure."

4. Engages in Circular, Nonlinear Thinking. This boy sees the cause and effect relationship between the bee and the flower. He **identifies the circular nature of complex cause and effect relationships.** "A systems thinker knows that the cause-effect relationships within dynamic systems are circular rather than linear."

5. Open-minded. These boys are looking at the same object from different perspectives. A systems thinker **changes perspectives to increase understanding.** "To understand how a dynamic system actually works, a systems thinker looks at the system from a variety of angles and from differing points of view, perhaps in collaboration with others."

6. Recognizes Assumptions in Self and Others. These young people have different assumptions about the cereal they are eating. One thinks it's full of sugar and the other thinks it's a source of vitamins. A systems

thinker **surfaces and tests assumptions.** "A systems thinker will rigorously examine assumptions in order to gain insight into a system. Insight put into action can lead to improved performance." The Ladder of Inference is a visual tool to use as you surface and test assumptions.

7. Controls Impulsivity. This young lady is frustrated by car trouble and has an impulse to use the hammer on it, but she resists. A systems thinker **considers an issue fully and resists the urge to come to a quick conclusion.** "A systems thinker is patient. S/he will take time to understand the system's structure and its behaviors before recommending and implementing a course of action. A systems thinker also understands that succumbing to the urge for a quick solution can create more problems in the long term."

8. Engages in Collective Inquiry and Dialogue about Assumptions. These young people are seeing the same event at the same time, but are forming different mental models. One sees snow and assumes he'll make a snowman while the other sees snow and assumes she will be shoveling it. A systems thinker **considers how mental models affect current reality and the future.** You know how your brain works and how perceptions are formed, so you understand the importance of this habit. "In any given situation, an individual perceives and interprets what is happening, thus creating a picture, or mental model, of some aspect of the world. Mental models are comprised of assumptions, beliefs, and values that people hold, sometimes for a lifetime. A systems thinker is aware of how these mental models influence perspectives and ultimately actions taken."

9. Searches for High-Leverage Solutions. This boy wanted to move a huge rock. He is using a simple tool, a lever, to move it. A well-planned small action can have big results. A systems thinker **uses understanding of system structure to identify possible leverage actions.** "Based on an understanding of the structure, interdependencies, and feedback within a system, a systems thinker implements the leverage action that seems most likely to produce desirable outcomes. Ideally, taking a small action at the leverage point can lead to significant improvements within the system.

10. Future Oriented. This boy has money in his hand. Will he put it in the bank or buy a donut? A systems thinker **considers both short and long -term consequences of actions.** Impulse control and delaying gratifica-

tion are aspects of this habit. "Before taking action to change a dynamic system, a system thinker weighs the possible short and long-term outcomes of the action. This practice increases the probability of the chosen action producing the desired outcomes."

11. Awareness of Uncertainty and Unintended Consequences. The mouse is getting away with the cheese. That was unexpected. A systems thinker **finds where unintended consequences emerge.** "Before any action is taken to change the outcomes of a dynamic system, a systems thinker uses proven strategies (e.g. systems archetypes or a systems dynamics model) to anticipate unintended consequences. If it is determined that probable unintended consequences are unacceptable, another course of action is explored."

12. Recognizes Change Over Time. This boy is having second thoughts about eating the candy because he is imagining himself at the dentist's office. A systems thinker **recognizes the impact of time delays when exploring cause and effect relationships.** "A systems thinker recognizes that when an action is taken within a complex, dynamic system, the outcome of the action may not be seen for some time. A systems thinker will account for the impact these delays may have within the system."

13. Works at Continuous Improvement. This artist has stepped back and is checking her painting. A systems thinker **checks results and changes actions if needed: "successive approximation".** "By definition, dynamic systems are constantly changing over time. A systems thinker, therefore, monitors and evaluates the behavior of the system and takes action when needed to assure the system continues to produce the desired results. By trying a situation and then assessing the results, understanding of the issue will increase. Over time, each cycle or successive approximation, of checking results and changing actions if needed, will move the system closer to the desired goal."

As you read through this list, I hope you recognized that the many of the mental habits listed here for systems thinking are also required for skillful thinking in general and critical thinking in particular. They include controlling impulsivity, delaying gratification, changing perspective and recognizing assumptions, considering alternatives, and being persistent. Let's continue to deepen your understanding of systems thinking by examining some systems visualization tools.

Visualization Tools

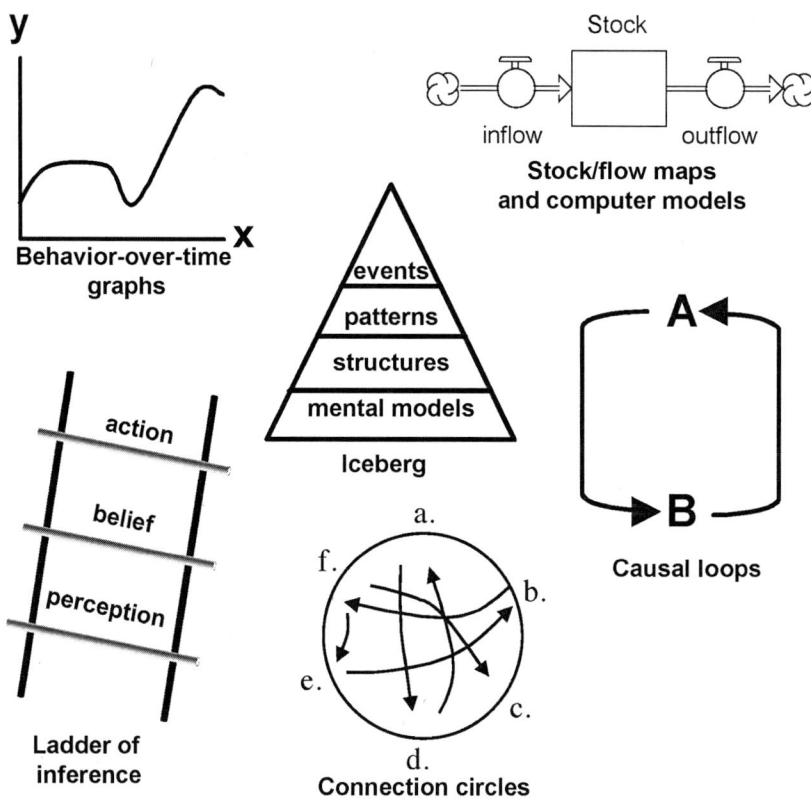

Image provided by Systems Thinking in Schools Waters Foundation, watersfoundation.org

Now that you have learned about stocks, flows, feedback, and feedback loops, you are ready to learn about some of the systems thinking visualization tools that are used to tell the story about a system. These tools create dynamic, visual models, which everyone can "see". Without these tools, the complexity of systems would be difficult, if not impossible, to visualize, understand, or explain.

The basic tools include the following: Behavior over Time Graphs (BOTGs); Causal Loop Diagrams (CLDs), and Stock-and-Flow Diagrams (SFDs). You can see the design of these tools in the previous graphic. Other visualization tools include the "Ladder of Inference" and the "Iceberg". The Ladder of Inference is a tool you learned about in chapter 6, critical thinking. It is a useful tool in systems thinking for identifying mental models. The "Iceberg" is a valuable systems thinking tool that is especially useful for people who are new to systems thinking. It is widely used in schools that teach systems thinking. This tool helps you probe into the hidden parts of a system where the real causes of systems problems, the mental models, usually lurk. In this section, the BOTG, CLD, SFD, and Ladder of Inference will be presented within the structure of the Iceberg.

The Iceberg—A Special Visualization Tool

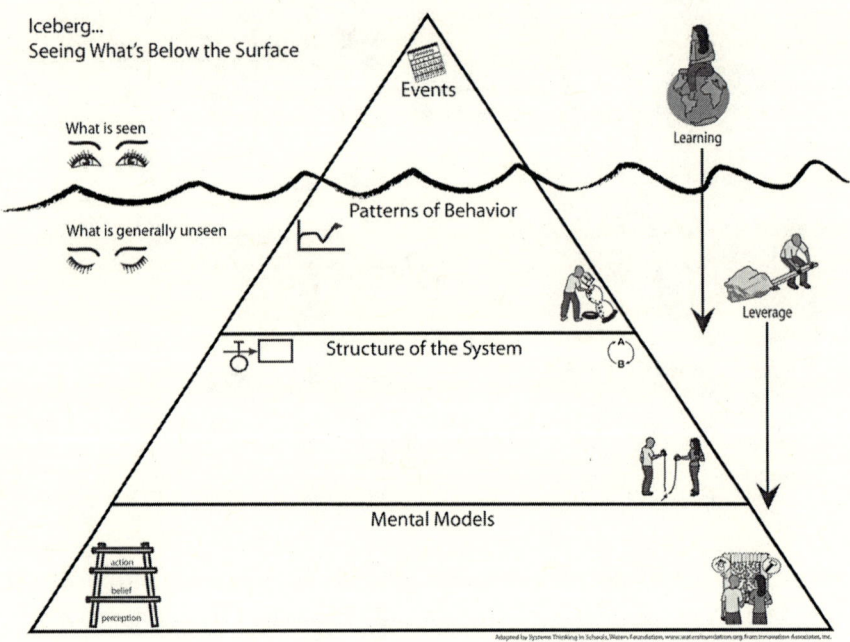

This "Iceberg" image is printed with the permission of the Waters Foundation [http://www.watersfoundation.org]. The "Iceberg" serves as a metaphor for the problems in systems thinking, since a systems problem and an iceberg have a lot in common. In both cases, all you see at first is the tip, which is perhaps only 20% of the total mass of the iceberg and 20% of the total problem. 80% of the mass of the iceberg is underwater and unseen, but this is where the action is; this is where the ocean currents act upon it. 80% of a systems problem may also be hidden from view. As the iceberg tool shows, there are four levels of a systems problem that need to be identified: events, patterns, structures, and mental models.[26]

You already know how important mental models are in driving your thoughts and behaviors. They also drive the action in a system. Since they are unseen, some people forget abut them. That's one of the values of the Iceberg tool; it reminds you of all the major components of a system. Although mental models are pictured at the base of the Iceberg, you can start looking for them in the beginning and at every level. Mental models permeate the entire structure. The Iceberg image emphasizes the huge role that mental models play in systems problems. They cannot be ignored.

The Iceberg also provides sets of questions that stimulate the communication skills of inquiry, dialogue, and reflection to help you get a complete picture of the total structure. You may wonder how a simple Iceberg image and its accompanying questions can help to reveal the patterns of behavior, the systemic structure, and the mental models that are below the surface. The answer is simple. Like Dr. deBono's "Six Thinking Hats", it provides a safe structure for dialogue. People need safe structures in order to communicate effectively. Let's examine the Iceberg.

FOUR LEVELS OF ICEBERG QUESTIONS

Whenever they are trying to solve a problem, systems thinkers are aware of and use the four levels of the Iceberg: Events; Patterns of Behavior; Structure of the System, and Mental Models. Unlike systems thinkers, some people only see the tip of the iceberg when it comes to finding the actual cause of problems, so they often impulsively jump to accept the first symptomatic solution that is offered at the event level. That may buy them some time, but it does not solve the problem. It will return. As a result, people keep treading water, sometimes barely surviving when a problem becomes overwhelming.

To solve twenty-first century problems, leaping at temporary solutions won't do. It is necessary to identify the fundamental causes of problems and seek long-term solutions. Let's examine each level of the Iceberg to learn how it can help you achieve that goal.

Level 1 - Events

Level 1 - Events: Events are the most visible elements in a system, but they are seldom the most important for problem solving. Seeing the world as a series of events is like seeing only the tip of an iceberg. Much analysis, like TV analysis, does not go deeper than the event level. People who are fascinated by events pay little attention to their history, so they neglect clues from history about the structure from which events and behavior flow. History is important because long-term behavior provides clues to the structure.[27] The Iceberg tool guides you to ask deeper questions, even at the events level.

Questions: Level 1. Events

- Name a critical event (such as a crisis) or problem that happened recently.
- Tell the story. What is happening?
- How have people responded?
- How have people tried to solve it?

What's the next step? You want to examine some of these events more closely to see if they provide any clues to the patterns of behavior within the system.

Level 2 - Patterns of Behavior

Events accumulate into patterns of behavior. How do you identify these patterns in a system? You use the "Behavior Over Time Graph (BOTG) to chart the course of related events over time. This simple tool enables you to plot on a graph the events that lead to changes in behavior within systems. Examining events on a time graph helps to clarify the key variables in a system and to suggest how they may be interconnected.[28]

Being able to identify the behavior of a system is very important. Remember, in order to tell the story of a system, you need to know its purpose. You learn its real purpose by studying its behavior over time. BOTGs reveal "what" is happening by gathering data about the systems history and examining these events.

The BOTG consists of a regular line graph with an x (horizontal) and y (vertical) axis. Time is always on the x axis. The y axis shows the behavior that is changing over time. It could be changes in population, changes in test scores, changes in infection rate, changes in profit, changes in computer use, etc. It is useful for any change over time that you want to examine. As you examine data and use real facts instead of opinions to draw the graph, you are learning important parts of the story. As you ask questions to plot the graph, you begin to see how the line depicts the pattern of change.

Questions: Level 2. Patterns of Behavior

- What is the history of the event described in level one?
- What has been happening?
- Have we been here before?
- What patterns or trends do you see emerging?
- What does the past say about our current situation? You can then answer questions like the following:
- What is changing?
- How is it changing?
- What caused the change?
- How did we get here?
- What's working well?

- During what time period have the changes occured?

If you have several BOTGs for different behaviors for the same problem, then ask: Do you see any connections or interrelationships between or among the graphs?

Economists often focus on this level. They examine patterns of behavior over time as they examine past trends for GNP, stocks, interest rates, etc. They see growth, collapse, and stagnation which provide clues to the structure, but they often don't go deeply enough to improve long-term performance.[29] To go deeper, move to level 3. At this level you begin to answer not only the question, "What is changing?" but also "Why is it changing?"

Level 3 - Structure of the System

If there is a problem within the system, it is most likely caused by the structure itself. It isn't a surprise then that this level is where systems thinkers spend a lot of time. Remember, the structure of the system is the source of the system's behavior. Systems analysts move back and forth between level two, patterns of behavior, and this level in their quest to identify and solve systems' problems. At this level they use two basic tools to help them identify structure: Causal Loop Diagrams and Stock-and-Flow Diagrams. Using these tools, nonlinear relationships, which are difficult to see, are easier to find.

The key to seeing the world systemically is to stop seeing linear cause and effect relationships and begin seeing looped relationships. When you look at one component in a system and then at another, and you can see the circle of influence between them, then you are beginning to "see" and think like a systems thinker.[30]

Causal Loop Diagram

Causal Loop Diagram

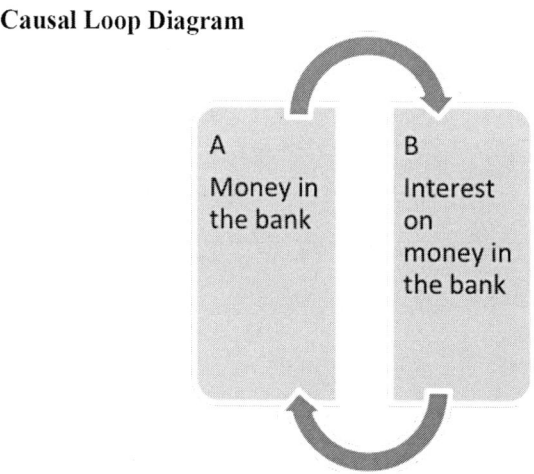

A

Money in
the bank

B

Interest
on
money in
the bank

Figure 8.1: Causal Loop Diagram

For example, Figure 8.1 is an example of a looped, nonlinear relationship with the two elements influencing each other. This Causal Loop Diagram (CLD) uses arrows and letters to represent the circular flow of the systems behavior. Arrows connect the variables that are changing over time, and the arrows create the image of circular feedback.

CLDs help to tell the story of a system, so let's read around the loop, starting at A to tell this story. Money in the bank (A) is the cause that leads to (B) the interest on the money in the bank which is the effect. Next, the original effect (B) then influences the original cause (A) money in the bank because now, with interest, there is more money in the bank, which influences (B) because more money means more interest which again influences (A) which again influences (B) and on and on in a causal loop. A: Money = B: Interest = A: more money = B: more interest = A: more money...

Basically, causal loop diagrams provide a sketch to show how feedback works. In this case, you have a reinforcing feedback loop. When the first variable changes, the second one changes in the same direction. Although this is a simple example, the bottom line is that this visual tool makes it a lot easier to communicate about feedback loops in complex systems than words alone can. The next tool, stock-and-flow diagrams is the most powerful of the basic tools.

Stock-and-Flow Diagram

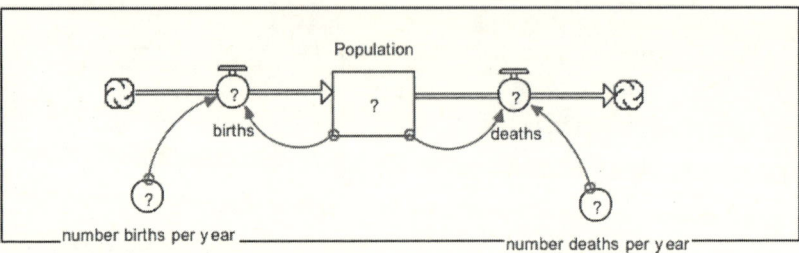

Figure 8.2: Stock and Flow Diagram

A stock-and-flow diagram (or map), pictured above, is the basic tool used to visualize the structure of a system. The structure itself is made up of stocks, flows, and feedback loops. One of the major values of a SFD is that it provides a concrete diagram that helps shift the mind into systems thinking by examining the inflows and outflows of a system. This simple structure tells a story regardless of a person's actual language, so it becomes a universal means of communication.

As you look at this image of a stock-and-flow map, you see several components. A rectangle represents the stock (an accumulation of something) which in this case is "population". The flow, the part of the diagram that shows the action, is represented by "flowpipes". Flowpipes have three parts: 1. the pipe itself with an arrow indicating the direction of the flow; 2. a cloud that represents a boundary—the boundary from which the flow emerges or the boundary where it ends, and 3. the flowpipe regulator. The regulator is located in the middle of the pipe. It looks like a tank with a spigot on top. The regulator can increase or decrease the rate of change in the stock.

This SFD represents a Population Dynamics Model. In this model, the inflow pipe represents births, and the outflow pipe, represents deaths. The stock (population) changes depending upon the number of births and deaths, which is the rate of change of the inflows and outflows.

Does the population itself influence the rates of change? Of course it does, so that influence is indicated by a "connector", a curved arrow. The connector represents "feedback". [31]The arrow leaving population and connecting to births indicates that just as the number of births changes the population, the size of the population itself influences the number of births. More people, or deer, or rabbits means more babies, fawns, or bunnies. There is a feedback relationship here. The same feedback relationship exists for deaths, so there is a connector from population to deaths. The size of the population also influences the number of deaths.

Systems analysts want more information to tell the real story regarding the stock. In this example, they will want to know how quickly the population reproduces itself or dies off. Another component is needed— a converter, which is represented by a simple circle. Converters capture details and perform algebraic operations. In this model, there are two converters— one for the number of births per year and one for the number of deaths per year. The converters influence the flows, and this is indicated by the connectors. As you can see, the SFD creates a visual image of the dynamic, nonlinear relationships in a systemic structure.

Questions: Level 3. Structure of the System

- What are the forces/causes that created the patterns and trends in level two?
- What are the consequences of these patterns and trends?
- Are there any unintended consequences of our actions?
- Do our responses cause more problems?
- How do these systemic elements seem to influence each other?
- If you want to change the patterns/trends, then what fundamental aspects of the organization must be changed? A Causal Loop Diagram is helpful for understanding "why" things are happening in a system. It shows how elements in a system influence each other through feedback loops. As a result, it highlights the circular nature of systems.[27]

Level 4 - Mental Models

Level 4 is the sweet spot in the system. It is the source of the mental models, assumptions, paradigms, and beliefs. Everything starts here—the purpose, goals, flows, feedback. Intervention at this level is most likely to change and transform a system.[32] This is an excellent time to use the Ladder of Inference. In addition, here are some key questions to ask at this level.

Questions: Level 4. Mental Models

- What is the thinking (beliefs, assumptions) that is leading to the choices being made?
- What thinking lets the system persist as it does?
- What is it about my own thinking that causes this structure to persist?
- What is it about other people's thinking that causes this structure to persist?
- How do other stakeholders view our situation?
- Do our assumptions about other stakeholders affect our decisions?
- Can the mental models of the different players be brought safely to the surface, so they can be discussed?

Overall, the Iceberg is a powerful tool that enables you to dig deeply into the structure of a system. The four levels of questioning provide a useful structure for investigation. This tool helps you tell the real story about what is happening within a complex system. It also will help you resist leaping to short-term, symptomatic solutions to problems.

The tools described here, BOTGs, CLDs, and SFDs, as well as the Ladder of Inference and the Iceberg, can be created by hand with paper and pencil for studying relatively simple systems problems. However, for complex problems, paper and pencil are not sufficient. Sophisticated computer simulations are required.

Computer Simulation Modeling

Computer simulations are the highest level of visualization tools in systems thinking. They are used to conduct rigorous analysis so systems thinkers can study and solve very complex problems. However, they use the basic tool that you have been reading about— the stock-and-flow diagram with its interrelated stocks, flows, and feedback loops. With a computer simulation, you work with a team to build a model of the structure of your system. You list the parts, the variables that are important in the problem you face. These variables are things that change over time. You work together to figure out how these variables interact and affect one another. In the process, you are clarifying assumptions and examining mental models.

The SFD model of population dynamics that I used was very simple, and it could have been created with pencil and paper. However, I used the STELLA software from isee systems [http://www.iseesystems.com] to make the model just to show you what a basic computer simulation model looks like.

With computer simulations, systems analysts can more easily study the behavior of feedback. The team assigns mathematical equations to the variables. The computer then runs the program. One part of the model can even be manipulated in a "what if" effort to see what the impact of a planned change would be on the whole system. This is one way to find out the intended and unintended consequences of solutions to problems before they are actually implemented. As a result of the concrete scientific study of systems, using computer simulation models, assumptions can be identified, and intelligent and informed approaches to complex problem solving can be found.[33]

The Hope and Reality of Systems Thinking

Systems thinking provides hope. Its tools enable systems analysts to create models of the structure of a system that has a problem. How is this helpful? The model of the structure forces people to stand "outside" the system and look objectively at the whole system. The people who create the models say that perceptions and paradigms are changed as people examine the structure and begin to question their mental models that created it. People learn that no mental model is 100% accurate. All mental models, all worldviews, are approximations of reality and not reality itself. As people learn this lesson, they may feel empowered to change their perceptions.[34] That is the hope. That is one reason that systems thinking is such a powerful way of thinking.

The reality of systems thinking has the same limitation. No matter how sophisticated a computer simulation model may be, it is not possible to capture in a model 100% of the structure of a system. Donella Meadows informed people that they would make a "terrible mistake" if they thought that systems thinking would finally fix the problems within systems and make them work. According to Meadows,

Self-organizing, nonlinear, feedback systems are inherently unpredictable. They are not controllable. They are understandable only in the most general way. The goal of foreseeing the future exactly and preparing for it perfectly is unreasonable. The idea of making a complex system do just what you want it to do can be achieved only temporarily, at best....Our science itself... leads us into irreducible uncertainty.

That statement makes it clear that systems thinking is not the cure-all for the world's problems. However, that statement highlights one of the most valuable lessons that systems thinking teaches. It recognizes that there are no absolutes. No one knows what is absolutely certain. Do you recall that in chapter 5, Common Sense Thinking, Daniel Kahneman, the author of Thinking Fast and Slow, stated that one of the signs of wisdom is admitting you do not have all the answers. You need to have a tolerance for ambiguity and an appreciation of uncertainty to be truly wise. You need to be willing to continue to learn and change. That is truly the hope and reality of systems thinking. Despite its limitations, systems thinking provides the best opportunity to avoid the catastrophe that Einstein predicted. As a systems thinker, you will come closer to solving complex problems than you would with other types of thinking.

Summary

In this chapter you learned the basics of systems thinking which includes a unique mindset, a specialized vocabulary, and some powerful visualization tools. You learned about systems, systems thinking, system dynamics, and how to become a systems thinker.

You now know that systems thinking enables you to see the big picture about how a system really works by revealing the interrelationships among all of its parts. With a systems thinking perspective, your mind shifts from seeing parts of a system to seeing the whole. You begin to see nonlinear looped relationships rather than simple linear cause and effect relationships.

You already knew about the importance of mental models, but the critical role that mental models play as a major part of systems problems has been reinforced. You know how important it is to examine your mental models and be willing to change them in order to solve complex problems. You stop seeking "one right answer" because systems thinkers do not fall into the trap of thinking that there is always a simple, quick-fix solution to problems. You are just beginning, but you are on your way to making this world a better place by learning this new way of thinking. In the next chapter, you will learn about self-control thinking which is valuable in every aspect of your life.

Questions for Reflection

1. **HEAD:** What did you learn? Imagine that you belong to a Book Club that is reading this book. Summarize the key points that you want to highlight during discussion.
2. **HEART:** How do you feel about what you learned?
3. **ACTION STEP:** What are you going to do now? Suggestions: learn more about the topic; share what you learned, or practice what you learned.

CHAPTER 9

Self-Control Thinking

When emotions dominate our actions, we make mistakes.
— Coach John Wooden

Self-control requires conscious thinking. Your thinking brain needs to be awake and alert. If Miss Amy G Dala, the queen of your emotional brain, is allowed to be the lead actor in your life, then you will have no self-control. In order to exercise self-control, you need to learn a few strategies to tame Miss Amy G.

Your prefrontal cortex (PFC), the CEO of your brain and its master brakes, is responsible for taming her, but only IF you activate it. That means in order to be a self-control thinker, you need to learn a few strategies to wake up lazy System 2. As you know, your PFC will not automatically work for you. It is content to let your survival and your emotional brains do most of the work.

When that happens, your impulses rule and you and your conscious brain have little involvement. That is unacceptable for a Mega-Thinker. In this chapter, you will learn a few strategies that will help you develop self-control thinking by activating your PFC, so you can make conscious decisions about what to believe and do.

What is Self-Control?

Let's begin with the definition of self-control provided by legendary college basketball coach, John Wooden.

Self-Control

- *Emotions under control.*
- *Delicate adjustment between mind and body.*
- *Keep judgement and common sense.*

Self-control is one of the fifteen personal qualities that Coach Wooden lists in his "Pyramid of Success [http://www.CoachJohnWooden.com]". He explains why self-control is important in the following statement:

To become our best, good judgment and common sense are essential. No matter the task—whether physical or mental—if our emotions take over, we're not going to execute near our personal level of competency, because both judgment and common sense will be impaired. When emotions dominate our actions, we make mistakes.[1]

Coach Wooden doesn't use the word amygdala, but you know he is talking about Miss Amy G when he talks about emotions. Coach Wooden states that controlling emotions involves a delicate adjustment between body and mind. Emotions rise up from your body's sensory experiences. At some point they trigger your brain to act upon them. If you have self-control, a part of your brain becomes aware of the tipping point between your feeling and your behavior. It acts like an inner voice to alert you to intervene by waking up your PFC. That's how you maintain emotional balance. There is powerful information emerging from a field of study called "Emotional Intelligence" that will help you understand how to achieve self-control and emotional balance.

New Intelligences

"Emotional Intelligence" is a hot topic today in the research lab, business world, and educational arena. There are many books, workshops, school programs, and websites dedicated to it. Once upon a time, but not too long ago, there was simply the concept of "Intelligence" as a human trait. The movement towards recognizing that there is more than one kind of intelligence started in 1983 with Dr. Howard Gardner of Harvard University when he first published his book, Frames of Mind: The Theory of Multiple Intelligences. In his book, he identified seven separate intelligences that people possess in varying degrees: logical mathematical; linguistic; interpersonal; intrapersonal; bodily kinesthetic; musical, and spatial. Since then two more were added: naturalist and existential which brings the number to nine.

Dr. Gardner believed that all of these intelligences can be strengthened and nurtured. Two of them, the intrapersonal and the interpersonal intelligences, can be viewed as components of emotional intelligence.[2] People who possess a high degree of intrapersonal intelligence exhibit the following characteristics: 1. they are excellent in self-awareness and can identify their own emotions; 2. they understand the basis for their feelings, and 3. they know what motivates them. People who possess a high degree of interpersonal intelligence exhibit the following characteristics: 1. they have excellent "people" skills so they interact well with others; 2. they understand the emotions, desires, and motivations of other people, and 3. they communicate effectively and manage their relationships with others well. All of these characteristics are also key aspects of emotional intelligence

Emotional Intelligence Defined

The term "Emotional Intelligence" (EI) was coined by two psychologists, Dr. John Mayer of the University of New Hampshire and Dr. Peter Salovey of Yale University in 1990. Their work influenced many people including Daniel Goleman, Ph.D. It wasn't until Goleman's book, Emotional Intelligence, was published in 1995 that the concept of EI came to the attention of the general public. In a more recent book, Working with Emotional Intelligence (1998), Goleman recognizes the important role that self-control plays in emotional intelligence. He states that self-control means "Keeping Disruptive Emotions and Impulses in Check".[3] People with this competence do the following:

- Manage their impulsive feelings and emotions well
- Stay composed, positive, and unflappable even in trying moments
- Think clearly and stay focused under pressure

Goleman recognizes that the ability to manage impulses depends on the brain's emotional centers working together with its executive centers. That means Miss Amy G and your PFC have to work together for you to gain self-control, and to get them working together requires emotional intelligence!

Definitions of Emotional Intelligence

Let's step back and examine two definitions of EI.

Definition 1 by Mayer and Salovey:

Emotional Intelligence is the ability to perceive emotions, to access and generate emotions so as to assist thought, to understand emotions and emotional knowledge, and to effectively regulate emotions so as to promote emotional and intellectual growth.[4]

The phrase "the ability to perceive emotions" in this definition focuses on the perception process in the brain. Remember that Dr. deBono calls perception the most important part of thinking. As you recall, perception takes place as sensory data enters your brain and your reticular activating system (RAS) admits it into the complex system of your brain. Perception happens early in the admission process, and it takes place at the unconscious level.

Definition 2 by Goleman:

Emotional Intelligence includes …*abilities such as being able to motivate oneself and persist in the face of frustrations; to control impulse and delay gratification; to regulate one's moods and keep distress from swamping the ability to think; to empathize and hope.*[5]

Doesn't this definition sound familiar? It emphasizes the importance of dispositions. Some dispositions are beneficial and some are not. Unlike an impulse that is brief and just triggers an action, dispositions are habits of mind and behavior that have been programmed into your brain. You developed many of them during your childhood. By now they have become well-traveled brain pathways created by the activity of your neurons as they fire and wire together. They are part of your normal temperament.

Sometimes people are described in terms of their dispositions, for example, he's very impulsive or he's very patient. If you have developed negative habits, and you keep practicing them, then you make the pathways stronger. If you begin to practice positive dispositions, then with effort, you nurture them, strengthen them, and eventually wipe out the old negative pathways. It takes a lot of will and effort to change your negative dispositions into positive ones, but it can be done. With emotional intelligence in general and self-control thinking in particular, you gain more control of your life. You identify your personal "hot buttons", so you focus on the emotional impulses that disrupt your life, and you respond to them using positive behaviors.

Self-awareness is the Key

With self-control thinking, you move from unconscious reactions to conscious responses. You do this because of your sense of self-awareness. Dr. David Sousa describes self-awareness as ...*the ability to see yourself with your own eyes and be aware of your beliefs, your goals, your values, your inner voice, the rules you live by, and the ways these contribute to your perception of the world you live in.*[6]

Without self-awareness, you are not in control. Miss Amy G and blind emotion will rule your actions. Self-awareness happens in phases. It follows the levels of Bloom's taxonomy: psychomotor, affective, and cognitive.

- **Phase 1** begins when your brain is **aroused** by physiological changes. It becomes **aware** of what is happening within your body as it is happening (psychomotor level). The symptoms may include a racing heart, faster breathing, rising blood pressure, tensing muscles, sweating hands, and blushing.
- In **Phase 2**, your brain is now **alert and paying attention** to a rising emotion (affective level). Will you unconsciously react or consciously respond to the emotion?
- **This is the key moment**.
- **Phase 3** begins when you take **conscious action**.

The key moment falls between Phase 2 and Phase 3. Do you or do you not have self-control? If you do, then your brain will **PAUSE** here. There will be a brief delay. It could be just a millisecond, but your brain will only pause if you have trained it to pause. If you have not trained it, then Miss Amy G, the queen bee of your brain, will take over and make you unconsciously react. You need to train your brain to pause before it acts.

As you can see, your self-awareness is the key to your self-control. Self-control does not start after you respond to an impulse from your body. Self-control needs to occur before the response. For self-control to work, there needs to be a delay, however brief, between the brain's physical perception, awareness, alertness, and attention to bodily signs and impulses, and phase 3, which is **action**. There needs to be a delay so you can wake up your prefrontal cortex. When you behave this way, you are using your self-awareness to self-regulate your body and brain in order to be in self-control.

Wake Up, PFC!

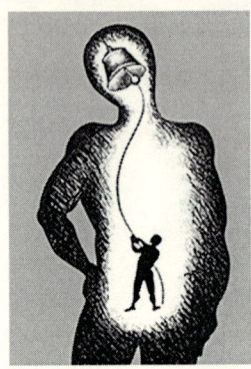

How do you train your brain? Most people do not know, because they do not know how their brain works, but you do. To train your brain, you need to develop new brain patterns. They need to become well-traveled neural pathways. Therefore, if you want self-control, then make it a personal goal. Keep your goal in mind. Think about self-control and talk to your brain about it. Talk with other people about it. Write it down as a goal. Most importantly, practice it. **Deliberately pause** before you emotionally respond to a situation. As the image above suggests, you need use signals from your "feeling" brain to wake up your "thinking" brain. Keep making yourself pause. Between the mental messages and the behavior changes, your brain will eventually **develop new brain patterns**. That's how you train your brain that something new has meaning for you.

Let me repeat. If you want to develop self-control, then you need to develop your self-awareness. You need to become **aware** of physical and emotional bodily changes. Once **alert**, you need to pay conscious **attention** to them and wake up your PFC to help you deal with your reactions to them. With the help of your conscious brain, you are less likely to leap into an unconscious response. You are more likely to **assemble your ideas** about how to respond and then take conscious **action**. Self-control thinking will help you develop a clear-headed response to an impulse. It will provide you with a reasonable ACTION, not a thoughtless, emotion-filled, impulsive REACTION.

Identifying Disruptive Emotions

VOCABULARY FOR EXPRESSING DISRUPTIVE EMOTIONS			
AFRAID	ANGRY	ANNOYED	AGGRAVATED
ANXIOUS	BORED	CONFUSED	DEPRESSED
DISAPPOINTED	DISGRACED	DISGUSTED	DISTURBED
DOUBTFUL	ENRAGED	ENVIOUS	EXASPERATED
FRUSTRATED	FURIOUS	HUMILIATED	HURT
INSECURE	INSULTED	IRRITATED	JEALOUS
MAD	NEGLECTED	PANIC	RAGE
REJECTED	RESENTFUL	REPULSED	SAD
SCARED	SHOCKED	SURPRISED	TENSE
TERROR	THREATENED	UNCOMFORTABLE	UNHAPPY
UPSET	WORRIED		

Since many people have difficulty naming their emotions, and since most problems arise from disruptive emotions, you may find the previous chart a helpful starting point for learning to name disruptive emotions that you may have. One of the most important steps you can take to develop self-control thinking is to learn to identify the signs that you are in dangerous emotional territory.

First, honestly examine your strengths and weaknesses in regard to emotions and dispositions. Be willing to admit to yourself what your "hot buttons" are, so your brain knows that you want to pay attention to them in new ways. Self-awareness involves not only the ability to name your emotional state as it is happening, but it also involves the ability to recognize your personal habits which may be causing some problems.

Why People Fail

As you engage in self-examination, you may find the following list helpful. Dr. Robert Sternberg developed this list of twenty reasons why people fail.[7] As you read down the list, some of the habits of mind and behavior should be familiar to you, since they interfere with your overall thinking ability, primarily critical thinking. Using your self-awareness ability, honestly examine the list and identify any that describe you. If you want to achieve 21st century success, then you must do everything in your power to eliminate these negative mental habits, these self-defeating behaviors, and to develop positive ones.

1. Lack of Motivation.
2. Lack of Impulse Control
3. Lack of Perseverance
4. Using the wrong abilities.
5. Inability to translate thought into action.
6. Lack of product orientation.
7. Inability to complete tasks
8. Failure to initiate.
9. Fear of failure
10. Procrastination
11. Misattribution of blame
12. Excessive self-pity
13. Excessive dependency
14. Wallowing in personal difficulties
15. Distractibility and lack of concentration.
16. Spreading oneself too thin or too thick.
17. Inability to delay gratification.
18. Inability to see the forest for the trees.
19. Lack of balance between critical, analytical thinking and creative, synthetic thinking.
20. Too little or too much self-confidence.

By examining the words that describe disruptive emotions and the list of reasons why people fail, you can identify specific areas where you may be weak. If you want to change, then let your brain know by setting goals to improve. Be specific. Teach RAS, your reticular activating system, what is important to you now. It will learn what you want to change and it will pay attention. In this way, you can help to eliminate negative emotions and dispositions and develop positive ones.

STRATEGIES FOR SELF-CONTROL THINKING

Now that you understand what self-control thinking means, you will learn a few strategies to help you develop it. Basically, you want to catch yourself as you travel between feeling and action. The best way to do that is to make yourself stop, however briefly, before speaking or acting. As you examine the strategies, select a few that you find appealing or make up your own. To become a self-control thinker, you must practice them!

Red Delay Button

This is the simplest strategy. It just provides a visual image. Do you recall the three phases in the self-awareness process? A delay needs to occur between phases two and three, so you can activate your PFC before taking action in phase three. Pretend there is a red button located right in the middle of your forehead in your PFC area. Call it your "red delay button". As soon as you feel your body responding to an emotional trigger, PRESS THE RED DELAY BUTTON! Hit your forehead, so you create a delay, and wake-up your PFC!

Remember that your prefrontal cortex, your PFC, is the master brake system to control your impulses. Dr. Amen says that using your PFC skillfully is "the essence of making unconscious, brain-driven behavior conscious...".[8] The more you use your PFC, the stronger and faster it will become. Your neurons will create new mental pathways that will soon become familiar mental roadways. Don't let your PFC be lazy. Use it. Pressing the imaginary red button is a simple strategy to consciously activate it. The act of pressing it causes a distraction and a delay. Give yourself

[handwritten annotations: PFC ... too repetitive? ... ʃC]

a few seconds before you speak or act, so you can prevent emotional trouble.

How much time do you need to activate your PFC to gain some control? No one knows for sure, but there are some suggestions. The "Six Second Rule" is one of them.[9] It will be most helpful in situations where you deal with disruptive emotions that get you riled up—especially anger. Once you are aroused and perceive your emotions (stimulus), you should take a deep breath and slowly count to six before speaking or taking any action (response). According to Dr. David Sousa, it takes six seconds for your prefrontal cortex (PFC) to "rebound from the emotional brain's agitation and reestablish rational control and prevent emotional hijacking."[10] Press the red delay button and count to six, breathing deeply between each number, so you can control negative impulses.

I mentioned earlier that one way to train your brain was to "talk" to it. This mental talk is called "self-talk" and it is very valuable. There are some established routines for self-talk that may help you develop self-control. Let's learn more about self-talk and some specific strategies to help you engage in it.

The following "Stoplight" and "SOCS" templates are two more visual strategies. Use one of these or make one up. The object is to design an image for yourself that will make you remember to pause before acting on impulses.

Stoplight Strategy for Impulse Control

The "Stoplight Strategy" is a very simple but effective strategy that was designed for the Social Competence Program for the New Haven, Connecticut public schools.[11] It is a skill for impulse control that was designed for fifth graders; however, this strategy can be used by people of all ages. It provides a concrete set of steps that are easy to follow. There was a poster of the stoplight strategy with its six steps displayed in all 5th grade classrooms, and it was directly taught to and practiced with the students. You can learn to use it by memorizing the steps and practicing it on your own.

Imagine a traffic light with its red, yellow, and green parts.

Red light:

1. **STOP**. Calm down, and think before you act

Yellow light:

2. **THINK**. Say the problem and how you feel

3. **THINK**. Set a positive goal

4. **THINK** of lots of options and solutions

5. **THINK** ahead to the consequences

Green light

6. **ACT**. Go ahead and try the best plan

Seeing the red light is like pressing the red button. It creates a delay. The yellow light provides guidelines for the kinds of self-talk questions your PFC should consider in phase two. Your response to these questions can be swift. For example, "I'm losing self-control and I'm angry; I want to maintain self-control; I can get physical and get into trouble or I can stay calm and avoid trouble. The green light represents the action you take in phase three— working hard to stay calm. As part of the Social Competence Program, an adult version of this strategy was developed. It is a problem solving strategy named SOCS.[12]

SOCS for Problem Solving

SOCS = SITUATION, OPTIONS, CONSEQUENCES, and SOLUTION

This simple strategy provides a mental roadmap when simple stopping is not enough. The main difference from the STOPLIGHT strategy is that you are not specifically setting a positive goal as part of the process.

1. STOP. Use self-talk to say what the **SITUATION** is and how it makes you feel.
2. THINK. Think about your **OPTIONS** for solving the problem.
3. THINK. Think what the **CONSEQUENCES** might be.
4. ACT. Pick a **SOLUTION** and execute it.

Self-Talk for Self-Control

Self-talk is a powerful way to regulate your emotions and gain self-control. Self-talk strategies emphasize the need to think about the consequences of your actions, and ask yourself: "Does my behavior get me what I want?" If the answer is "No", then you are probably reacting to your unconscious emotions and letting your unconscious brain control your life. You need to change your behavior. How? Using "self-talk"! In his book, <u>Magnificent Mind at Any Age</u>, Dr. Daniel Amen calls self-talk "…internal logic…one of the most important brain skills we will ever need…. Yet nowhere are we ever taught how to question our own thoughts…"[13]

I am hopeful that this message is beginning to sound familiar to you. With self-talk, you are letting your brain know that you want to change. The basic message in self-talk is "Help me, Brain!" Remember, when you are actively acknowledging mentally or verbally that you want to stop one behavior and start another, your brain is paying attention and learning what has new meaning for you. It will eventually rewire if you make a deliberate effort to change. With self-talk, lazy System 2 becomes a trainer. It consciously lets leaping System 1 know that you want new pathways to develop and old pathways to fade away.

With self-talk, System 2 can stop you from impulsively speaking and acting. It makes you focus on thinking consciously about what to do. It directs you into positive thinking patterns. As a result, self-talk can help you to change your dispositions. In chapter 6, critical thinking, you learned some slogans to help you change your dispositions. Using the slogans is self-talk. Repeating the word patterns can help eliminate negative dispositions and develop the positive ones. The importance of developing positive dispositions cannot be emphasized enough! In the process, you will be developing more self-control.

Another advantage of self-talk is that it will help you control the release of chemicals that make you feel bad or angry. You know how the brain works. With every thought, the neurons in your brain release chemicals, neurotransmitters, which cross the synaptic gap to be received by a dendrite. The chemicals trigger an electrical transmission through the neuron.

If your thoughts are negative, your brain releases chemicals like cortisol that make you feel bad. If your thoughts are happy, your brain releases chemicals like dopamine and seratonin to make you feel good. Try to use positive self-talk. Remember, change the way you speak and you change the way you think! Simply the act of smiling can help you feel better. If you need a boost but don't feel like smiling, then just bite on a pencil with the eraser end towards one ear and the point end towards the other ear. You could even use a stick. When you do this, your muscles make your face into a smile, and you may feel better! Now let's examine some specific strategies.

Controlling Anger with STARR

Guiding Good Choices is a research-based drug and alcohol prevention program for parents of children between the ages of 9 and 14. One of its goals is to enhance family competency in conflict management. It has developed some useful strategies that can be used by people of all ages. Its STARR strategy is an excellent example of a self-talk skill.[14] It consists of five steps with a key phrase to say to yourself at each step. It provides a useful template for expressing disruptive emotions. It provides a direction for action as well as a distraction from reacting immediately.

1. **STOP.** Say "I'm getting angry." *This is the most important step.*
   [You are experiencing self-awareness. What physical symptoms do you feel?]
2. **THINK.** Think about what could happen if you lose control. Say "If I lose control..."

[Have you had angry outbursts before? Think about times when you might have lost control and had an angry outburst. What happened? How did you feel?]

3. **ASK.** Ask yourself what you want to happen here. Say "I really want…"
[What do you want the other person to do? What do you really want to happen?]

4. **REDUCE.** Reduce the anger. Say "I need to cool down. I'm going to…"
[You need a distraction:." You could say, "I'm going to count to six, or lie down, or take a brief walk, or do a chore, or exercise, or take deep breaths. Use a distraction to reduce your anger.]

5. **REWARD.** Reward yourself. Say "Good job! I'm going to …"
[You controlled your anger and avoided conflict. Treat yourself to something you enjoy.]

As you can see, this is a metacognitive process. The individual, parent or child, learns to use a recipe for self-talk that helps to reduce anger.

A.N.T Therapy

A.N.T. therapy is a self-talk strategy developed by Dr. Amen to help children get rid of "Automatic Negative Thoughts". For children with ANTs, their brain pathways have become stuck in negative emotions and negative behavior. The goal is to get kids "unstuck" and move them toward positive thoughts which promote positive emotions and positive behavior with self-talk. Like ants at a picnic which can ruin the fun, ANTs in your head can ruin your day or your life. Dr. Amen identifies the following nine different types of ANTS in his book, Magnificent Mind at Any Age:[15]

1. Always Thinking — Overgeneralizing a situation and usually starting thoughts with words like always, now, everyone, every time
2. Focusing On The Negative — Preoccupying yourself with what's going wrong in this situation and ignoring everything that could be construed as positive
3. Fortune Telling — Predicting the future in a negative way
4. Mind Reading — Arbitrarily believing you know what another person thinks, even though they have not told you

5. Thinking With Your Feelings — Believing your negative feelings without ever questioning them
6. Guilt Beatings — Thinking with words like should, must, ought, I have to, that produce feelings of guilt
7. Labeling — Attaching a negative label to yourself or others
8. Personalization — Allowing innocuous events to take on personal meaning
9. Blame — Blaming other people for the problems in your life

These ANTS can lead to self-defeating behaviors like being inflexible, argumentative, holding grudges, and worrying excessively. He teaches his patients that when they become aware of an ANT causing negative emotions like being angry, scared, disappointed, or nervous, they should write down the thoughts going through their heads. Notice that the action of writing delays an automatic reaction. That alone is helpful.

Dr. Amen lets the children know that ANTS are automatic; they just happen. The children may not be able to control the thought, but they can control their reaction to it. He teaches them that they do not have to believe or accept every thought that comes into their brain. Many negative thoughts are not true, so they need to question the negative thoughts and evaluate them to find out if they are true. When the thoughts are not true, he teaches them to talk back with ANTeaters! He provides them with key phrases to use. With ANTeaters on patrol inside their brains, they can fight the ANTs by talking back to the lies they tell. Did you realize how powerful self-talk is? Use self-talk to eliminate the ANTs in your life!

FEWW Strategy for Expressing Anger

"FEWW" is another strategy provided by Guiding Good Choices. "FEWW" (Phew! Relief) is a strategy for expressing anger or other disruptive emotions to others.[16] This strategy goes beyond self-talk. It provides a verbal template that enables a person the opportunity to express anger to another person in a controlled manner. However, self-talk is still involved because you need to say to yourself, "I better tell this person how I feel and why".

1. **F = FEEL** Tell the person how you **FEEL**. (match feeling level to situation)
   "I'm feeling…."
2. **E = EVENT** Identify the specific **EVENT** that produced the feeling. (observable)
   "I'm feeling… because…."
3. **W = WHY** Explain **WHY** that specific event produced that feeling. (effect on you)
   "The reason I feel… is that…."
4. **W = WHAT** Explore **WHAT** the options are, and make a plan to solve the problem.
   "What are some ways we could solve this problem?"

Having a specific script to get you through a difficult emotional confrontation can be very helpful. It helps people stay in control by focusing on the step-by-step design. It is a strategy that keeps Miss Amy G under control.

DISTRACTION AS A SELF-CONTROL STRATEGY

Beyond visual cues, self-talk, and specific scripts, there are other ways to maintain self-control and distraction is a good one. It is particularly helpful as a strategy to delay gratification. You learned in Chapter 5, Common Sense Thinking, that your brain has a bias toward immediate gratification. As a result, people do not have an innate tendency to plan for the future. As a result, the focus on long-term planning needs to be developed through culture and education. This is an important brain habit for success in the 21st century. The following study demonstrates this point.

The Marshmallow Study

During the late 1960s and early 1970s, Dr. Walter Mischel, a psychology professor, conducted studies to examine the ability of children to delay gratification. The experiments took place at the Bing Nursery School on the campus of Stanford University and involved 653 little children (ages 4 -6) and a selection of treats. A child could select one of three treats: a marshmallow, an oreo cookie, or a pretzel stick. The researcher then told the child that he was going to leave the room for a few minutes. In the meantime, he told the child that she could eat the treat right away if she wanted to, or if she waited for the researcher to return, she could have two of the treats. With that instruction, the researcher stepped out of the room. Would this child be able to delay her gratification?

The researcher in this study not only stepped out of the room, he did not return for fifteen minutes! That's an eternity for little ones. During that time, 70% of the children gave in. Only 30% were able to delay their gratification and enjoy the reward of two treats. Did these 30% have anything in common? Yes, they used strategies to distract themselves, so they could resist the temptation. Instead of focusing on the "hot stimulus", the treat, these children turned their attention to other things like singing songs, playing hide-and-seek underneath the desk, covering their eyes, and turning around. They distracted themselves. They did not forget about the treat. They really wanted it, since they were willing to delay their gratification in order to get a bigger reward. Somehow, during their young lives, they learned how to use their minds to control a little bit of their world. Somehow, somewhere in their environment, someone taught them that having a goal means you just have to wait, even if you don't want to. They learned some self-control.

13 years after the original experiments, researchers conducted a follow-up study of these children and examined their SAT scores. The patient children who delayed their gratification had higher SAT scores. This demonstrated that there is a correlation between patience and intelligence. In fact, the ability to delay gratification is a sign of emotional intelligence.

In a 2009 article in The New Yorker magazine by Jonah Lehrer,"Don't! The secret of self-control", Dr. Walter Mischel, the psychologist in charge of the marshmallow experiments, calls the crucial skill that these children possessed the "strategic allocation of attention". Dr. Mischel explained that he continued his delay-of-gratification study with different groups including poor children from the Bronx. Overall, he found the children from the Bronx had a below average ability to delay their gratification. He states:

When you grow up poor, you might not practice delay as much. And if you don't practice, then you'll never figure out how to distract yourself. You won't develop the best delay strategies, and those strategies won't become second nature.[17]

Did he just gather this information and leave? No. As he and the members of his research team worked with different groups of children, they taught them "a simple set of mental tricks". For example, they told the children to pretend the marshmallow was a cloud, or to pretend it was only a picture of a marshmallow and to put a mental picture frame around it. Once the children learned about these "mental transformations", they could easily wait for fifteen minutes.

They were learning strategies to redirect their attention and distract them-selves in order to delay gratification and to develop self-control. Like intel-ligence, self-control is not a genetic quality. It is a combination of genetics + knowledge + environment + skills. Dr. Mischel thinks that every child in kindergarten should be given a marshmallow and taught some strategies for self-control. He states, "We should say, 'You see this marshmallow? You don't have to eat it. You can wait. Here's how'." Teaching kindergart-ners the mental tricks for self-control and delayed gratification worked—at least during the experimental period, according to Dr. Mischel. Do these informal findings transfer over to the real world? Do students use these strategies at home to make choices? At this point, no one knows. Let's hope so.

Goal Setting: Keep Your Eyes on the Prize

There is widespread agreement about the importance of goals. Dr. Amen believes that one of the most important things you can do to gain control over your impulses is to have goals. This focus on goals enables you to maintain self-control. According to Dr. Amen:

Your brain is the most powerful organ in the universe. It has the ability to direct your life in a positive way or create a living hell. To harness your brain's power it needs direction and vision. It needs a blueprint. [18]

You need to be the architect for that blueprint. Your brain needs to know what has meaning for you. You need a way to tell it what your goals are. In his book, Dr. Amen provides a form that is called "My One Page Miracle". [19] You complete it after asking yourself some questions including:

- What do I want for my life?
- What am I doing to make it happen?
- What's important to me? He provides a list of ideas to get you started including the following: Happiness; Fun; Wealth; Health; Fulfilling relationships; Fame; Individual accomplishments; Legacy; Making a difference in the lives of others, and Faith in a higher power.

There are several categories including

- Relationships: Family; Friends
- Work/Career
- Finances: Short term and Long term
- Myself: Physical health; Emotional health; Spirituality; Character

In this book, The 7 Habits of Highly Successful People, Stephen Covey makes a similar suggestion. Habit 2 states that to be successful, you need to "Begin with the End in Mind". [20] He recommends that you write out a personal mission statement indicating what is important in your life. His categories are similar to Dr. Amen's.

The authors of The Winner's Brain recommend that you map out a route that becomes a roadmap for you to reach your goals. Your goals then become a mental GPS for your thinking brain, your PFC, to use when it is making decisions about what to believe or do. [21] As you can see, there is wide consensus about the value of goal setting. Whether you use My One Page Miracle, a Mission Statement, a Road Map, or something else of your choosing, you need to make it clear to yourself what is important, and you need to keep reminding yourself about it. As you reread and restate what has meaning for you, you are letting RAS know what is important to you, so your brain will be learning and your pathways for goals will grow stronger.

What happens if you change goals? Write the changes down and read it to yourself. If you are deciding to make changes in your life, the physical act of writing your thoughts down and then reading them aloud to yourself is a way to let your brain know that new things are important and have meaning and some old things have lost meaning. As your brain learns that these changes are permanent, it will rewire. As you begin to practice new habits, your brain will grow new pathways. As you no longer practice old habits, those old neural pathways will be pruned and decay.

More Tactics for Self-Control

Creative Tension Elastic Band

To resist impulses and maintain self-control, remember your goals. Pause and ask yourself, "Will my behavior help me reach my goals?" To trigger your memory about your goals, put your hands together, and then pull them apart as if you are pulling on an elastic band. That should remind you about the "creative tension" tool where you think about where you are now and where you want to be. Goals help maintain self-control.

TTT—Things Take Time

Scribble TTT mentally and repeat the phrase "things take time". It serves to remind you that you need to wait to have what you really want. Don't give in to impulses. Delay gratification by saying this phrase or simply writing

"TTT". Post "TTT" notes all over the place to keep you focused on your goals.

Take a Break

Step away from a situation where you might lose your self-control. Make up an excuse. Say you need a bathroom break. Take a little time so you do not act impulsively. Take a short walk; get a drink of water; play Candy Crush, take six deep breaths, or meditate.

Change the Channel

An adorable, smart, and active three year old boy named Sam taught me this technique. I was spending some time with him. He was a lot of fun, but after a few hours I was getting tired; however, he was becoming more spirited. I asked him to calm down. He said, "OK. I'll change the channel." He then calmed down and changed his activity. I couldn't believe how easy it was for him, and how good it was for me.

This little man had already started to develop self-control skills. He was able to think about his behavior and come up with a thinking strategy that affected his actions. Someone in his life used that simple sound bite, "change the channel", to let him know when he needed to change his behavior. He understood it, and he used it. That's simple, skillful, self-control thinking. The phrase "change the channel" is an excellent example of the fact that none of these strategies is written in stone. Someone made them up, so don't get stuck forcing yourself to memorize any of them if you can create a better one that works for you.

National Priority

Before completing this chapter, Daniel Goleman made an important point that I want to emphasize. He sees the need to develop the skills of emo-

tional literacy as a national priority. He believes that to promote democracy, students must learn how to break down bias and stereotypes—also called perceptions and mental models. They need help in avoiding disputes. He writes:

Emotional literacy goes hand in hand with citizenship... as a society we have not bothered to make sure every child is taught the essentials of handling anger or resolving conflicts positively – nor have we bothered to teach empathy, impulse control, or any of the other fundamentals of emotional competence.[22]

The Time Has Come

I agree with Goleman that developing emotional literacy is a national priority. That's one of the reasons that there is a chapter on self-control thinking in this book. While emotional hijacking and emotional intelligence may be relatively new terms, the need for self-control has been known for a long time. American educators have known about the problem for a long time. In 1910, John Dewey wrote:

Passions overwhelm reason time and time again; it's part of our biological design. It's part of our basic neural circuitry... when passions surge the balance tips: it is the emotional mind that captures the upper hand, swamping the rational mind.[23]

The time has come for more direct attention to the development of self-control and emotional intelligence. It is needed in schools and workplaces. In my opinion, it is the leverage point for powerful change. Unfortunately, it is not a national priority at this point. However, it is a priority for a Mega-Thinker, so you have a role to play. You have the "power of one" to use your brain to learn how to achieve greater self-control and to model the behavior for your friends, classmates, teammates, family, and co-workers. In addition, you may also be in a position to introduce a program to teach self-control at your school or workplace. If you can make a bigger difference, do it! Please.

Summary

by developing new habits + eliminate old habits

In this chapter you learned how to develop your self-control thinking. Basically, you develop it by practicing and developing new habits and eliminating old habits. You learned the meaning of self-control, when it is activated in your brain, and some strategies to help you use it. Here are some points to remember:

- *Know Yourself* — begin w/ *invert*)c Self-awareness is the cornerstone of self-control.
- Recognize the physical signals of emotional impulses.
- Identify your triggers. Know your hot buttons. Look for patterns in your behavior to help you find them.
- Exercise self-management.
- Use your master brakes (PFC); Wake up your conscious brain.
- Press the Red Delay Button!
- Practice the "Six Second Rule".
- Engage in self-talk; Remember the key question: Does this behavior get me what I want?
- Discard negative dispositions, and develop positive ones. Rewire your brain.
- Learn some strategies or make up some strategies.
- Use the strategies.

Finally, I want to end this chapter with a powerful message. In his book, <u>Magnificent Mind at Any Age</u>, Dr. Amen lists characteristics of a magnificent mind. They include personal responsibility, clear goals, good attention, consistent effort, effective social skills, impulse control, motivation, integrity, and creativity. Many of these match beautifully with emotional intelligence and self-control thinking. It's an uplifting thought to consider that you are not just learning to develop your thinking skills, but you are developing a magnificent mind. In the next chapter you will learn some strategies that will help to train your memory, so you can achieve school success. The focus with be on memory tricks called mnemonics.

Questions for Reflection

1. **HEAD**: What did you learn? Imagine that you belong to a Book Club that is reading this book. Summarize the key points that you want to highlight during discussion.
2. **HEART**: How do you feel about what you learned?
3. **ACTION STEP**: What are you going to do now? Suggestions: learn more about the topic; share what you learned, or practice what you learned.

School Success Thinking

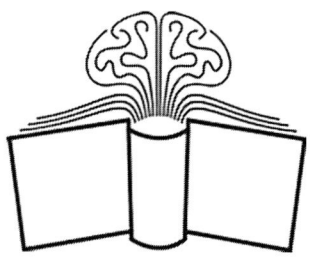

*One of the most depressing facts in all of education: people usually forget
90% of what they learn in class within 30 days....The majority of this forgetting occurs within the first few hours after class.*
— Dr. John Medina

The depressing quote at the top of this page is based on solid research conducted by Hermann Ebbinghaus, a German psychologist in the 1800s, who
is famous for discovering the "forgetting curve". His research was repli-
cated by many others throughout the years. It shows that forgetting is easy;
remembering is hard. School success, however, depends on remembering,
and remembering depends on how your brain works.

Do you remember that your brain searches for patterns and makes associations with the data that enters it? If the data has no meaning or cannot be

connected to previously stored information, then it is deleted. Unfortunately, school-based data is often not meaningful to students, so their brains do not make long-term connections, and the information is forgotten. If you want to achieve school success, then you need to take action and learn some strategies to train your brain to remember difficult and sometimes forgettable information.

The purpose of this chapter is to supply you with tools to develop a trained memory. You will learn about the journey method, the house method, the link method, peg systems, the story system, acronyms, acrostics, rhymes, and songs to help you remember. You will also learn a few study habits to help you develop your school success thinking. You may already know and use these tools, because they are tried and true. In that case, this chapter will be a refresher for you or you can simply skip it.

Remembering Semantic Information

You learned in chapter 4, Memory Matters, that information that is easy to forget is primarily connected to your semantic memory pathway, the one that handles impersonal facts, words, and knowledge. Semantic information is often difficult to remember because it can be unfamiliar, hard to understand, boring, or it may not be connected to anything you already know or care about. Remember, your brain is wired to keep you alive, so it responds to danger and emotion. It loves novelty, movement and excitement. Semantic information does not usually meet these criteria, so it will not make it into your sensory/working memory or long-term memory using regular memory processes.

That causes a huge problem, because semantic information is at the core of school learning. One of the main purposes of the school-success memory tools is to get the semantic information into your brain and keep it there for as long as you need it—short term or long term. What do you need to do? You need to add some tools to your thinking skills toolbox to trick your memory into remembering semantic information. The tools will make you a skillful memorizer. School success, especially in traditional learning environments, is more likely to happen if you are a skillful memorizer.

Natural versus Trained Memory

Before learning about the tools for school success thinking, I want to make a distinction between natural and trained memory. Although your brain encodes, stores, and retrieves memories the same way in either case, "natural" memories come easily. You are hardwired to remember. Your brain seeks patterns and makes associations rapidly, so you remember faces and places, your favorite foods and your favorite movies, and all sorts of things that enable you to live your life. Memory is also the ability to replay, in your mind today, events that took place in the past. Significant episodic memories are also naturally formed by your brain. For you to remember meaningful things, you do not need to train your memory. You simply use your natural memory on a daily basis with little or no effort.

A trained memory, however, does not come naturally. Developing a trained memory is only possible because you use the brain's natural process of making associations. You need to create artificial associations between things. Although developing a trained memory may not be a natural process, it builds upon a natural process—the knowledge of how your brain naturally works. It looks for patterns and makes associations. In The Memory Book: The Classic Guide to Improving Your Memory at Work, at School, and at Play, Harry Lorayne and Jerry Lucas make this point very clear when they state, "If you know how to *consciously* associate anything you want to remember to something you already know, you'll have a trained memory. It's as simple as that".[1] The memory tools will guide you in making associations that provide novelty, movement, and excitement, so your brain can remember difficult or easily forgettable information. In addition, these strategies can be used by people at any age to help them remember. Since learning is a lifelong process, once you learn them, you can always use them to remember new things. Use your imagination to make associations. Have fun and think like a child. Children have great imaginations.

Memory Tricks

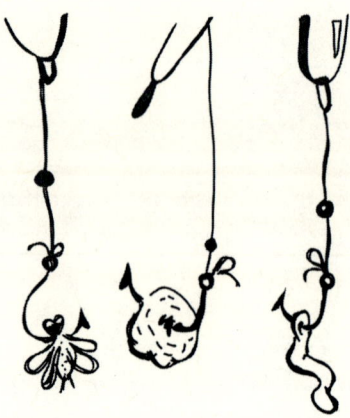

Memory tricks are learning techniques that aid memory. In many ways, they are like fishing lures. Fishermen select lures based on the type of fish they want to catch. The lures use color and movement to attract the curiosity of fish, so a fish will bite the bait and get hooked. A memory trick uses different mental lures to "hook" different kinds of information, so it is not forgotten. These memory tricks are not new. Some are thousands of years old! However, many people do not know about them. Now you will.

Mnemonic Devices

The proper name for these memory tricks is "mnemonic devices" or simply "mnemonics". The word comes from the Greek language. "Mnema" means remembrance, and Mnemosyne was the goddess of memory in Greek mythology. Mnemonics is based on the fact that your brain is always seeking to link information in some way, so it has meaning and will be remembered. Let's step back in time to learn about the first known example of a memory trick.

Memory Palaces

The Memory Palace is a very visual and very powerful mnemonic technique. The "Memory Palace" technique became famous in ancient Greece after a horrible event. Around 516 BC, a wealthy nobleman named Scopas won a boxing match in the Olympic Games and celebrated by having a feast in the banquet hall at his palace. Scopas hired a well-known poet named Simonides to entertain the guests by reciting a poem in his honor. Simonides was also famous for his superior memory ability. For example, he was able to remember the names of all the guests at any event he attended. He did this by creating a visual image in his mind that associated a person's name and some facts about the person, based on where they sat —their location.

On the day of Scopas' banquet, after reciting his poem, Simonides was called out of the banquet hall. While he was out, the roof of the palace collapsed, and everyone inside was crushed to death beyond recognition. Since the families of these victims wanted to give them a proper burial, they asked Simonides to help them identify the bodies. By using his memory "trick", he did. He was able to identify everyone who was killed based on where they were sitting. The "Memory Palace" is the first known trained memory technique, and Simonides is credited with inventing mnemonics. For most people, the kind of information that Simonides remembered is easy to forget. That's why the guests were so impressed when he did remember it. The Memory Palace strategy today is also called Method of Place, Method of Loci, House Method, and Journey Method.

Visual memory tools are very helpful for remembering information that is not naturally memorable. In his book, Moonwalking with Einstein: The Art and Science of Remembering Everything, journalist Joshua Foer relates his experiences as he covered and competed in a national memory competition.[2] He won! He says that skilled memorizers, who call themselves memory athletes, use visual memory techniques all the time. It is a basic skill for them. The idea is to be creative and have fun, so the images stick and you remember.

Making Memorable Associations

You strengthen your visual memory by making the mental picture ridiculous. That helps to explain the title of Foer's book, <u>Moonwalking with Einstein</u>. Imagine doing that! In <u>The Memory Book</u>, Lorayne and Lucas list the following four rules for making ridiculous and memorable associations: 1. Substitution- where you picture one item instead of another; for example, you might make a tree fly instead of an airplane to make a memorable link; 2. Out of Proportion- where the size of things is larger than life; for example, they frequently use the word gigantic; 3. Exaggeration- where you will verbally magnify the image; for example, they use the word millions a lot, and 4. Action- because actions are usually easy to remember.[3] It takes conscious mental effort to make a strong memorable association. The conscious effort is the reason why you will remember the information.

Strategies for School Success

Like a fisherman, you are now going to examine some lures, some mental hooks to help you remember. You may find that you like a few of these hooks. If you do, use them to help you remember, but don't force yourself into a choice. If you are not comfortable with a technique, then you won't use it. Don't limit yourself to the ones I list in this chapter. I am including some basic but powerful tools, but there are more choices for memory techniques in books about memory skills as well as on the Internet. You can Google "mnemonics" or memory tools to access some. The basic process, however, is the same for most of the tools. Since memory is associative, you will create artificial, memory associations or "hooks" to connect what you need to memorize with one of your hooks. Some tools have built-in frameworks and some don't. Let's get started with the "Link" Method. Making associations is the key strategy. It links together two items that have nothing in common with ridiculous associations to help you remember things.

The Link Method

In this method, there is no framework. You simply use your imagination to link one item to the next item on a list in a wild and crazy way. Each individual link needs a powerful image to hold it in your memory as you connect it to the next unrelated link. The links become part of a memory chain. Step: 1. Have a list to be memorized; 2. Create an absurd picture in your mind that links the two items you want to remember. Use as many senses as possible to create vivid mental images. Use Lorayne and Lucas' four rules. Include colors, smells, tastes, sounds, tactile sensations, and movements. 3. Take a second to really see the image of the linked items in your mind's eye. It's almost like a mini-movie. 4. Link the next item. 5. Continue until you finish the list.

Here is a list of ten random words that Lorayne and Lucas used to explain the Link Method in their book, <u>The Memory Book:</u> airplane, tree, envelope, earring, bucket, sing, basketball, salami, star, and nose.[4] These words have nothing in common, but the trick is to link them, so they can be remembered in order. I'll list the associations that they used in their book for linking the items together. After you read the associations that they make, see if you can remember the items. The associations are so vivid and crazy, that you may be surprised about how much your brain remembers. Once you start creating your own links, it will be even easier for you to remember.

The real trick is to remember the first word, because you do not link it with anything. In this sample of the link method, you start with the word "airplane". That means you need to link airplane and tree, so you make an association, using a ridiculous image. Don't forget, you do not want a logical picture. It must be absurd and can even be impossible. Just make it memorable. Make a link in your mind right now between airplane and tree before reading the following links to see if you understand what to do. As you read about each link, take a few seconds and try to picture it. Let your brain see the association and watch the action.

- Airplane and tree
  Picture an airplane with hundreds of trees boarding it.
- Tree and envelope
  Picture a tree. Instead of leaves growing on it, there are millions of envelopes covering the branches.
- Envelope and earring
  Picture yourself picking up an envelope. Open it, and hundreds of earrings fly out and hit you in your face.
- Earring and bucket
  Picture someone wearing an earring that is shaped like a gigantic bucket.
- Bucket and sing
  Picture these buckets singing.
- Sing and basketball
  Picture someone singing and millions of basketballs fly out of their mouth.
- Basketball and salami
  Picture a basketball player dribbling a dried salami instead of a basketball.
- Salami and star
  Picture the salami twinkling in the sky instead of a star.
- Star and nose
  Picture someone with a twinkling star on his face instead of a nose.

Did the link method work for you? Let's see if you can remember the list of unconnected words. Go back and remember the first item. Since the first word can be the most difficult because it is not associated with anything, I'll provide it. The first word was airplane. What does that bring to mind? Do you remember the next link in the memory chain? Try to list all the words now before you read any further. If you cannot do it, then you may need to read the silly links a few times to put them into your memory. If your mental movie was good, then you'll remember airplane's association with tree. Tree should remind you of envelope, and so on, and so on.

Did you remember them? If not, it may be because you did not relate to the links listed. That's why it is much better to use your own mental images. As Lorayne states, creating links will force the "Original Awareness" that is needed to remember anything at all.[5] Original awareness forces you to observe because if you want to remember something you must first observe it. Does this remind you of self-awareness? Remember, in order to develop self-control, you must be aware of what is happening within your body as it is happening. For the link method, you become aware and observe. You concentrate; you use your imagination, and you consciously make associations. The silly associations that you read about here should help you understand the nature of the crazy associations you can make with the rest of the tools. Next, you will learn about a relatively simple and useful tool, the Journey Method.

The "Journey Method"

The journey method is a strategy that is similar to the Memory Palace. In the journey method, you take a mental journey along a route that you pre-select. It does not matter what the route is. You can use any route you like, including your route to school or to work, your route through an amusement park or a campground. It can even be an imaginary route. The only essential factors are that the route is very familiar to you, and you follow it exactly every time you use it. It has to be easy for you to remember.

Next, you identify designated stopping points along your route. These become the locations where you will place the items you want to remember. For example, one location could be a specific bench in a park that is on your route. It cannot simply be a bench. It must be very specific like the metal bench at Harmony Park to the right-front of the bandstand.

You have now completed the design structure that will help you remember things. Next, take the items you need to memorize and put one item at a time at each stopping point along your journey's path. Use novelty, surprise, and visual images to make the connection. Use whatever else works for you to associate what you want to remember with that particular stopping point on your route. Later, at test time, for example, your goal is to mentally complete the journey following your route exactly. As you stop at the assigned spots, you will remember what you put there. It will be easy to retrieve the information if you have done a good job of making powerful associations so the information is encoded strongly in your memory.

If you need to remember seven things, select seven stopping points on your route. If you need to remember fifteen things, then select fifteen stopping points. The easy part is that you must be very familiar with the journey, because you select the stops and the order of the stops. You then put one piece of the information that you need to remember at each stopping point. That's the tricky part. This is where a youthful brain can help. The sillier and more interesting you make the associations between the stopping point and the item to be remembered, the easier it will be to retrieve the item.

Steps for using the Journey Method

1. DRAW the framework for your journey. It is helpful to physically draw it, so you clearly visualize it. Draw the route from your start to your finish and label the landmarks.
2. Take the Route: Mentally walk, ride, or fly the route you selected to fix it firmly in your mind.
    PAUSE
    These first two steps are critically important, so review them. Don't rush. Be very specific about the route and the locations for stopping points. Designing your route and selecting stopping points should not be hard, since you selected the journey. Practice the journey in your mind. Check your memory against your drawing. Did you forget anything? If not, go on. If you did forget a stop, then take the journey in your mind until you get it right. It's worth taking the time, because any time you need to remember a list for a short time, you can use the same journey over and over to remember new things. Now the "fun" begins.

What do you need to remember? Whatever it is, your journey method memory tool will work to help you.

3. IMAGINE your journey. Start moving along your predetermined route. As you reach your first stopping point, you will place the first piece of information to be remembered on that location.

4. GO CRAZY making a mental picture. Associate the first piece of information with the first landmark. Use your senses. Use color, action, novelty, exaggeration, and substitution. Make the information items unique or comical and out of proportion.

5. REPEAT this step. Follow your route to the next stopping point. Place the second piece of information at the second landmark. Go crazy again making an association between the stopping point and the second item and create a vivid mental picture.

6. CONTINUE your journey until everything you need to remember has been placed at a specific stopping point along your predetermined route.

7. REMEMBER by walking around. Sit back. Relax. Your heavy lifting work is over. When you want to remember the items, simply recall your mental journey. In your mind, start taking your predetermined route. Stop at each predetermined stopping point and pick up the piece of information that you placed there.

Reusable Tool

Since a great deal of the information that you learn in school is placed in working memory, as soon as a test is over, it is forgotten. If that is the kind of information you are studying, then you can use the same "journey" over and over for new information, because creating a new list usually wipes out the old one. Just change the images at the stopping points to match the new information. On the other hand, if your goal is to put something into long-term memory, then you should have a special journey just for that information, so create a new one.

Overall, this is a flexible strategy and it's easy to use. Whenever you have to remember something, you have a mental template of a journey that you can take. The only change will be the information you put at the stopping points. In the beginning, it may take practice to make strong and memorable associations, but eventually you will be able to remember what you want to remember. You will become like the poet Simonides who used a memory trick to remember where people were sitting in the palace.

The House Method

The House Method is basically the same strategy as the journey method, only now you focus on one building. It is more like the memory palace in that regard. For the house method, step one is to imagine the floor plan in your house or in another house that you know well. You place information that you need to remember at very specific locations within the house. Again, you need to use your senses, details, and novelty to make associations using vivid images. The crazier the better! With this trick you are giving yourself a hint, a trigger that helps you retrieve the information from your memory. When you need to remember this information, you will retrieve it as you mentally walk through the "house" on your predetermined route.

Any time you need to remember a list for short term use, you can use the same set of locations in your house, just as you could use the same journey over and over. However, if you have many different things you want to put into long-term memory, then you'll need new locations within your house for each set of things you want to remember. For example, you could remember math items in different locations within the kitchen like refrigerator, stove, microwave, sink, etc. and history facts at different locations in your in the living room, and English literature characters at different locations in the bedroom. Remember, this tool is limited only by your imagination. Try these tricks when you have to remember a list of things — whether it's a memory assignment for school or a grocery list — and see if your memory improves!

Peg Systems

A peg system is a great tool for memorizing lists. It differs from the journey and house tools in several ways. First, it comes with a built-in framework. The framework is something you know very well. Some common frameworks for peg systems include numbers, the body system, and the alphabet. Second, the major drawback with the journey and house methods is that you need to remember the entire sequence even if you only want to remember something that happened in the middle. With the peg system, as you will see, you can directly recall a specific item without going through the whole list.

Four peg systems are included in this chapter: 1. a "number rhyming" peg; 2. a "number image" peg; 3. a human body peg, and 4. an alphabet peg. Basically, peg systems use three steps: 1. a framework (that is provided), 2. unique images that you create to associate the items to be memorized to the framework, and 3. information recall using the associations you make with the framework. The peg becomes a "hook" onto which you will place information that you want to remember. The rhyming peg system is easy to use for most people. The keyword associated with a number rhymes fairly closely with the name of the number.

Number Rhyming Peg System

1. sun
2. shoe
3. tree
4. door
5. hive
6. sticks
7. heaven
8. gate
9. vine
10. hen

If you have a rhyming word that you prefer, for example "bun" instead of "sun" for one, or "pen" instead of "hen" for ten, or "wine" instead of "vine" for nine, then use it. Use what you will remember best. Now read the numbers and their keywords once or twice. If you close your eyes, can you recall all of them? If the answer is yes, you are ready to use this tool.

Next, you take the list of items that you must remember in sequence. Link the first item to number one with the keyword "sun". The usefulness of this tool depends on what it is you have to remember. If you are remembering the human body systems, for example, it might take too much effort to make an association with endocrine or lymphatic, so you would not use this tool. Use what works for you. The goal is to make school material easier to remember—not harder.

Number Image Peg System

For this system, I included the number zero with its keyword "cloud". Cloud is selected because it resembles the shape of the number itself— 0. You may have to stretch your imagination to see the resemblance of each of the numbers to its image, but it is there. Actually, if you "see" a different "image" for a number, use your own image. For example, the number eight in the following list is a snowman; however, it could also be an hourglass. Use the word that works for you because it is easy for you to remember.

0 = cloud; 1 = pencil; 2 = swan; 3 = bird; 4 = sailboat (Note: the number 4 looks like a sail); 5 = hook; 6 = golf club; 7 = edge of a cliff; 8 = snowman; 9 = balloon on a stick, and 10 = bat and ball.

I think that this number "image" peg system is also a useful tool for remembering numbers. That's why I included the zero. In this case, the number you need to remember drives the order of the images. For example, try to memorize the number 1926380547 in order. Most people cannot remember ten numbers in a row, so this is a difficult task. However, if you turn the numbers into the images used in this peg, and use the images to tell a story, then perhaps you could! Try to make up a crazy story that substitutes an image for the number. See if you can do it; see if it works for you, and see if you like it. If you don't want to try to make one up, then here is a ridiculous story that you can use. First, review the numbers and their keyword images. You must be able to translate the image back into a number. Next, read the ridiculous story and see if it helps you remember numbers.

A pencil (#1) shot out of a cannon and blasted through my sky-high balloon (#9) while I was being chased by gigantic swan (#2) that was swinging a golf club (#6). Big Bird (#3) came to my rescue, but I crashed into a snowman (#8) that was as white as a cloud (#0) but decorated like a pirate with a huge hook (#5) for a hand. Instead of a pirate ship, he had a sailboat (#4). I climbed into it, but unfortunately, sailed over a cliff (#7).

Read the story again, but this time it will not include the actual numbers. A story will not have numbers in it. I did that initially to help you see the connections.

A pencil shot out of a cannon and blasted through my sky-high balloon while I was being chased by gigantic swan that was swinging a golf club. Big Bird came to my rescue, but I crashed into a snowman that was as white as a cloud but decorated like a pirate with a huge hook for a hand. Instead of a pirate ship, he had a sailboat I climbed into it, and unfortunately, sailed over a cliff.

Close your eyes, picture the story happening in your mind's eye, and write down the numbers in order. If you practice reading the silly story a few times, then you'll probably get it. Naturally, it will be better for you if you create the silly story. This tool, as with all tools, may seem awkward and hard to use, but when you really need to remember something, especially for a short time, it is valuable to have a tool like this in your thinking toolbox. You can use pegs for all kinds of things you need to memorize in school as well as for remembering things like grocery lists.

The Human Body Peg System

You can use whatever body parts you want to help you remember, but here are fourteen basic ones to use as pegs for attaching information to remember. They start at your head and end at your feet.

1. Forehead
2. Eyes
3. Nose
4. Mouth
5. Neck
6. Waist
7. Right elbow
8. Left elbow
9. Right hand
10. Left hand
11. Right knee
12. Left knee
13. Right foot
14. Left foot

There's an alphabet peg system too. With the alphabet system, you can use sound-alikes or concrete words. The sound-alike alphabet pegs rhyme with the letter they are associated with, for example, A – Hay, B – Bee, C – Sea, D – Deed, E – Eve, etc. For a complete list, you can Google "alphabet peg system".

STORY SYSTEM

You already know that linking visual images is a good way to learn lists. Another strategy is to make up a story by linking ideas. Another name for this is "narrative chaining". What if you needed to remember the rights of all Americans that are listed in the First Amendment to the Constitution? Here is an example using the first amendment in the Bill of Rights.

Actual words: *Congress shall make no law respecting an establishment of* **religion**, *or prohibiting the free exercise thereof; or abridging the freedom of* *speech, or of the **press**; or the right of the people peaceably to **assemble**, and to **petition** the Government for a redress of grievances.*

Your assignment is to remember the five freedoms: religion, speech, press, assembly, and petition, but they do not have to be in order. You could use the following story which I found on the ~~Internet.~~ *greataurs* ?   *n not say*

A large group of people walked through the town and <u>assembled</u> in front of their <u>church</u> where they set up microphones so everyone, including the <u>press</u>, could hear them giving <u>speeches</u> about their right to <u>petition</u> the legislature to raise ~~the driving age.~~ *the min wage to 9.50 /hr.*

When you use the "Story System", you are triggering your brain to remember the five freedoms: assembly, religion, press, speech, and petition. The story system is a technique that you can use to link ideas in any subject. Make up a story that you can easily remember. No one else needs to know your story, so you can make it as amusing or bizarre as you want. Your goal is to remember the semantic information. Use what works for you.

ACRONYMS

Acronyms are single words that are made up from the first letters of the words to be remembered. Here are some examples, and they may be familiar to you.

HOMES for the Great Lakes: Huron, Ontario, Michigan, Erie, Superior.

SPA for the "Big 3" Greek Philosophers in teaching order: Socrates, Plato, Aristotle. Socrates taught Plato, and Plato taught Aristotle. You can add another A (SPAA) if you want to add Alexander the Great, Aristotle's pupil.

KISS for the design principle "Keep It Simple Stupid" ?   *No*

HONC for the four elements that are life's building blocks: Hydrogen, Oxygen, Nitrogen, Carbon. As you can see, the "word" does not have to be spelled correctly. You make up whatever works for you. The goal is to recall information.

ACRONYMS plus VISUALS

You can also use an acronym with a visual aid to help you remember. For example, the image of a hand with a ring on it (HAND-R) is an acronym/visual reminder for some of the major components of the brain involved in thinking and memory:

Hippocampus, Amygdala, Nucleus accumbens, Dopamine—Reticular activation system (RAS)

If you wanted to remember the 6 pathways for long-term thinking, then you could use the PEACE sign. Since you hold up two fingers when you make the sign, that will help you remember that there are two Ps. You would pronounce it as "peace" because that's the mental trick, but you would write "P^{2}EASE" or "PPEASE" to remember the pathways:

Procedural, Perceptual Representation, Emotional, Automatic, Semantic, and Episodic. While an acronym is a useful memory tool, it is limited because it can only be used for one specific set of data. Nevertheless, it can lead to school success and that's your goal.

ACROSTICS

An acrostic is a simple and fun technique. You simply make up a sentence using the first letter of every word or thing that you need to remember. It can be a silly or profound sentence. The point is to remember it. I frequently used this technique in high school and college. If I just remembered the first letter of a word or concept, then that was enough to trigger my memory. Here are some examples, and they may be familiar.

"**Kids prefer candy over fried green spinach**" for zoological classifications in descending order: **k**ingdom, **p**hylum, **c**lass, **o**rder, **f**amily, **g**enus, **s**pecies.

"Please Excuse My Dear Aunt Sally" for the order of operations in solving algebraic equations in math: parenthesis, exponents, multiplication, division, addition, subtraction or simply, "My Dear Aunt Sally" for the order of basic math operations.

"My very elegant mother just served us nachos" for the planets: Mars, Venus, Earth, Mercury, Jupiter, Saturn, Uranus, Neptune. The commonly used sentence used to be "My Very Elegant Mother Just Served Us Nine Pizzas" when Pluto was still a planet.

"Eat an aspirin after a nasty sandwich" for the continents: Europe, Asia, Africa, Antarctica, Australia, North America, South America.

"Every good boy does fine" for the musical staff: EGBDF.

"Eighty pizzas smell marvelous" for the four levels of the "Iceberg Image": Events, Patterns, Structure, and Mental Models.

The benefit of acrostics is that it can be used in all subjects. Although the sentence you create is limited to the set of data you are studying, you can use the technique to make up sentences for everything in all grades.

RHYMES

Rhyming strategies are usually easy to remember and very useful. Remember the rhyming number pegs (one = sun)? The "30 days" rhyme has helped many people remember how many days are in each month.

30 days hath September,

April, June, and November.

All the rest have thirty-one

Except February, with twenty-eight days clear,

And twenty-nine each leap year.

The following rhyme helps you remember how to spell difficult words like "receive".

I before E, except after C.

Or when sounded like "A"

as in neighbor and weigh.

If you feel creative, you can have fun and make up your own rhymes for things you need to memorize.

SONGS

Did you realize that when you sing the alphabet song, you are singing to the tune of "Twinkle, Twinkle Little Star"? Using familiar songs as the structure you use to remember information is a useful thinking tool. For example, another way to learn the continents is to sing the words to the tune of the Oscar Meyer bologna song. I remember it well, but many young people probably don't! If that's your situation, then ask an older person to help you.

Oh, I know seven continents

I'll tell you what they are

Asia is the biggest

Antarctica is really far

Europe and Australia

North and South America

Africa- where lions roam

I think I'll stay right here at home!

Here is a song idea that I made up to remember Dr. Edward deBono's Six Thinking Hats strategy. Sing "The Gears in My Brain" to the tune of "The Wheels on the Bus".

"The Gears in My Brain"

The gears in my brain go round and round, *round and round, round and round. The gears in my brain go round and round, all through my head.*

The gears in my brain say "stop & think", *stop & think, stop & think. The gears in my brain say "stop & think", all through my head.*

The white gear asks, "What are the facts?" *What are the facts? What are the facts? The white gear asks, "What are the facts?" all through my head.*

The red gear asks, "How do I feel?" *How do I feel? How do I feel? The red gear asks, "How do I feel?" all through my head*

The black gear asks, "What are the dangers? *What are the dangers? What are the dangers? The black gear asks, "What are the dangers?" all through my head.*

The yellow gear asks, "What are the strengths?" *What are the strengths? What are the strengths? The yellow gear asks, "What are the strengths?" all through my head.*

The green gear asks, "What are new ideas?" *What are new ideas? What are new ideas. The green gear asks, "What are new ideas?" all through my head.*

The blue gear asks, "What thinking is needed?" *What thinking is needed? What thinking is needed? The blue gear asks, "What thinking is needed?" all through my head*

STUDY SKILLS

To be a successful learner at any age involves hard work. However, there are strategies you can use to work smarter, not harder. These include memory aids like chunking, study time recommendations like spacing, reading strategies like SQW3R, prediction strategies like KWL, and priority setting tools like a time management chart. Let's begin with chunking.

CHUNKING

Chunking is a learned skill. You increase the amount of information held in short term memory by dividing a large group of things into smaller "chunks" of information. The chunks are designed around patterns, common characteristics, and categories to help the brain remember. Actually, chunking is something you see all the time, although you may not be aware of it. For example, do you remember that I asked you earlier if you could remember this list of ten numbers—1926380547? You read a silly story that linked visual images with each number. Well, there is another technique that you could use. Try dividing the numbers up like this: (192) 638-0547. It probably looks familiar, because it is the pattern used for telephone numbers. Now there are three chunks of numbers, instead of ten separate numbers. It may have been easier for you to remember the numbers by chunking than by making up a story using image pegs. You need to find what works best for you.

Since the 1950s, the rule of thumb about how much information could be put into short-term memory and retained for a few seconds is the "magical number 7— plus or minus 2". That means 5 to 9 bits or chunks of information. It depends on what is being held in memory and the ability of the individual learner. When numbers are in a recognizable pattern, they are easier to learn and remember. Do you recognize this pattern 000 00 0000? It's the Social Security Number pattern- 3 chunks. How about this one— 0000 0000 0000 0000? It's the credit card number pattern- 4 chunks.

Chunking helps you to remember. Therefore, if you do need to memorize numbers, you could use a number peg system to create amusing mental images or you could try chunking them into a familiar pattern. That may be enough to help you remember. You could also create an amusing visual for each chunk.

SPACING: Using Study Sessions Effectively

Spacing (also called "distributed" practice) is a study strategy that improves your memory, so you can be a more successful thinker. Spacing is the opposite of cramming, which is also called "massed" practice.

- Spacing/Distributed practice = practice over time to assure retention—to learn and remember.
- Cramming/Massed practice = frequent practice in a very short time-frame—to pass a test and frequently forget.

The basic strategy is that several short study sessions are better than one long one. Why does it make a difference? It's all about how your brain works. The technical phrase is the "primacy-recency effect".[6] I first learned about this strategy in 1995, when Dr. David Sousa, presented a professional development workshop in my school district in Massachusetts on the topic, "How the Brain Learns". Dr. Sousa has written many books about the brain and learning, and I highly recommend his work. He is a former educator, so he connects with the real world of teaching and learning.

First and Last Method: The Primacy-Recency Effect

Prime time 1— what comes first

Prime time 2—what comes last

Down time—what comes just past the middle

When you study, your best memory is about the information that comes *first*. After that, your second best memory is for information that comes *last*. The information in the middle is the hardest to remember! Therefore, if you study hard for 60 straight minutes, then you have one first part of information and one last part. You'll remember these best. However, if you divide your 60 minutes of study time into three chunks of twenty minutes apiece, then you have three firsts and three lasts. In between the chunks of time, you can take deep breaths, stretch, or take a quick break for a couple of minutes. Spacing means that you space out, you distribute, you separate your study and review periods versus cramming to learn. If you really want to get information into long-term memory (LTM) then you need to break the information into chunks to study it. Cramming under stress may help you to pass a test, but you will not learn the information. If you want to learn information, not just remember it briefly, then it helps to know how your brain works and to use the information wisely.

READING TEXTBOOKS: SQW3R

Reading textbooks is a great way to practice spacing and the primacy-recency effect. Do you recall the learning pyramid? Within 24 hours, you forget 90% of what you read—unless you have a strategy! Try reading for twenty minutes or half an hour and take a brief break, then read for another twenty minutes or half hour. Ask yourself when you stop each time, "What did I just read?" See if this strategy helps you to remember. Another terrific tool for reading textbooks is SQW3R. It helps you build a framework to understand your reading assignment. It focuses your brain's attention, and it primes it for learning and remembering. SQW3R stands for six steps: Survey, Question, Write, Read, Recite, Review.

1. **Survey**
   a. Read the title, headings, and subheadings
   b. Read the first and last paragraph.
   c. Read the summary.
   d. Read captions under pictures.
   e. Examine every chart, graph, or map.
   f. Pay attention to highlighted vocabulary.
   g. Read the questions at the end of each section as you survey the chapter, and read the questions at the end.
   h. Review any questions the teacher gave you.

2. **Question**

   Start questioning as soon as you start surveying. What does it mean? Do I already know anything about this? Questioning keeps your brain active. As you survey, write some questions down and leave some space to answer them. This could be the beginning of an outline for you.

   a. Turn chapter title, headings, and subheadings into questions.

   b. As you survey, ask yourself, "What do I already know about this subject?" Keep your brain active, try to make connections as you survey.

   c. As you read the questions at the end of a section or chapter, ask yourself, what will I need to know to answer this question? Awareness of what you need to know will help keep your brain engaged.

3. **Write.** As you survey and ask questions, you write some of the questions down. You are focusing on what is important. You will continue to write as you read in detail next.

4. **Read.** You should now be an active reader with a purpose.

   a. Answer questions as you read. Answer questions you made as well as those at end of sections and chapter.

   b. Reread all captions for pictures and all graphic aids: maps, charts, graphs.

   c. Pay attention to anything that is italicized or highlighted.

5. **Recite.** Putting it all together on paper.

   a. As you read over your notes, write them over in your own words if necessary.

   b. Don't be afraid to ask the questions out loud, and state the answer out loud as you write it. You'll be making the process multi-sensory which helps memory.

   c. If you can, use visualization techniques to make your memory of the text stronger.

6. **Review.**

   Your brain has been active, so you should have gathered a lot of useful information that you can review as needed. You should have a good set of meaningful notes which you can review for a test. Using this approach, you should not reach the end of a chapter, and ask yourself, "What did I read?" You are taking charge of your learning, and it will help you experience school success.

KWL, a Prediction Strategy

KWL fits into a category of learning tools that are called "advance organizers" or graphic organizers. They are usually used before you start to learn a new topic. I asked you to use the KWL strategy before you began to read each of the three parts of this book. You may or may not have understood its value. KWL is very useful because it provides an opportunity for you to activate your prior knowledge about the topic in the column "What I Know". If you already know something about the topic, it is easier for your brain to make connections to new information. In addition, the "What I Want to Know" column provides an opportunity for you to focus on your learning goal and to predict what you hope to learn, so you will be actively searching for that information. Finally, the KWL presents a useful structure for summarizing new information and it may help build long-term memories as you fill in the column "What I Learned".

This is a simple yet effective strategy to help you achieve school success. I hope you returned and filled out the "What I Learned" column after part 1, and I hope you will do it again now that you are finishing part 2. When you take that action, you will be practicing a strategy that will help you remember and learn.

Priority Setting & Time Management

The final tool in this chapter comes from Stephen Covey's book, The 7 Habits of HighlyEffective People. The habit described here is Habit 3: "Putting First Things First".[7] Remember that your goal in reading this book is to become a more skillful thinker who makes intelligent decisions about what to think and do. To accomplish this goal, you need to have your priorities in order and you need to use your time well. Covey's "Time Management Matrix", which is pictured here, helps you to learn how to put first things first.

FIRST THINGS FIRST: TIME MANAGEMENT MATRIX	
QUADRANT 1 URGENT AND IMPORTANT	QUADRANT 2 NOT URGENT BUT IMPORTANT
QUADRANT 3 URGENT BUT NOT IMPORTANT	QUADRANT 4 NOT IMPORTANT AND NOT URGENT

Covey believes that success does not come from managing time as much as it comes from managing ourselves. That means you must make choices about getting involved in different activities. You must focus on those activities that help you reach your priorities and bring you personal satisfaction; therefore, you must say "No" to some activities. Covey provides a quote by Goethe to make his point:

Things which matter most must never be at the mercy of things which matter least.

Activities and Results

Covey uses the key words "urgent" and "important" in each of the four quadrants to describe the kinds of activities that take place there. As a result, the matrix describes activities in terms of their combined urgency and importance. Let's examine the kinds of activities he places in each section and how he describes the results of these activities.

- **Quadrant 1** consists of "Urgent and Important" activities like deadline-driven projects, pressing problems, and crises. Immediate attention is definitely needed.

As a result of spending time here, you can expect stress and burnout because you are always in crisis management mode and continually putting out fires. You may feel the need to escape to quadrant 4.

Because it is necessary, you will spend some time here, but strive to be here only some of the time and not all of the time.

- **Quadrant 2** consists of activities that are "Not Urgent but Important" like planning new projects, building relationships, preventing problems, and recognizing new opportunities. Recreational activities and family activities that keep you healthy and well-balanced also fit in here.

As a result of spending time here, you can expect that your goals will be met and your vision may be realized. You are able to act in a disciplined and balanced way with few crises. You are able to see new opportunities and you have time to build relationships. You feel in control. **Try to be here most of the time.**

- **Quadrant 3** consists of "Urgent but Not Important" activities like interruptions from some phone calls, some mail, some meetings, and some unexpected visitors. It also includes some pressing problems as well as some popular activities. Often, the urgency in quadrant 3 activities comes from other people. You try to meet the expectations of others.

As a result of spending time here, you can expect to feel victimized. You may have weak relationships. You have a short-term focus, so you may end up in crisis management situations. You are willing to ignore plans and goals to meet short-term needs that feel urgent. You need to limit your time here.

- **Quadrant 4** consists of "Not Urgent and Not important" activities including trivia, busy work, some mail and phone calls, and time wasters. It also includes pleasant activities which today often means playing video games or watching movies.

As a result of spending time here, you can expect to have some fun, but at what cost? This is a place to escape to when you feel overwhelmed, but it is leading nowhere. You will not reach any goals. It can be an area of total irresponsibility. Drastically reduce your time here.

As you can see, this is a powerful tool to help you decide which activities matter and which need to be avoided. Take a few moments to think about how you spend your time. You probably spend some time in each quadrant, but how much time? Covey emphasizes that highly effective people spend much of their time in Quadrant 2, Important but Not Urgent. Let's learn why.

According to Covey, to be successful, you need to focus on relationships and results— not just things and time. You focus on what is important because it contributes to your goals and values. It has to do with the results you want. You avoid urgent activities if possible because urgent means immediate attention is needed. Sometimes you do not have sufficient time to think, so you react, and the outcome may be less than desirable. It may not meet your goals and values in the long run. There will always be urgent situations, and you will need to act, but you do not want all situations to be urgent. If you can work within quadrant 2, you can get important things done, so they do not become urgent. As the habit is named, you are putting first things first.

I am hopeful that this brief visit to time management will help you to focus on your goals and your plans for reaching them. It can guide you towards paying attention to important things and not being distracted by unimportant things. If you try to spend more time in quadrant 2, then it will help you to achieve school success and it will help in all other areas of life as well. You will still need a calendar or appointment book, but it more likely to be filled with Quadrant 2 activities.

Summary

In this chapter, you learned the difference between natural memory and trained memory. In addition, you learned that you can train your brain by providing it with artificial associations to help you remember semantic information, the kind presented in school that is essential for school success. You learned some tools to help remember this information because semantic information is the most difficult kind to recall, since it is frequently not associated with other things in your brain.

The tools you learned included the following: the Link Method, the Journey Method (similar to the House Method); the Peg System; and the

Story System. These tools helped you form associations among unrelated items so you could remember them. You learned other tools that trigger your brain to remember. They include acronyms, acrostics, rhymes, and songs. In addition, you learned some study strategies that will help you achieve school success. These include chunking, spacing, SQW3R, KWL, and priority setting/time management.

You have now completed part two of this book, Train Your Brain. After you complete your questions for reflection, take some time to return to the KWL sheet and summarize the key points that you have learned about the six dimensions of thinking: common sense, critical, creative, systems, self-control, and school success. I hope what you have learned makes a difference in your life. You are well on your way to becoming a Mega-Thinker. In the final part of the book, you will learn how to care for and maintain your brain. This is definitely information that you will use for the rest of your life.

Questions for Reflection

1. **HEAD**: What did you learn? Imagine that you belong to a Book Club that is reading this book. Summarize the key points that you want to highlight during discussion.
2. **HEART**: How do you feel about what you learned?
3. **ACTION STEP**: What are you going to do now? Suggestions: learn more about the topic; share what you learned, or practice what you learned.

CHAPTER 11

Brain Care: Eat, Play, Sleep, Balance Stress, Stay Youthful

HEALTHY ICONS

Exercise boosts brain power. To improve your thinking skills, move.
— Dr. John Medina

Your brain is a living, growing, and changing part of your body. It requires care, and only you can guarantee that it gets what it needs. It is never too early to take charge of your brain's health. Nutrition, exercise, and sleep are the brain's troika according to Dr. Richard Restak, author of <u>Think</u>

Smart: A Neuroscientist's Prescription for Improving Your Brain's Performance.[1] Troika is a Russian word meaning a collection of three. Not just any random three things, but three things that belong together because each is good alone, but when united, they work best. Nutrition, exercise, and sleep work together to keep your brain healthy, and as Dr. Daniel Amen, author of A Magnificent Mind at Any Age states, "a magnificent mind starts with a healthy brain."[2] In this chapter, you will learn how to take care of your brain with three physical things: food, exercise, and sleep. In addition, you will learn the importance of two mental requirements for brain care: balancing stress and maintaining a youthful mindset.

EAT: Feeding your Body and your Brain

You might enjoy a dinner with roast chicken, a crunchy salad, and a slice of hot apple pie. The sight, smell, and taste combine to bring you pleasure, and you may even get a dopamine burst. However, it doesn't matter what foods you use to feed yourself, they all break down into the atoms and molecules that make up the amino acids, proteins, carbohydrates, and fats that feed your body and your brain. Your job is to make sure that the foods you eat have the right ingredients to please your body and your brain, not just your taste buds.

Which of the following four words is seldom used in conversations about meal planning: carbohydrates, amino acids, proteins, or fats? Answer: amino acids. "Amino acids" may not be a familiar term in the kitchen or on cooking shows, but they are absolutely indispensable and essential for life!

Amino Acids

To start a formal dinner, many people have an appetizer as a first course. Think of amino acids as appetizers. They are the first course in healthy eating. Without amino acids (AAs) your body could not function. Your body can produce some amino acids, but not all. You must obtain at least eight of them, called "essential" amino acids, by eating protein. Some proteins are better suppliers of amino acids than others. The following foods are "complete" proteins: lean meat, fish, poultry, eggs, milk, cheese, and yogurt. Each one of them supplies all of the necessary amino acids that your body needs. In addition, each of these protein foods provides amino acids in the correct proportion that your body needs, so you should try to incorporate at least one of these into your daily meals.

There are other foods that provide all of the essential amino acids, but not in the right proportion. Unlike fats and carbohydrates which can be stored in your body, amino acids cannot be stored, so you need to eat foods that provide the essential, amino acids on a daily basis. The following chart includes the "essential", indispensable amino acids listed in alphabetical order and some of the food sources for each.

Amino Acid Chart

Eat these for all 8 amino acids	Lean meat, fish, poultry, eggs, milk, cheese, yogurt
Isoleucine	lentils, seeds, soy/tofu, whole grain wheat, almonds
Leucine	Cottage cheese, sesame seeds, peanuts, lentils
Lysine	Beans, lentils, soy/tofu, spinach, amaranth grain, nuts, apples
Methionine	Cottage cheese, whole grains, lentils, peanuts, sesame seeds
Phenylalanine	Cottage cheese, soy/tofu, lentils, nuts, beans, seeds, asparagus
Threonine	Beans, nuts, seeds
Tryptophan	chocolate, oats, bananas, dried dates, cottage cheese, soy/tofu, peanuts/peanut butter, brown rice, sesame seeds, potatoes, beans, lentils, turkey
Valine	Whole grains, mushrooms, nuts, soy/tofu, brown rice, lentils, cottage cheese

Figure 11.1: Amino Acid Chart

Searching for a Brain Diet

There is no such thing as a specific brain diet, but Dr. Restak provides lots of useful information about what components should be included.[3] Your diet will help with your brain care if you do the following: reduce the intake of calories to maintain a healthy and preferably low weight; cut down on saturated fats; eat less red meat; eat fish and foods with high Omega-3 fatty acids, and eat more fruits and vegetables, particularly leafy green vegetables. With knowledge about amino acids, proteins, carbohydrates, and components of a diet that keeps your brain healthy, you can make informed choices about what to eat.

I am not presenting this information to you, so you can have better overall health, although that is a good goal. My main point in presenting this information to you is to emphasize that what you eat has additional consequences for you beyond your physical health. Food impacts your brain which impacts your behaviors and emotions too. Here's an example. Let's pretend you have two breakfast choices tomorrow. Choice one is a high carbohydrate breakfast like pancakes. It will increase the amino acid tryptophan in your body, which causes your brain cells to produce the neurotransmitter, serotonin. Serotonin promotes a sense of well-being, calmness, and sleepiness. Choice two is a high protein breakfast like scrambled eggs. It will increase the amino acid tyrosine in your body, which causes your brain cells to produce the neurotransmitter norepinephrine. Norepinephrine promotes alertness.

Which breakfast will help you prepare for your day? Think about the activities you have planned. Remember, your food is actually a chemical feast for your brain. Food is involved in producing the brain chemicals, the neurotransmitters that have an impact on your behaviors. Therefore, choice one, the high carbohydrate breakfast, is probably better if you are on vacation and relaxing, and choice two, the high protein breakfast, is probably better if you have a test at school or a presentation at work.

Top 10 Power Foods

According to Dr. Restak, these are the top 10 foods, in alphabetical order, to enhance your brain's performance:

Almonds; Bell peppers—all colors; Blueberries; Broccoli; Grapes; Olive oil; Spinach; Strawberries; Tomatoes, and Whole grains

If you combine this list with the essential amino acids list of lean meat, fish, poultry, eggs, milk, cheese, and yogurt then you would have a powerful shopping list for foods that promote both body and brain health.

Serotonin Seekers

Serotonin is a neurotransmitter that contributes to well-being and happiness. Foods high in serotonin give you an emotional boost! In doing the research for this book, I discovered that I was a "serotonin seeker"[4] I didn't realize the biology behind my food choices. The following list of high carbohydrate foods increases the tryptophan in the bloodstream, which within thirty minutes is used to produce serotonin in the brain. I learned that I was seeking serotonin when I reached for, yes craved, some of my favorite sweet, salty, delicious, "comfort" foods: Bagels; Bread; Candy; Chips; Chocolate; Cookies; Ice Cream; Pasta; Pizza; Popcorn, and Pretzels.

Eating these high carbohydrate foods to get the emotional boost provided by the serotonin is a good thing in moderation, but these foods can become addictive and lead to health problems, especially obesity. Now that you know how your brain works, you are able to understand that dessert and snack foods bring people pleasure not only because they taste good, but also because of the neurochemicals they release that actually provide that sense of pleasure. You already know that the way you look at things and the way you speak can impact the way you think. Now you know that the way you eat, your food choices, can impact your thinking, your behavior, and your emotions too.

Water, Water...

What you drink is also an important part of your nutrition, especially water. One of the biggest threats to your brain is dehydration, which occurs when the amount of fluids leaving your body is greater than the amount going into it. Your body is about 60% water and your brain is about 75%-80% water. You need to drink about a half-gallon (approximately two liters or 8 glasses) of healthy fluids each day to replace the fluids your body loses. Healthy drinks keep you hydrated, which means that you maintain the right balance of water in your body. Beware of drinks that dehydrate you. Many advertised energy drinks are high in caffeine which will dehydrate you if you drink too much. Limit your intake of high caffeine drinks including coffee and soda. Alcoholic drinks also dehydrate you, so use them cautiously. If you drink anything that dehydrates you, offset its effect by drinking additional healthy fluids— especially water. It is essential that you properly "hydrate" your body and your brain.

PLAY: The Fountain of Youth

"Physical activity is cognitive candy",[5] according to Dr. John Medina, author of Brain Rules. If you want to feel younger, then get a good helping of physical activity, the brain's candy. There is widespread agreement among scientists about its value. Dr. Daniel Amen believes that you will uncover your "fountain of youth" if you just "boost your blood flow".[6] How? Move! Get active and play. Have fun! Get involved in recreational activities that you enjoy. Pick something that gets you moving, and you will get your heart pumping faster, which boosts your blood flow.

You may be wondering why your brain needs more blood flow. Your blood is what delivers the oxygen to your brain. Your brain may be only 2% of your body weight, but it uses 20 to 25% of your body's oxygen supply. Without oxygen from fresh air, your brain can only "live" for about five minutes.[7] How does the oxygen get to your brain? Hemoglobin is the hero. It is the protein in your blood that makes it red. As your red blood cells travel around your body, they pass through your lungs that are filled with fresh oxygen. The oxygen attaches itself to the hemoglobin, and together they travel to your brain and all the other parts of your body. The more you exercise, the faster your heart rate goes up, and the faster you breathe. The faster you breathe, the more frequently hemoglobin passes through your lungs and gets fresh oxygen. When you engage in physical activity, you are helping hemoglobin do its job of carrying oxygen to your brain.

Stopping the Flow

What is bad for blood flow? You already know that caffeine and alcohol can cause dehydration, and that inhibits blood flow. In excess, the following factors also limit or disrupt blood flow to your brain:

- Stress
- Nicotine
- Drugs
- Artery disease/heart disease
- Diabetes
- Environmental toxins
- Lack of exercise
- Lack of sleep

Exercise is Medicine for Your Brain

The word more commonly used to describe how to increase your blood flow is "Exercise". In his book, Spark: The Revolutionary New Science of Exercise and the Brain, Dr. John Ratey writes that "... exercise is the single most powerful tool you have to optimize your brain function".[8] Based upon hundreds of recent research reports published (most within the past ten years), Ratey states that "Exercise is medicine".[9] Exercise is also important for neuroplasticity, the ability of neurons to grow and change.

The key to the brain's plasticity is the family of brain chemicals called neurotrophic factors. The word comes from the Greek words "neuro" which stands for brain and "troph" which stands for nourish. The neurotrophin

BDNF, which stands for "Brain-Derived Neurotrophic Factor", has become the most studied of all the brain factors. It is central to preservation of brain cells and their actions. Dr. Ratey calls BDNF "miracle grow" for the brain, because it nourishes neurons. It is the fertilizer that helps new brain cells grow and survive. He writes that you can increase your BDNF by exercising. That means by simply taking a walk or a run, you can boost the power of your brain and maintain a healthy brain.

Combo Pack: Aerobic Exercise + Skill Development

Although walking and running are good, Dr. Ratey writes that research is finding that your brain benefits the most when you learn something new, so the combination of aerobic exercise and a complex skill-building activity is best. Examples of a complex skill-building activity include tennis, gymnastics, swimming, basketball, figure skating, hockey, karate, and all kinds of dancing. You could combine ten minutes of aerobic exercise before rock climbing, or juggling, or golf. The bottom line is to find something you enjoy and play! Have fun, and in the process you will be helping your heart and your brain.

PE Class: Creating Brain Cells

In Spark, Dr. Ratey describes a physical education program in Naperville, Illinois that has been in place since 1991. This program operates on the principle of fitness rather than sports. It teaches a lifestyle by showing the students how to monitor and maintain their fitness and health. The program combines a sense of fun with developing healthy habits that gets students hooked on moving. The fitness program is also a cornerstone of the academic achievement of the students. Paul Zientarski, PE coordinator states: "In our department, we create brain cells. It's up to the other departments to fill them".[10] This is an amazing statement that shows that the scientific evidence that connects exercise with brain growth is reaching a wide public audience.

SLEEP: "Syn-naps"

Let's review. You need to eat protein in order to get the amino acids you need to produce the brain chemicals called neurotransmitters which are responsible for brain activity — for thinking. Exercise is essential to maintain good blood flow and also to produce BDNF. The opposite of exercise is sleep. What is the connection of sleep to your brain? As listed above, lack of sleep interferes with blood flow, but it has other connections as well.

Fill Her Up!

Just like gas in an automobile or food in your belly, you need to "refill" the neurotransmitters in your brain. You eat to get the amino acids; you move to produce BDNF, and you sleep to replenish your neurotransmitters. After concentrating for a long time, people get unfocused, fidgety, and distracted. That's a sign that their levels of serotonin, dopamine, tryptophan, and epinephrine are running low. The evidence for this is provided by neuro-imaging. What can a person do to fix this? Dr. Judy Willis, a neuro-scientist and a middle school teacher, explains the need for a nap. In her book, How Your Child Learns Best: Brain-Friendly Strategies You Can Use to Ignite Your Child's Learning and Increase School Success, she states that neurotransmitters rebuild with time but only when the brain is rested. Willis cleverly states that "It is neuro-logical" to plan "syn-naps".[11] She believes that after just 15 minutes of sustained, complex brain activity, your brain might need a break.

It is commonly accepted that judgment and performance are impaired if people do not get enough sleep. Sleep is restorative, so performance is better in any activity after a period of rest. However, sleep is more than restorative. Findings in neuroscience are showing that you consolidate what you learn and you form your memories when you sleep by "replaying" them in your brain. A PET scan of someone sleeping matches the PET scan of that same person that was recorded during the day while the individual was actually learning something new. This demonstrates that what a person learns during the day is practiced or replayed while sleeping.

Dr. Willis quotes Matthew Walker, the director of the sleep and imaging lab at Beth Deaconess Medical Center in Boston, stating that "… the more the brain learns, the more it demands from sleep at night…. in short, if you learn something while awake, you can increase your chances of remembering it by 'sleeping on it' ".[12] What is the message here? When you feel tired, try to rest. Your body is telling you what your brain needs, so "log off". A 20 to 30 minute "power nap" may be all you need. Now that you understand the value of sleep, I hope you will be more likely to give your brain a rest.

Coping with Stress

You have learned about some *physical* requirements needed to maintain a healthy brain. Now you will learn about a *mental* requirement for brain care. You must learn to cope with stress. Stress is a part of life that will not go away. Some stress is good because it can heighten alertness, which can lead to improved performance. Some stress is bad because it can interfere with the brain making new connections, interfere with memory formation, limit mental flexibility, and lead to lack of motivation and emotional burnout. It is the negative side of stress that you hear about the most. I think it is important that you develop a balanced sense of stress to help you maintain a healthy brain.

One of the best presentations that I ever heard about stress was given by Kelly McGonigal, a Health Psychologist specialist, who gave a "TED" talk (Technology, Entertainment, and Design) on stress.[13] She explains that stress is not the enemy. The enemy is your reaction to stress. She explains that if you can change the way your brain thinks about stress, then you can change your body's response to stress. If you change your mindset and think about stress in new ways, then you can help reduce its negative impact on you.

Do you remember that job #1 for your brain is to keep you alive? Your brain's main job is your survival, so when your brain thinks that you are threatened, it triggers an alarm. Physical symptoms of stress appear including increased sweating, a pounding heart, and faster breathing. Your body releases hormones including cortisol, which is sometimes called the "stress hormone". This hormone prepares your body for action, and it responds with "fight or flight" and sometimes "freeze" activity. In this case, the stress response is a good thing. Your body becomes energized to meet a challenge. If you have this mindset that stress is good, then once the challenge has passed, your body will recover from the stressful event by releasing different hormones like oxytocin. Oxytocin works on your cardiovascular system to help your heart recover from stress.

If your mindset is that stress is bad, then your body may not recover as quickly from the threatening experience. It will continue to release cortisol and too much of this hormone is dangerous. Dr. Ratey agrees that stress is not the enemy when he writes that "stress is not a matter of good and bad — it's a matter of necessity".[14] It keeps you alive. He considers your body's stress response to be built-in gift of evolution. That is definitely a new way to think about stress.

Learning to cope with stress is an important part of brain care. In Brain Rules, Dr. Medina warns that the very worst kind of stress can overwhelm you and make you feel helpless. It leaves you with the feeling that you have no control of a problem. Try not to let stress reach that point in your life by learning some strategies to cope. Many good suggestions for managing stress and building resilience are found in the book, The Sharpbrains

Guide to Brain Fitness: How to Optimize Brain Health and Performance at Any Age. They include the following lifestyle solutions:[15]

- Exercise. Aerobic physical exercise not only releases BDNF but also endorphins which are called "feel-good" brain chemicals. They promote a sense of well-being. It also promotes better sleep.
- Relaxation. Relax by doing something calming that you enjoy. A nature walk is helpful like a walk in a park, in a forest, or along a beach. Even looking at a series of pictures of nature can help.
- Socialization. A few close social relationships with friends, family, or even pets foster trust, support, and relaxation. This enhances mental and physical health.
- Empowerment. This means feeling in control over important areas of one's own life, including brain health. Your effort to improve your thinking ability and to care for your brain definitely put you on the path to empowerment.
- Positive Thinking. If you face a stressful situation, it is helpful to have positive thoughts about it. For example, the book referred to students who were coached into believing that feelings of nervousness before a big test could improve their performance. It did. Coached students performed better than the non-coached ones. Putting a positive spin on a stressful situation helped.
- Meditation. There are various ways to meditate, but the goal is the same. You want to control your attention and control your emotional arousal. You want to get beyond your automatic unconscious and subconscious responses and move to a higher level where you have some control. The book covers five types of meditation.
  - Basic meditation. Try to think about nothing.
  - Focused meditation. Focus on something outside of your body like a sound, a candle flame, or a mantra. Focus on something within you like deep breathing.
  - Activity-oriented meditation. Engage in a repetitive activity like yoga or walking.
  - Mindfulness meditation. Becoming fully aware of the present moment rather than thinking about the past or future.
  - Spiritual meditation. Engaging in a spiritual practice like prayer.

The sooner you learn how to cope with stress, the better! As you just read, it does not need to be complicated. An additional step you can take to prevent yourself from being overcome by stress is to limit your use of the different types of media including the television and radio. The 24/7 cycle of news makes people aware of every scary and tragic event in the world. It makes some people think they live in a world that is more unsafe and dangerous than it really is. Miss Amy G can go into overdrive with fear and this creates a state of chronic stress. The simplest step is to shut off the media. Don't listen to it.

Maintain a Youthful Brain

27 TRAITS OF A YOUTHFUL MIND			
Sense of Wonder	Curiosity	Imagination	Playfulness
Need to Organize	Joyfulness	Love: Need for love & to love	Sensitivity
Flexibility	Experimental-mindedness	Explorativeness	Resiliency
Laughter and Tears	Optimism	Honesty and Trust	Compassionate Intelligence
Open-mindedness	Creativity	Enthusiasm	Friendship
Dance	Song	Sense of Humor	Need to Know
Need to Think Soundly	Need to Learn	Need to Work	

The second *mental* requirement to keep your brain healthy is to maintain a youthful brain. This point is clearly made by Dr. Ashley Montagu, a world-renowned anthropologist and the author of Growing Young. In his book, he identified 27 youthful qualities that are listed in the chart above. He believes that people need to keep these qualities if they are to grow and develop into mentally and physically healthy individuals.[16]

Do some of these qualities describe you? I hope so. If you want to maintain these qualities, then it will require effort, just as growing your intelligence does. Why? Sadly, for many people these qualities are easy to lose. Dr. Sigmund Freud captured the loss in the following quote: "What a distressing contrast there is between the radiant intelligence of a child and the feeble mentality of the average adult." Did you ever wonder what happens to the brain as it makes its journey from childhood to adulthood? According to Dr. Montagu, most adults develop a dreadful disease as they make the journey. He calls it psychoschlerosis or the "hardening of the mind". It is very hard to cure, because most adults don't even know they have it.

Danger of Phychoschlerosis

Although it isn't a real disease in the medical world, the concept of psychoschlerosis is very real. It is dangerous because it locks people into mindsets that stop them from learning. You learned about the characteristics of this "disease" in Chapter 1, The Power of Perception. Back then, I did not give it a name, but you learned that people make inferences and develop perceptions, viewpoints, stories and other "mental models" about how the world works. They believe that their schooling and their personal life experiences have provided them with all they need to know, so they resist new information. They have a personal worldview, formed by their unique perceptions, that they believe is true, and they won't consider changing it. People who are locked into rigid, inflexible mental patterns resist new ideas. They are mired in the "obsoledge" that the Toffler's wrote about. As a result, it is difficult for people with "hardening of the mind" to be skillful thinkers. You must exert effort to maintain some of those 27 youthful qualities to avoid psychoschlerosis.

Awakening Genius

12 QUALITIES OF GENIUS		
HUMOR	WONDER	VITALITY
SENSITIVITY	IMAGINATION	JOY
PLAYFULNESS	WISDOM	CREATIVITY
FLEXIBILITY	CURIOUSITY	INVENTIVENESS

Dr. Montagu is not alone in believing in the importance of youthful traits of mind. Consider the twelve words in the previous chart. These words are similar to the ones Dr. Montagu used, but these were identified by Thomas Armstrong in his book, Awakening Genius in the Classroom. They describe twelve "Qualities of Genius".[17] Armstrong uses the word "genius" to represent the potential within each student. He believes that students need to be in environments where these qualities can thrive. Ideally, all people need to be in environments where these qualities can thrive.

Scientific Attitude of Mind

I want to add one more source to the argument that people need to maintain a youthful state of mind. In his book, How We Think, Dr. John Dewey wrote that:

... the native and unspoiled attitude of childhood, marked by ardent curiosity, fertile imagination, and love of experimental inquiry, is near, very near to the attitude of the scientific mind.[18]

To be playful and serious at the same time is possible, and it defines the ideal mental condition. Absence of dogmatism and prejudice, presence of intellectual curiosity and flexibility, are manifest in the free play of the mind upon a topic.[19]

Look at the words that capture the same message that Montagu and Armstrong sent: curiosity, imagination, experimental inquiry, playful, and flexibility. The evidence is clear. You must make the effort to retain the qualities of a youthful brain if you want to be mentally and physically healthy and happy.

Summary

Most people realize that food, exercise, and rest are essential for good physical health. However, many are unaware of the importance of each of these factors on their brain's health. You are now aware, so take action. Become "your own brain fitness coach."[20] Eat a balanced and nutritious diet. Include amino acids and foods that keep your brain healthy! Exercise and play to get plenty of oxygen to your brain, so it can grow BDNF, and reduce stress! Rest well. Take "syn-naps" and replenish your neurotransmitters and consolidate your learning. In addition, take action to meet the two mental requirements for brain care. Work at balancing and coping with stress, and have fun maintaining a youthful mindset.

I cannot leave the topic of maintaining your brain without addressing technology, a staple of 21st century life, and a potential trouble area for brain health. In the next chapter, you will learn about technology's impact on your brain.

Questions for Reflection

1. **HEAD:** What did you learn? Imagine that you belong to a Book Club that is reading this book. Summarize the key points that you want to highlight during discussion.
2. **HEART:** How do you feel about what you learned?
3. **ACTION STEP:** What are you going to do now? Suggestions: learn more about the topic; share what you learned, or practice what you learned.

CHAPTER 12

Technology and Your Brain

The current explosion of digital technology not only is changing the way we live and communicate but is rapidly and profoundly altering our brains.
— Dr. Gary Small and Gigi Vorgan

Technology is changing the human brain! That's what Dr. Gary Small and his wife Gigi Vorgan write about in their fascinating book, <u>iBrain: Surviving the Technological Alteration of the Modern Mind.</u> Since you now understand how the brain works, you won't be surprised that they say the explosion of digital technology is rewiring people's brains. You know that your brain changes all the time based on its experiences. It makes new connections and deletes old ones. Since many technology devices and games provide novel, stimulating, and pleasurable experiences which brains love, many brains are enjoying the technology boom and rewiring like crazy. The result is not just a generation gap but a brain gap.[1]

In this chapter, you will learn about one of the main issues that this brain gap raises— the decline in interpersonal skills. You will also learn some of the pitfalls associated with technology like technology addiction, "video-game-brain", and the dangers of multi-tasking. In addition, you will learn some actions that you can take to help you safely maneuver within this technological world.

Rewiring Your Brain

You know your brain is rewiring as you learn new things including technology, but wouldn't it be great to have a specific, real-world example of this rewiring and how quickly it occurs? Dr. Small thought so. He wanted to know how quickly the brain can rewire itself when it uses a new technology tool. Together with some associates at UCLA, he conducted a study to demonstrate the impact of technology on the brain's ability to rewire as a result of neuronal activity. In this case, the technology tool was a computer. The research team enlisted three adults skilled in using computers, which the researchers called the computer-savvy group, and three adults with absolutely no computer experience, which they called the computer-naïve group.

The researchers used fMRI scans to detect changes in the brain's neuronal pathways as each volunteer completed two different types of mental tasks: 1. reading pages from a book (as a control task), and 2. conducting an Internet search for specific topics using Google (as the experimental task). In case you are shaking your head because you know you cannot read a book or use a computer to conduct a Google search inside an fMRI scanner, just relax. You are correct, but the researchers figured out a way around this. They had the participants wear a special set of goggles that presented images of the website and they did a few other things as well. The procedure is detailed in Dr. Small's book.

The baseline scanning session revealed no differences in the brain circuits used by any of the participants as they read pages from a book. However, during the Google search, the scans of the two groups were distinctly different. The computer-savvy group used a pathway in the left prefrontal cortex (PFC). As you know, that's your brain's executive function area where your higher-order thinking takes place. There was little, if any, activity in this PFC region for the computer-naïve group.

For the next part of the experiment, the three computer-naïve participants received one hour per day of computer search-engine training for five days. The computer-savvy group were on their own conducting their own searches for the same amount of time— one hour a day for five days. Then they all had their brains scanned again.

The results of the scans showed that after only five hours of training, the computer-naïve group was now using the exact same pathways as the savvy group. The activated brain circuits in the left PFC were the same. Their brains had rewired with just five hours of training! Are you surprised it happened so fast? Keep this experiment in mind as you learn more about technology and your brain. You have concrete evidence that the brain changes when technology is used. On the positive side, it demonstrates that using technology can sharpen your cognitive abilities.[2] However, an important question arises. How much technology use is beneficial to your brain and how much is detrimental? The information in this chapter will help you to make up your own mind.

Technology Brain Gap

One of the biggest differences among people today is in the way they communicate. This is particularly true among the generations. Older generations engage in more traditional, personal, face-to-face interactions while the newer generations communicate using technology devices. This is leading to a decline in basic interpersonal and social skills. In the history of the human race, most communication was done on an interpersonal, face-to-face level. People are born with brain wiring already developed for this.

Over the years, communication patterns slowly changed as different technologies developed from the telegraph in 1839, to the telephone, the radio, television, electronic mail (only called email since 1993), and the home computer in 1972. Each of these inventions changed the way people communicated, but face-to-face social interaction was still a dominant form of communication.

Today that has changed. A person can be "connected" with many others, yet seldom engage in a live connection. Skype, Facebook, Tweets, instant messaging, email, and cellphones make communication easy but real human connection hard. This creates a real 21st century problem. If a person spends too many hours communicating using social media instead of personal interaction, then the brain is not using the patterns, the neural circuitry for social interaction that humans developed over several hundred thousand years. You know that neurons need to fire to keep mental pathways strong. Remember the phrases, "neurons that fire together, wire together" and "use it or lose it". If the neurons don't fire and the pathways are not used, then the path deteriorates.

The difference in the amount of technology a person uses in a day is also very great among the generations. You may have heard the terms "digital native" and "digital immigrant". These terms help to describe the technology generation gap. They were coined in 2001 by Marc Prensky as he described the radical changes that characterized students in grades K through college who "think and process information fundamentally differently from their predecessors".

Since Prensky considered the younger group to be "…'native speakers' of the digital language of computers, video games, and the Internet", he called them digital natives. Everyone not born into their digital world, but have chosen to enter it are called digital immigrants.[3] Then there are the non-digitals. These are the people, usually older, who choose not to enter the digital world at all.

In what ways are these groups different? The obvious answer is in their use of technology, but that's not what Prensky highlighted when he coined the two terms. He said the difference was in the way people "think and process information". The generations do it differently. What does that mean?

You know that the process of thinking starts when your brain is stimulated by sensory experiences in your environment. That does not change. What changes is the source of the stimulation, and that's where technology comes in. As a result of the different types of stimulation that the generations experienced as they lived their lives, their brain circuits became wired differently. You saw evidence of this is the study described earlier. Exposure to just five hours of technology use changed the wiring. This raises a societal concern. If brains are wired differently, will people from different generations still be able to communicate?

This is not a theoretical question, because research is finding that because of high technology usage, there is a real decline in face-to-face communication. Reduced face-to-face communication is leading to a decline in non-verbal communication skills like reading body language. This is a serious issue, because body language signals can provide a great deal of information that is not verbally communicated. You may be surprised to learn that about 70% of face-to-face verbal encounters involve non-verbal communication like eye contact, facial expressions, and different aspects of body language.[4]

Words obviously count in communication, but it is the combination of verbal and non-verbal aspects of communication that make a message clear. It is important, especially if you are a digital native, that you maintain and practice your non-verbal skills. The way to do that is to avoid spending too much time using technology. However, that becomes increasingly difficult as the use of technology expands.

Crazy Busy

A 2005 study conducted by the Kaiser Foundation and Stanford University with over two thousand young participants between the ages of 8 and 18 found that they spend 8 ½ hours per day using technology including TV. As a result, they are getting much of their sensory stimulation from nonhuman devices and their human contact skills are declining.[5] Dr. Edward Hallowell, a psychiatrist who specializes in ADD and ADHD agrees. He believes that young people today are leading "crazy busy" lives character- ized by impulsivity, hyperactivity, and inconsistent attention span. The rise in technology is affecting how students learn and this could become a problem. Technology can get them into an "F" state — frantic, frenzy, and forgetful where many mistakes are made. They need to be in a "C" state — careful, cool, calm, and caring to do their best work. Therefore, technology use needs to be controlled.

Disconnection

In addition to its role in keeping people "crazy busy", Dr. Hallowell explains that over the past twenty-five years, technology has enabled humans to become super-connected with other people; however, the rela- tionships are often shallow and some people are experiencing a heightened sense of disconnection. He says people are neglecting traditions and are feeling "alone", not lonely, but alone. Technology has given people the chance to "live at a distance" and this can lead to societal problems.

Dr. Hallowell believes that the state of connectedness is the single most important cause of health, happiness, and longevity. People need the warmth and security of connectedness to thrive personally. As a result, Dr. Hallowell calls this problem of feeling disconnected while being more "connected" than ever before the "Central Modern Paradox".[6] It is a problem that you may face as you weigh the value of your technology time with the value of your human connections time. Which is more important? How will you resolve the paradox for yourself?

Tools for Learning

Prior to the Digital Age, technology had little or no impact on the way the brain processed information. The delivery systems for information were much slower and not as stimulating as they are today. I am a digital immi- grant, and my brain was wired as I interacted with an environment that directly supported thinking and learning with textbooks, teachers, and talk. Social interaction, books, school, and television used to be central drivers of brain activity, and they are huge factors in how my brain is wired. For more recent generations, they are not. Technology is taking over.

The brains of digital natives are used to receiving information from a delivery system that is fast and fun. It would be difficult to find digital immigrants who describe their early information delivery systems that way. Perhaps they would say interesting and challenging, maybe boring, but certainly not fast and fun. As years go by, people will have even more opportunities to participate in an informational delivery system that is fast, fun, stimulating, and pleasurable. A danger may occur if a person, especially a student, decides that he likes the way his brain feels when it is engaged in digital activities. He could become addicted to technology and his real learning would suffer.

Technology Addiction

You've heard of alcohol addiction, drug addiction, gambling addiction, and food addiction. Almost anything that gives people what they consider "pleasure" can become addictive, so it is not a surprise that there is technology addiction. Like other addicts, technology addicts report feeling a rush of good feelings when they engage in their addiction. Do you recall what causes that rush? It's the neurotransmitter dopamine. Researchers, who conducted fMRI studies on people playing video games, saw increased activity in the basal ganglia area where dopamine exerts it pleasurable influence.[7]

Dopamine, as you know, activates the brain's pleasure centers, so it is responsible for the euphoric feelings that an addict chases whether it's an alcohol, drugs, gambling, food, or technology addiction. Addiction usually develops gradually as the future addict repeats his actions over and over again to get the feeling he craves. However, after continued repetition of the activity, the feeling isn't as strong, so he plays more and more, hoping for a stronger dopamine boost from his emotional brain. In the process, the "thinking" part of the brain, the pre-frontal cortex, loses ground. Like all addictions, this leads to people neglecting their priorities and responsibilities.

"Video Game-Brain"

Brains love novelty and excitement, so it comes as no surprise that brains enjoy videogames. However, people who play videogames from two to seven hours a day risk developing what Dr. Small calls "video game-brain", and that's not good. Video game-brain is a syndrome that basically turns off the pre-frontal lobes of your thinking brain. Video-game brainers are the people who already are, or who will become, technology addicts. While playing videogames, activity in the brain's pleasure center, the nucleus accumbens, increases. Unfortunately, the activity in the thinking center, the prefrontal cortex, declines. What cause this? You guessed it—dopamine. While playing, people get a dopamine burst that makes them feel good.

Sometimes, they get so wrapped up in a game, they forget where they are, and they physically sense the danger involved in an artificial world. When that happens, their blood pressure and heart rate increase as they get a thrill from being scared. Their body responds to their sense of danger by releasing—what? Yes, more chemicals. In this case, stress-related chemicals like adrenaline. There's danger here, since too much stress can damage the body and the mind. In addition, some video games, especially violent video games, can impact behavior. One result from playing violent videogames is that people become more comfortable with violence. They enjoy the thrill that the violent games produce, so they are less sensitive to the pain, horror, and death involved in the action. One research study demonstrated that playing violent video games for as little as ten minutes a day increased aggressive behaviors. This is an unwanted side effect.[8]

Multitasking Dangers

The term, multitasking, originated in the computer industry. It referred to the computer's ability to complete more than one task simultaneously. In actuality, a regular, one-core computer can only complete one task at a time. However, one-core computers are designed so different tasks are done at different times, but because of the computer's speed, the tasks just appear to be completed simultaneously. In a dual-core computer, two tasks can actually be processed at the same time, since there is a single core for each task. Some computers today have many cores; so many tasks are completed simultaneously.

The bottom line with computers is to get the jobs done efficiently, effectively, and error free. Anything less is unacceptable. Isn't that what you want too? Wouldn't you like to get your jobs done efficiently, effectively, and error free? Yes, but as you know, the human brain is not designed like a computer. Remember that its new parts are built on top of old parts. You cannot change the design, so you need to work with what you have. What you have is a brain that multi-tasks well in some areas and horribly in others. Let's learn why.

Let me begin with a question. Do you think you can multitask? Most people think they can. It's true in some cases. For example, you can take a shower and sing at the same time. You can read a book and eat a meal. How about walking and talking? Of course you can do both, but notice that these activities can be categorized into two groups. Group 1 involves cognitive/thinking skills and mental activities like singing, reading, and talking that involve your cerebrum; Group 2 involves motor skills and physical activities like showering, eating, and walking that involve your cerebellum. It would be helpful if you could think of your brain like a computer with a two-core processor: Core1. the cerebrum for thinking skills and Core 2. the cerebellum for motor skills. As long as you multitask using the two different processors, you can multitask effectively.

Problems occur when you give two tasks to the same processor to be completed at the same time. Your brain cannot do it. Let's use some examples found in Dr. David Sousa's book, Brainwork, and let's start with an amusing motor skill activity. Sit down, lift your right leg up, and move it in a clockwise rotation about four times. Stop and put your foot flat on the ground. Now take your right arm and extend it with your right index finger in a pointing position. With your finger, draw the number eight in the air four times. Stop. Now try to move your right foot in a clockwise rotation **at the same time** that you try to draw figure eights with your right finger extended in the air. You cannot do it. You cannot ask your cerebellum to complete two unrelated motor activities simultaneously and get good results. Now try doing only one motor activity at a time. Draw circles in a clockwise rotation using your right leg and right arm at the same time. Now try drawing figure eights with both at the same time. What happened? You could do it. Your brain could handle doing one related motor activity at a time.[9]

Alternate and Sequential Tasking

You are probably thinking that you know you can do more than one thing at a time, so this is a good time to make a distinction among multi-tasking, alternate-tasking, and sequential-tasking. With alternate-tasking, your brain shifts its focus back and forth between two tasks at incredible speeds. With sequential-tasking, your brain shifts its focus among three or more tasks at incredible speeds. Dr. Sousa provides an interesting example for alternate-tasking. Count from one to ten as fast as you can. If you timed yourself, you are aware that it took about two seconds. Now recite the alphabet from A to J as fast as you can. That's approximately two seconds also. If you do them back-to-back, count to ten and then recite the letters A to J, then four or five seconds seconds passed.

Now try alternate-tasking where you shift your attention from one task to the other. Try saying the first number followed by the first letter, the second number followed by the second letter, the third number followed by the third letter like this: 1, A, 2, B, and so on until you reach 10, J. That took a lot longer than 5 seconds— perhaps 15. Why? Your brain kept shifting its focus between the counting task and the alphabet task. Your brain can do it, but it cannot do it well. You can complete each task skillfully when done alone, but when you alternate the tasks and switch between them, you become less skillful. Researchers have a name for this: task switch cost. Your attention to one task is distracted by the attention you give to the other task.[10] Sometimes you have no choice and you must engage in alternate or sequential-tasking. Just be aware that when you try to do more than one thing at once, your brainpower will suffer.

Cell Phones and Driving

Let's get very serious now, and examine what happens when your cerebrum, your conscious thinking brain, tries to multitask and complete two unrelated cognitive tasks *at the same time*. Without even knowing the tasks, can you predict the result? Will both tasks be completed effectively and efficiently?

The tasks include 1. talking on a cell phone and 2. driving a car. Can you effectively, efficiently, and safely talk on a cell phone while driving? This is an excellent example of multi-tasking, because you cannot alternate between them. You are doing them both at the exact same time, and both activities are cognitive and involve your cerebrum.

Functional MRI studies have found that when you make a cell phone call, the following three brain regions are activated and work together to complete the task: the left prefrontal cortex (PFC); the anterior cingulate, and the parietal lobe. Your brain is working to find meaning in the spoken word. However, when you talk on a cell phone, it is more difficult to determine the true meaning of the caller's words. You have no body language to assist you. As a result, your brain has to work a lot harder to analyze the caller's voice including tone, pacing, and pitch to determine the true meaning of the words. fMRI studies show that about 37% of a driver's attention is focused on the call. That means that when a person makes a call while driving, he is paying partial attention (only 63%) to the road.

Focusing on a cell phone call results in your brain missing out on very important information related to driving. Peripheral vision in particular is affected. As a result, the driver is in a dangerous situation because his ability to respond and make quick decisions is impaired. Recent studies show that the level of impairment caused by driving while using a cell phone is equivalent to drunk driving.

Some people think that hands-free, voice activated devices are better. Studies show that there is little difference in the driver's level of distraction. Texting and driving is even worse. Dr. Sousa states, "This combination is not only dangerous, it is insane!"[11] The end result is that there are many traffic accidents and deaths as the result of cellphone calls and text messaging while driving. Now you know why.

You **cannot** multitask if the tasks involve the same part of your brain needing to pay attention at the same time (cerebrum/cerebrum or cerebellum/cerebellum). The human brain cannot do it. It is a myth that it can. Multitasking with the same brain part leads to an increasing number of mistakes as well as reduced productivity.[12] That will not make you more successful. You **can** multitask effectively and complete two tasks at the same time if they involve different parts of your brain (cerebrum/cerebellum). What is the message here? If something is important to you and you want to avoid problems, then pay full attention to it! Do not multitask!

Continuous Partial Attention

Society's infatuation with technology has led to a new problem which Dr. Gary Small calls CPA — continuous partial attention. CPA means trying to pay attention to everything without being focused on anything. When this occurs, your brain misses important information which can lead to dangerous situations. With CPA, a person often anticipates communicating with others with various technology tools— cellphones, text messages, instant messaging, and Facebook. People with CPA are on alert for the latest news and keep scanning for contacts. This constant anticipation can lead to a form of mental stress that Dr. Small calls "techno-brain burnout." This stress causes the body to release stress hormones like cortisol and adrenaline. They don't do much harm in the short-term but over the long-term these hormones can change the neural circuitry in the parts of the brain that control thinking and emotions— the hippocampus, the amygdala, and the prefrontal cortex.[13] You are now alerted to some of the dangers that technology holds. Be cautious in your use of exciting technology tools. You do not want to harm your brain.

Actions Needed

Technology is here to stay. It will only become more powerful, faster, less expensive, and more exciting. In the 21st century, you will be living with it as a constant presence, but you cannot let it take over your life. You need to protect yourself and your brain by approaching technology as a useful tool but not the center of your life. One of the very real problems with technology devices is that people get such intense emotional feelings from using them on a regular basis. Unfortunately, they do not get the same emotional thrill as they engage in normal life activities like school or work. How can real life compete with all the bells and whistles of technology tools that are always available? Instant gratification is only a video game or an IPad away. This is where your conscious, thinking brain comes in.

You learned how it worked so now you can use it effectively. You can now use your brain to make decisions and take actions that will lead you to a successful life in the 21st century. These actions include the following:

- Remember that technology products are a set of tools. You use them. Don't let them use you, no matter how exciting they are. Activate your pre-frontal cortex, the CEO of your brain , so it can maintain emotional control. Don't let Miss Amy G hijack you.
- Visualize the "Creative Tension" image. Where are you now and where do you want to be? Use technology to help you succeed. Don't let it be a trap to lure you into distraction, and don't let it replace real human connections.

- Beware of becoming addicted. Monitor and control the time spent playing these games. Remember, they are only games. They should be a small part of your real game of life.
- Maintain live face-to-face contact to keep your social skills and your connections to the real world intact. A balance is needed between technology communication skills and human contact communication skills. Make a conscious effort to connect in person with real people.
- Be patient and try to understand the people on the other side of the technology generation gap. Just because you did not learn in the same way they did, it does not mean that you do not have the same priorities and want the same outcomes. Make sure you work together with, and value the talents of people across the generations.
- Do not trust your ability to multi-task if the tasks involve the same part of your brain. Do not try to do two important cognitive activities at the same time. In this case, it has nothing to do with "will". You may want to complete two cognitive tasks, but your brain does not have the 'skill" to do it.
- Multitasking and CPA are different, but they have something in common. They both can serve as substitutes for setting priorities. Make sure that doesn't hapen to you. If you aim for success, then you need to have priorities. If you do not set priorities, then you can waste a lot of time and even end up drifting through life. Do not let technology interfere with setting priorities.
- Make sure you focus on important things and avoid distractions. Technology is making this harder to do. Use the "time management matrix" that you learned about in chapter 11, School Success Thinking. It may help you focus on what is important but not urgent. In today's crazy, busy world with all of the technology tools and toys, it is becoming more difficult to focus and easier to become distracted. Focus requires mental energy. Use it to complete your important tasks.

Summary

You learned that technology has created a brain gap. People learn and communicate very differently. The digital natives are changing the ways they communicate with others so drastically that interpersonal skills are declining, and that is a cause for societal concern. You can play a role in solving this "Central Modern Paradox" by maintaining face-to-face personal relationships, continuing to build empathy so your neural circuits do not deteriorate, and establishing connections with people in other generations because you have a lot to teach each other.

You also learned that digital natives are so in love with their technology devices that some spend a full eight hour day engaged in using them, so they may be in danger of becoming technology addicts. To avoid this and also video-game-brain, you know you need to make informed choices about your use of technology. Keep track of the time you spend with technology devices. Don't let it interfere with your goals and priorities.

You also learned that digital natives love to multi-task, so they may be putting themselves in danger. You now understand the reasons for this danger, so can make conscious choices about what multi-tasking activities are safe for you. Remember that you cannot complete two tasks that involve the same part of your brain at the same time. Avoid CPA, continuous partial attention, by paying attention to important things.

If you do these things, then you should be able to avoid technology pitfalls like a decline in interpersonal relationships, technology addiction, video-game-brain, and multitasking dangers. Avoiding pitfalls will make it easier to be successful.

Building Better Brains

You now have the big picture about how to care for your brain. It includes good nutrition, plentiful aerobic exercise, adequate sleep, reduced stress, and the proper use of technology. Your job is to keep your brain healthy, so it can adapt well to this ever-changing world. In the next chapter, everything is put together, and we complete our journey.

Questions for Reflection

1. **HEAD**: What did you learn? Imagine that you belong to a Book Club that is reading this book. Summarize the key points that you want to highlight during discussion.
2. **HEART**: How do you feel about what you learned?
3. **ACTION STEP**: What are you going to do now? Suggestions: learn more about the topic; share what you learned, or practice what you learned.

CHAPTER 13

Putting It All Together: A Mega-Thinking Toolbox

The difference between a successful person and others, is not a lack of strength, not a lack of knowledge, but rather a lack of will.
— Coach Vince Lombardi

The goal of this book is to help you achieve 21st century success by becoming a Mega-Thinker. Since the introduction to the book started with a quote about success, I want to end with a quote about success. The quote above was made by the legendary professional football coach, Vince Lombardi. Every year, the team that wins the Super Bowl receives the "Lombardi Trophy", which is named in his honor. Notice the word "will" in his quote. **Success requires will.**

Legendary college basketball coach John Wooden also defined success. He stated: "Success is peace of mind which is a direct result of self-satisfaction in knowing you made the effort to become the best of which you are capable". Notice the word "effort". **Success requires effort.** These great coaches know that effort and willpower are needed to achieve success in any area.

Now let's revisit the quote which started this book: "…success is defined not by where you are born, how smart you are, or how much money you have — or even by dumb luck. **Success is attained by using your brain's faculties** to respond to the circumstances and challenges you face in life". Putting it all together, success in life does not depend on your zip code, your IQ, or your pocketbook. It also does not depend on your gender, race, ethnicity, age, religion, language, or nationality. Your success depends on your **will,** your **effort,** and your **use of your brain's faculties.**

Using your brain's faculties to achieve success requires both effort and willpower. Skillful thinking definitely requires hard work. In fact, Henry Ford, the great American industrialist, said "Thinking is the hardest work there is, which is probably the reason why so few engage in it." However, you now have some knowledge to make the hard work of thinking a little easier.

Knowledge is Power

In 1597, over 400 years ago, Sir Francis Bacon, an English author and philosopher, said "Knowledge is power". Your basic knowledge about brain science and thinking skills has given you power. It has prepared you to understand how your powerful brain works, how it can be trained, and how it can be maintained. It is time now to summarize what you have learned. Let's begin the wrap-up of your journey by recalling some of the big ideas in this book. In the following pages, I'll highlight key points and tools from this book, so it can serve as a handy reference guide for you.

The Mega-Thinking Toolbox

MEGA-THINKING TOOLBOX	
Section 1: KNOW YOUR BRAIN • PERCEPTION • NEURONS • BRAIN BASICS • MEMORY	Section 3: MAINTAIN YOUR BRAIN • BASIC BRAIN CARE Nutrition Exercise Sleep Understand Stress
Section 2: TRAIN YOUR BRAIN • WILL: Dispositions • SKILLS: Common Sense Thinking Critical Thinking Creative Thinking Systems Thinking Self-Control Thinking School Success Thinking	• WISE TECHNOLOGY USE

Key Points from Part 1: Know Your Brain

The Power of Perception

- Your brain is bombarded with data from the "outside" world. It allows very little of this data to get "inside" your brain.
- Your experiences with the world are based on, and limited to, the external sensory data, in the form of atoms and molecules, that enter your brain through your sensory organs. You learn about the real world from the limited sensory data that enters your brain.
- Your survival is you brain's number one job. Your brain works fast as it searches the sensory data to make sure you are not in danger. It leaps to

make sense of the data for you. In the process, your brain is forming perceptions of the world.

- Your perception of the world is limited to the sensory data that provides your individual life experiences. As a result, your world view is actually your "perceived" world; it is not the "real" world.
- Perceptions are powerful. The way you perceive the world impacts everything you believe and do.
- **Your perceptions can make you prisoners of your own beliefs. You can become STUCK in your perceived world!**
- The power of perception is an obstacle to skillful thinking. Other words for perception include mental models, assumptions, paradigms, stories, biases, worldviews, prejudices, cliches, and myths.
- You need to overcome your perception problems.
- Learning how your brain works makes you aware that your perceptions of the world, your worldview, is flawed—just like the worldview of every other person on earth.
- Solutions to problems cannot be reached when flawed perceptions dominate.
- There will never be a perfect perception. Accepting uncertainty is a sign of wisdom. It keeps the mind open to other worldviews and new possibilities.
- You need to learn to become unstuck. Efforts need to be made to get out of flawed perceptions, brain ruts, and mental models that interfere with the skillful thinking needed for 21st century success.

Neurons Rule

Your perceptions are formed as your neurons work together to create mental pathways. You control whether or not pathways are added or deleted. You control whether or not you get into brain ruts, which are very well-worn mental pathways. Many people have no idea about the role of their neurons in shaping their brains, but you do. You know that neurons rule. Let's review some key facts.

- Neurons are the fundamental building blocks of the brain.

- Neurons are brain cells with four main parts: dendrites, cell body, axon, and axon terminals.
- Neurons seek meaning for you by finding patterns in your experiences.
- Finding patterns causes the neuron to fire. Neurons that "fire together wire together". That's how brain pathways and perceptions are formed.
- Neurons communicate with each other by releasing special brain chemicals called neurotransmitters into the gap, called a synapse, between axon terminals and dendrites.
- When the chemical is received by a dendrite, it "fires" and generates an electrical signal that travels to the cell body, down the axon, and when it reaches the axon terminal it causes a sac with a brain chemical in it to explode. That releases the brain chemicals into the synapse. This action repeats when another dendrite receives a neurotransmitter. Remember, you can use your hands and arms to demonstrate this action.
- If a chemical is released and no dendrite accepts it, then a connection is not made.
- If a dendrite accepts a chemical and "fires" it, the nucleus in the cell body may choose not to send it. Again, a connection is not made.
- Your experiences and your choices determine whether or not connections are made. Most of your decisions are made at the unconscious level.
- Your brain is not static. It is continually changing and being reshaped by growing new brain cell connections or pruning old or unused connections between neurons. This is called brain plasticity or neuroplasticity.
- You have the opportunity to grow your brain and grow your intelligence by making more connections among your brain cells throughout your lifetime.
- Your brain grows in predictable phases: fetal development; birth-3; 4-12, and after 12. Your brain is not fully developed until your twenties.
- When brain pathways are no longer used, they decay or are pruned. As a result, your brain is the ultimate "use it or lose it" machine. So use it!

Brain Basics and the Cast of Characters

Your neurons are communicating so you can make sense of the world and live your life. However, they do not operate in isolation. You learned that there is an entire cast of characters that work together to make up your brain. Let's review some of them.

- The **Amygdala** is presented first, naturally, because she is the character that prefers the center of the stage. Miss Amy G Dala is the Queen Bee and the drama queen that specializes in emotion, especially fear, so she always carries a "Panic Button". She also has one of the two "delete" buttons in the brain. She deletes information she doesn't want, so it won't get into your thinking brain. In many ways, she is your brain's boss if you don't stop her.
- The **Hippocampus** is the Memory Keeper and the Architect combining received, processed, and stored memories into new designs and directing them into either sensory/temporary, working, or long-term memory.
- **Reticular Activating System (RAS)** in the brain stem is the Bodyguard. It is your attention center, and it never sleeps. It is the first part of your brain with a "delete" button. It determines what sensory information is allowed into the brain. It is always on alert for threats to your survival. It keeps unwanted information out of your brain. It prevents information overload.
- **Thalamus** is the control tower of your brain. Once RAS lets sensory information in, the thalamus routes the successful sensory data to their proper brain destinations using either a regular route to your PFC or an emergency route to your amygdala.
- The **Prefrontal Cortex** is part of the frontal lobe of your cerebrum. It is the CEO, the Chief Executive Officer with intellect and judgment. It specializes in planning and decision making and works in frontal lobe of your cerebrum. Like an automobile, it not only has a steering wheel, but it also has brakes. It helps to control your emotional impulses. However, it is not fully developed until age 25 in many people.
- The **Parietal Lobe** section of your cerebrum is your Masseuse. It specializes in touch and movement.
- The **Occipital Lobe** section of your cerebrum is your Cameraman. It specializes in vision.

- **The Temporal Lobe** section of your cerebrum is the Band Leader. It specializes in speech, language, and sound.
- **Insular lobe** (only lobe not visible from the outside) is like a Chef, since it specializes in taste. Research is also finding connections with consciousness, self-awareness, homeostasis, and emotions such as disgust.
- **Nucleus Accumbens** is explosive. It specializes in releasing dopamine which provides you with pleasure, motivation, and magical moments of feeling good.
- **Dopamine**, the **Happy Chemical**- the neurotransmitter that brings pleasurable feelings. It is important to remember the power of dopamine, because it also plays a role in addiction.
- **VTA** (ventral tagmental area) is a very primitive part of the brain that acts like a Chemist and synthesizes dopamine.
- **Cerebellum** is the Personal Trainer that specializes in physical movement and coordination.

You also learned that many of these brain parts are used in making your memories. Let's review why memory matters.

Memory Matters

Memory matters because "you are what you are" as a result of what you remember. What is memory?

- Most people think about memory as the mental capacity of a person to encode, store and retrieve information such as facts, details, impressions, remembrances, and recollections from life experiences. These are basic memory processes; however, it is more than that.
- Memory is the connection among neurons. The basic building block of your memory is the neuron. The connection among neurons is what makes memories.
- Memory is evidence of learning. If you cannot remember something, then you have not learned it.
- The complete definition of memory has three components: 1. Encoding, Storage, and Retrieval of Information; 2. Connections among Neurons, and 3. Evidence of Learning.

- There are Natural and Trained memories. Memory itself is natural. People are born with the ability to remember. People can learn to train their memories using skills and strategies when they need to learn semantic, school-type information that is not easily recalled.

Learning about Memories

Scientists learned about memories in three ways:

1. Studying people. For example, studying a man (H.M.) who no longer had long-term memories due to a serious bicycle accident during his childhood.
2. Studying animals. For example, studying the large neurons in the sea slug, Aplysia, that demonstrated the biological basis of memory and learning.
3. Using technology. For example, using specialized tools for brain scans.

Stages of Memory

There are three stages of memory.

1. **Sensory/immediate memory** is a temporary memory that works at the unconscious or subconscious level and is located in your right PFC area. It can retain information for up to 30 seconds.
2. **Working memory** is a temporary memory that works only at the conscious level. It is also located in your right PFC. It usually retains information for 20 to 30 minutes but attention and interest can make it last for hours or days.
3. **Long-Term Memory** is what it says- a long-term memory. Long-term memories can last days, weeks, or a lifetime. They are located in your cerebrum in the area of the brain lobes where they were formed.

Six Long-Term Memory Pathways

There are six pathways to memory storage, and they each store different kinds of information.

1. The **Semantic Pathway** involves learned, school-type information. It usually requires a trained memory. This is also a conscious and declarative pathway. Semantic memories are stored in the Hippocampus and the Cerebrum.

2. The **Episodic Pathway** involves personal experiences and it develops through natural memory. This is also a conscious and declarative pathway. Episodic memories are stored in the Hippocampus and the Cerebrum.

3. The **Emotional Pathway** involves emotions such as love and fear. It can be Conscious or Unconscious and Declarative or Non-Declarative. Emotional memories are stored in the Amygdala.

4. The **Procedural Pathway** involves muscle movement and skills like bike-riding, swimming, and walking. It is unconscious and non-declarative. Procedural memories are stored in the Cerebellum.

5. The **Perceptual Representation System Pathway** involves the structure, form, and sound of words and letters. It is also unconscious and non-declarative. Perceptual Representation System memories are stored in the Cerebellum.

6. The **Automatic Pathway** involves sensory experiences like sounds and smells that automatically trigger involuntary reactions. It too is unconscious and non-declarative. Automatic memories are stored in the Cerebellum.

- It is important to remember that you are **consciously aware** of forming memories along the semantic and episodic pathways and only sometimes along the emotional pathways. Otherwise, your memories are formed unconsciously.

Memory Retrieval

- Memory retrieval is complex and not fully understood. However, attempts are made to explain it in two ways: 1. The Library Model, and 2. The Crime Scene Model.
- The barriers to a good memory include distraction and failure to pay attention to the initial sensory experiences which is also called your "original awareness".
- The keys for improving you memory include the following:

1. **ATTENTION**. If you pay attention to something, then you increase your chances of remembering it. If you cannot maintain attention, focus, or concentration, then you won't be able to improve memory or brain performance in any other area.
2. **SHARPEN YOUR SENSES**. If you pay attention to what you see, hear, smell, taste, and touch, then you increase your chances of remembering it.
3. **POWERFULLY ENCODE DATA.** Elaborately encode data using sensory details and associations.

This concludes the summary for Part 1, Know Your Brain.

Key Ideas for Part 2: Train Your Brain

Part 2 covered six chapters, and the focus was on dispositions and skills. Let's start with dispositions. They are essential.

Dispositions

You need to possess certain dispositions to be a Mega-Thinker. Think of it as developing a scientific mindset. The following is a useful summary of the dispositions needed for Mega-Thinking.

- **Self-Awareness**: Paying attention to emotional impulses, physical sensations, and thoughts.
- **Self-Control; Self-Regulation; Self-Discipline; Impulse Control:** Delay gratification; Emotional balance; Take time to think.

- **Will**: Desire; Choice; Desire and Choice to value thinking. Desire and Choice to take time to think.
- **Effort**: Work done by the mind or body; Force; Conscious exertion.
- **Curiosity**: Desire to know; Inquiry; Questioning; Open to continuous learning.
- **Humility**: Modesty; Humbleness; Awareness that you are a lifelong learner. Awareness that no matter what your expertise is, sometimes you can be wrong.
- **Attention**: Awareness; Interest; Observation; Avoid distractions; Power of the brain to focus on important things.
- **Courage:** Brave; Mental strength to persevere through difficulty. It takes courage to ask tough questions and examine other points of view.
- **Flexibility:** Adaptable; Open-minded; Surfaces and tests assumptions; Willing to change perspective; Willing to ask if there is another way; Willing to break out of brain ruts; Considers alternatives.
- **Suspends Judgment:** Appreciation of uncertainty; Truth Seeker; Scientific Mindset; Seeks reasons and facts; respect for evidence; faith in reason.
- **Inquiry:** Asks challenging and essential questions; Curiosity.
- **Persistence:** Endurance; Continuity; Perseverance; Accepts the fact that thinking is hard work.; Works through obstacles and frustrations; Keeps at it. Einstein stated this quality best when he stated: "It's not that I'm so smart, but I stay with the questions longer".

Strategies for Mega-Thinking

I am using a hard hat image here to represent the hard work of Mega-Thinking. In part 2, each category of thinking had its own chapter. I'll summarize the strategies here using the colors of the hats in Dr. Edward DeBono's "Six Thinking Hats". The colors provide a useful structure to help distinguish and organize the strategies.

YELLOW: COMMON-SENSE THINKING

CUE: The yellow sun is a common sight.

KEY: AWARENESS THAT THE BRAIN NATURALLY HAS LIMITATIONS & BIASES

- Knows how to activate System 2, conscious thinking.
- Recognizes triggers for **Jumping to Conclusions** which includes "Framing" and "Priming" and for **Taking Shortcuts** which includes "Similarity", "Availability", and "Anchoring".
- Avoids Poor Brain Habits like Mental Laziness; Inability to Delay Gratification, Not Paying Attention to Important Things.
- Avoids Overconfidence— the feeling that he cannot fail.
- Is less vulnerable to Neuromarketing.

BLACK: CRITICAL THINKING

CUE: A judge wears black robes.

KEY: SUSPENDS JUDGMENTS AND ASKS QUESTIONS—WHY?

- Develops Positive Brain Habits: Managing Impulsivity; Persisting, and Thinking Flexibly.
- Uses Skillful and Socratic Questioning.
- Uses The Six Thinking Hats.
- Uses Bloom's Taxonomy.
- Uses The Ladder of Inference.
- Uses the Scientific Method.
- Uses the 5 A's of Mega-Thinking.
- Uses Graphic Organizers.

GREEN: CREATIVE THINKING

CUE: Green grass signals renewal, new life and new patterns.

KEY: BREAK OUT OF ESTABLISHED PATTERNS OF THINKING

- Change Perception.
- Change Language.
- Use Lateral Thinking Tools (PO-provocative operations): Escape Method; Reversal; Random Input.
- The Three B's
- SCAMPER
- BRUTETHINK
- False Faces
- Conceptual Blending

BLUE: SYSTEMS THINKING

CUE: The blue sky provides the big picture.

KEY: SEEING CONNECTIONS AMONG ALL PARTS LEADS TO THE "BIG PICTURE".

- Develop Habits of Systems Thinkers.
- Learn vocabulary of systems thinking: system; feedback; balancing feedback loops; reinforcing feedback loops; structure; leverage; mental models.
- Use skills of inquiry, dialogue, and reflection to examine mental models.
- Use Visualization Tools including the following: BOTGs (Behavior Over Time Graphs); CLDs (Causal Loop Diagrams); SFDs (Stock and Flow Diagrams); Creative Tension Tool; the Iceberg; the Ladder of Inference, and Computer Simulation Modeling.
- Become Looped-for-Life.

RED: SELF-CONTROL THINKING

CUE: A red heart symbolizes emotion.

KEY #1: DEVELOP SELF-AWARENESS TO RECOGNIZE EMOTIONAL IMPULSES AND PHYSICAL SIGNALS.

- Know Emotional Triggers
- Recognize and Avoid Emotional Hijacking
- Develop dispositions essential for self-control including persistence, flexibility, and the ability to delay gratification

KEY #2: DEVELOP SKILLS FOR SELF-DISCIPLINE AND SELF-REGU-LATION

- Goal Setting
- Red Delay Button
- Stoplight: Red = Stop; Yellow = Think; Green = Act
- SOCS: (for problem solving) Situation; Options; Consequences; Solutions
- Self-Talk
- STARR: (for anger) Stop; Think; Ask; Reduce; Reward
- FEWW: (for expressing emotions) Feel; Event; Why; What
- ANT Therapy
- Distraction
- Goal Setting
- Elastic band- Creative Tension
- Things Take Time
- Take a Break
- Change the Channel

WHITE: SCHOOL SUCCESS THINKING

CUE: White paper represents school.

KEYS: PAY ATTENTION; AVOID DISTRACTIONS; ENCODE DATA POWERFULLY

- Use Memory Tricks including the Journey Method and the House Method, the Link Method, the Peg System, the Story System, Acronyms, Acrostics, Rhymes and Songs
- Use Study Skills like Chunking, Spacing, SQW3R, KWL, and the Time Management Matrix

All of the tools and strategies that you are learning about in this book form a basic mental toolbox. It is a solid start, but it's only the beginning. Keep adding new tools as you continue on your journey to become a Mega-Thinker. You could start by reading some of the resources cited in this book.

Key Ideas in Part 3: Maintain Your Brain

Nutrition, Exercise, Coping with Stress, Sleep, and Technology are factors that affect the health of your brain. You need to maintain your brain so it can work at its optimum level. You need to make sure you stay healthy by having proper nutrition, adequate exercise, and plenty of sleep. You need to know how to cope with stress by having a balanced view of it, and you need to try hard to maintain the qualities of a youthful brain. In addition, you need to use technology tools wisely. As you do these things, you will be making wiser decisions about the actions you take. These actions will help you maintain your brain, so it can help you to achieve success in all the roles of your life.

Basic brain care begins with the following:

NUTRITION:

- Feed your brain with amino acids.

Here is a grocery list that includes complete proteins plus the *top 10 brain power foods

- eggs, milk, cheese, cottage cheese, yogurt.
- apples, bananas, *blueberries, *grapes, *strawberries
- asparagus, beans, potatoes, mushrooms, *broccoli, *bell peppers, *spinach, *tomatoes
- lentils, oats, *whole grains, seeds, sesame seeds, brown rice, *almonds

EXERCISE:

- Boost your blood flow to your brain.
- Play is the fountain of youth.

- Exercise is medicine for your brain.

COPE WITH & BALANCE STRESS:

- Too much stress can be bad for you, but
- Some stress can be good for you.

SLEEP:

- Replenish your neurotransmitters.
- Consolidate what you learned during the day.

Wise Technology Use

Using technology wisely is also an important part of brain care.

- Use technology wisely; do not let it use you.
- Remember that your brain is being rewired when you use technology, and you are the one allowing the rewiring. Be consciously aware of what you are doing!
- Rewire cautiously; Avoid technology addiction.
- Avoid "video game-brain".
- Be aware of the brain gap between digital natives and digital immigrants.
- Work hard to maintain personal face-to-face relationships.
- Do not allow your brain pathways for personal relationships to decay.
- Remember the dangers of multi-tasking. When you try to do two or more things at once with the same part of your brain, you will make errors.
- Avoid cell-phone use and texting while driving. It engages you in CPA-continuous partial attention — which is dangerous.

Ready for Action

The review of key ideas is now complete. You are now prepared to take action as a Skillful Thinker who is on the road to becoming a Mega-

Thinker. You know that 21st century problems cannot be solved with common-sense, automatic, and sometimes lazy thinking. You know that if you do not make a deliberate effort to engage yourself in the hard work of slow, effortful thinking, that your brain will take the fast, easy, intuitive, unconscious route to decision making and problem solving—leaping all the way. It can't help it. As a pattern-making, prediction machine, it is designed to take shortcuts. In order to achieve success, you need to develop more self-awareness and self-control and activate your conscious brain to help you decide what to believe and do. As you take these actions, you are preparing for success in all of your life roles.

Life Roles

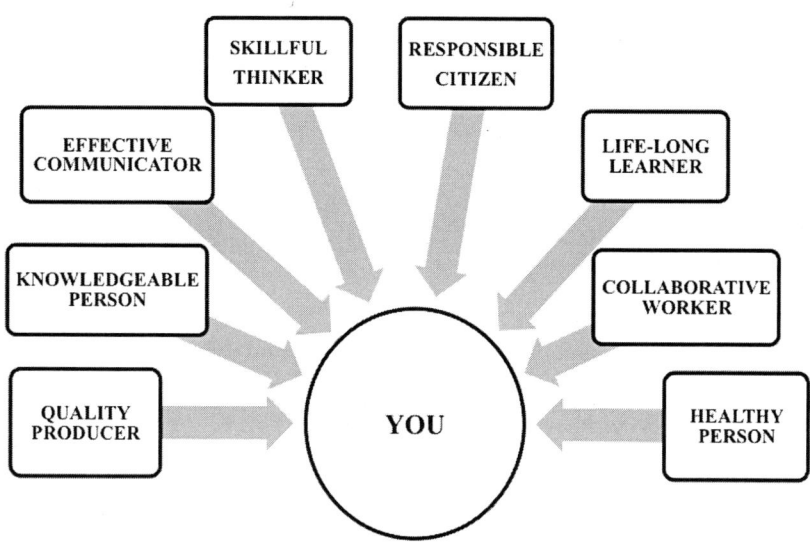

Figure 13.2: Life Roles Requiring a Healthy Brain

Learning to know your brain, train your brain, and maintain you brain will help you live a successful and productive life in all the roles that you play.

Skillful Thinker

1. Acquires and demonstrates skillful critical, creative, common-sense, systems, self- control, and school-success/mnemonic thinking.
2. Effectively uses a variety of thinking strategies to make decisions, solve problems, and create plans in everyday life.
3. Develops habits of mind that promote skillful thinking including inquiry, reflection, and self-control.
4. Skillfully evaluates and uses information to decide what to believe and do.

Responsible Citizen

1. Acquires the knowledge and skills necessary for effective participation as a citizen in a democratic society.
2. Understands individual rights, rules, and responsibilities.
3. Understands the privilege and knows the significance of voting.
4. Understands how the principles of democracy, equality, freedom, law, and justice work in society.
5. Is law-abiding and accepts responsibility for one's own behavior and actions.
6. Volunteers as a community contributor in meaningful community activities.
7. Develops and displays positive character traits including responsibility, honesty, kindness, courage, loyalty, fairness, self-discipline, truth, and integrity.
8. Respects cultural diversity and individual differences.
9. Acts as a steward of the environment.

Knowledgeable Person

1. Acquires a core of essential knowledge.
2. Acquires strategies and dispositions for skillful thinking.
3. Effectively integrates and applies knowledge using strategies and skills.Learns important concepts and basic skills of content areas including the following: English Language Arts/Literature; Mathematics; Science and Technology; History, Geography, and Social Sciences; World Languages; Visual and Performing Arts, and Health and Wellness.

Healthy Person

1. Acquires the knowledge and skills necessary for physical well-being: hygiene, diet, exercise, avoids harmful substances, etc.
2. Acquires the knowledge and skills necessary for the emotional well-being: self-control, rational behavior, adaptability, persistence, flexibility, positive self-image, etc.
3. Has a positive vision for self and future.
4. Copes effectively with personal challenges and frustrations.
5. Participates in satisfying leisure activities.
6. Maintains a youthful mindset. Avoids psychoschlerosis.

Life-Long Learner

1. Is motivated to learn — seeks and values learning experiences.
2. Is intellectually curious.
3. Studies and learns effectively.
4. Recognizes the need to continue to learn because of the inevitability of change

Effective Communicator

1. Reads and listens critically for information, understanding, and enjoyment.
2. Writes and speaks clearly, effectively, factually, and persuasively.
3. Communicates with diverse audiences for a variety of purposes.
4. Communicates clearly using the most appropriate medium (voice, print, technology, video, the arts, etc.).

Collaborative Worker

1. Works hard, perseveres, and acts with integrity.
2. Acquires skills needed to participate in work environments that may be culturally and organizationally diverse.
3. Works cooperatively in groups to achieve group goals.
4. Demonstrates effective interpersonal skills.

Quality Producer

1. Creates/develops products that achieve a purpose.

2. Creates/develops products appropriate for audience.
3. Creates/develops products that reflect craftsmanship.
4. Creates/develops products that use resources/technology.
5. Creates/develops artistic, intellectual, and practical products which reflect originality, high standards, and the use of current technology.

Striking it Rich with Brain Power

In addition to helping you live a successful and productive life, your effort to become a Mega-Thinker will pay off in a number of ways— including your pocketbook. People who can use their brains well, and who can engage their effort and will in the hard work of thinking, will be in demand in the 21st century.

In their book, Revolutionary Wealth, the futurists Alvin and Heidi Toffler predict that knowledge is becoming the new wealth of the 21st century. They predict that knowledge may be the "oil" of the future, but even more valuable. Why? Oil is a resource with a limited supply which requires rigs, pipes, and tankers to get it to its destination. The more the world uses it, the less there is. Knowledge, however, is unlimited. The more people use it, the more they create!

Here is a key question. What makes a person "knowledgeable"? The Tofflers explain that there are many things including "...knowing about our own bodies and brains, how they perform and when they let us do our best work".[1] You now have a basic understanding about how your brain performs, so you are meeting an important requirement of their definition. Use your knowledge and brainpower wisely to achieve 21st century success.

The Biggest Idea

Before you finish this book, I want to re-emphasize what I think is the BIGGEST idea in it. Your perceptions, your mental models, are the most important part of your thinking. Your perceptions have created your personal worldview which is uniquely yours. No one else on Earth has exactly the same worldview as you. Your perceptions make you who you are; they determine what you believe and do.

I hope this information keeps you humble as you realize that neither you nor anyone else on Earth has a worldview that is 100% correct. As a result, each of us needs to be at least a little open-minded (preferably a lot), so we question our own mental models and consider other peoples' points of view.

A skillful thinker, a Mega-Thinker, recognizes the danger of people getting stuck in their personal perceptions. People who are stuck are convinced that their worldview is correct, and they refuse to consider other points of view. When this happens, "thinking" and learning stop. Complex and serious problems cannot be solved when people stop thinking and learning.

The good news is that you have acquired some knowledge, skills, and dispositions to help you become unstuck. Your thinking and learning will continue to grow. You can play a role in making the "real" world a better place.

Final Thoughts

I wish you success as you continue your life's journey using your powerful brain. Remember, breakthroughs in brain science are occurring at a rapid pace. Pay attention to these scientific breakthroughs, so you can continue to learn how to unleash your brain's power. Never stop learning. Never stop growing your brain. Never stop growing your intelligence. Maintain a youthful mindset. Keep using the knowledge and skills of Mega-Thinking. Prepare for success in the 21st century!

Questions for Reflection

1. **HEAD**: What did you learn? Imagine that you belong to a Book Club that is reading this book. Summarize the key points that you want to highlight during discussion.
2. **HEART**: How do you feel about what you learned?
3. **ACTION STEP**: What are you going to do now? Suggestions: learn more about the topic; share what you learned, or practice what you learned.

Notes

Part One: KNOW YOUR BRAIN

Introduction

Quote. Brown, Jeff & Mark Fenske with Liz Neporent. (2010). <u>The Winner's Brain: 8 Strategies Great</u> Minds Use to Achieve Success. Philadelphia, PA: Da Capo Press, 193-184.

1. Smith, Frank. <u>to think</u>. NY: Teacher's College, Columbia University, 1990: 9.
2. Among the resources that state thinking is a skill that can be improved are the following: Dewey, John. <u>How We Think.</u> Boston, MA: D.C. Heath, 1910 and deBono, Edward. <u>DeBono's Thinking Course, revised edition</u>. NY: Facts on File, Inc., 1994, and Ferron, Mary Fennessey. <u>Creating a Community of Thinkers: A Case Study of the Implementation of a Program to Teach Thinking in a Middle School.</u> Unpublished Doctoral Dissertation, School of Education, University of Connecticut, Storrs, CT, 1994: 34-35.
3. Dewey, John. <u>How We Think.</u> Boston, MA: D.C. Heath, 1910, 28.

4. Caine, R. N. & Caine, G. (1991). <u>Making Connections: Teaching and the Human Brain.</u> Alexandria, VA: ASCD, 134.
5. Many scientists agree that the brain remains a mystery, including the following: Buonomano, Dean. <u>Brain Bugs: How the Brain's Flaws Shape Our Lives</u>. NY: Norton, 2011; Kandel, Eric R. <u>In Search of Memory: The Emergence of a New Science of Mind</u>. NY: Norton, 2006; and Medina, John. <u>Brain Rules: 12 Principles for Surviving and Thriving at Work, Home, and School</u>. Seattle, WA: Pear Press, 2008.
6. Kandel, Eric R. <u>In Search of Memory: The Emergence of a New Science of Mind</u>. NY: Norton, 2006: 7-8.
7. Fullan, M. <u>The New Meaning of Educational Change</u>, 4th ed. NY: Teachers College Press, Columbia University, 2007.
8. Sousa, David. <u>How the Brain Learns, 3rd ed.</u> Thousand Oaks, CA: Corwin Press, 2006: 89-94.
9. Eames, Ray & Charles. *Powers of Ten,* a Documentary Film, 1977.
10. Trilling, Bernie & Charles Fadel. (2009). <u>21st Century Skills: Learning for Life in Our Times</u>. San Francisco, CA: Jossey-Bass, 157.

Chapter 1. The Power of Perception

Quote: deBono, Edward. <u>DeBono's Thinking Course, revised edition</u>. NY: Facts on File, Inc., 1994: 8.

1. Medina, John. <u>Brain Rules: 12 Principles for Surviving and Thriving at Work, Home, and School</u>. Seattle, WA: Pear Press, 2008: 32.
2. Kahneman, Daniel. <u>Thinking, Fast and Slow</u>. NY: Farrar, Straus, and Giroux, 2011.
3. deBono, 1994: 9.
4. Brooks, David. <u>The Social Animal: The Hidden Sources of Love, Character, and Achievement</u>. New York, NY: Random House, 2011: 285.
5. Sousa, David A. <u>How the Brain Learns, 3rd ed.</u> Thousand Oaks, CA: Corwin Press, 2006: 52.
6. Kandel, Eric R. <u>In Search of Memory: The Emergence of a New Science of Mind</u>. NY: Norton, 2006: 226-227.
7. Senge, Peter, M. (1990). <u>The Fifth Discipline: The Art and Practice of the Learning Organization.</u> NY: Doubleday: 185.

8. Toffler, Alvin and Heidi. <u>Revolutionary Wealth</u>. NY: Currency Books, 2006: 122-129.
9. Kahneman, Daniel. <u>Thinking, Fast and Slow</u>. NY: Farrar, Straus, and Giroux, 2011: 263.
10. Senge, Peter M., et al. (2000). <u>Schools That Learn: A Fifth Discipline Fieldbook for Educators, Parents, and Everyone Who Cares About Education</u>. NY: Doubleday: 68.
11. Senge, Peter M. (1990). <u>The Fifth Discipline: The Art and Practice of the Learning Organization.</u> NY: Doubleday: 8.
12. Smith, Frank. <u>to think</u>. NY: Teacher's College, Columbia University, 1990: 132.

Chapter 2. Neurons Rule

Quote. Kotulak, Ronald. (1997). <u>Inside the Brain: Revolutionary Discoveries of How the Mind Works</u>. Kansas City, MI: Andrews McNeil Pub: 6.

1. Medina, John. <u>Brain Rules: 12 Principles for Surviving and Thriving at Work, Home, and School</u>. Seattle, WA: Pear Press, 2008: 56.
2. Sprenger, Marilee. <u>Learning & Memory: The Brain in Action.</u> Alexandria, VA: ASCD, 1999.
3. Kandel, Eric R. <u>In Search of Memory: The Emergence of a New Science of Mind</u>. NY: Norton, 2006, 66.
4. Newquist, 2004: 85-96.
5. Howard, Pierce J. <u>The Owner's Manual for the Brain: Everyday Applications from Mind-Brain Research</u>. Austin, Texas: Bard Press, 2006: 50.
6. Kandel, 2006: 99-102.
7. Kotulak, 1997: 13-16.
8. Newquist, H. P. <u>The Great Brain Book</u>. New York: Scholastic, 2004: 98-99.
9. Armstrong, Sarah. <u>Teaching Smarter with the Brain in Focus</u>. New York, NY: Scholastic, Inc., 2008: 14.
10. Kandel, 2006: 3.
11. Kandel, 2006: 58-59; Medina, 2008:57.
12. Kandel, 2006: 146-147
13. Kandel, 2006: 198-205.

14. Kandel, 2006: 59-60.

15. Kandel, 2006: xiii.

16. Willis, Judy, MD, M.Ed. <u>How Your Child Learns Best: Brain-Friendly Strategies You Can Use to Ignite Your Child's Learning and Increase School Success</u>. Naperville, IL: Sourcebooks, Inc., 2008: 278.

17. Restak, Richard, M.D. <u>Think Smart: A Neuroscientist's Prescription for Improving Your Brain's Performance</u>. NY, NY: Riverhead Books, 2009: 19.

18. Kotulak, Ronald. <u>Inside the Brain: Revolutionary Discoveries of How the Mind Works</u>. Kansas City, MI: Andrews McNeil Pub, 1997: 6-11.

19. Restak, 2009. 70-78.

20. Sprenger, 1999: 10-14.

21. Restak, 2009: 73.

22. Plucker, J.A., Ed. <u>Human Intelligence: Historical Influence, Current Controversies, Teaching Resources</u>, 2013. Retrieved April 27, 2014 from http://intelltheory.com.

Chapter 3. Brain Basics and the Cast of Characters

Quote. Begley, Sharon. (2010). "The Human Brain: Marvel or Mess? [http://www.newsweek.com/human-brain-marvel-or-mess-97675]" 2010.

1. Information about the triune brain from Sprenger, Marilee. <u>Learning & Memory: The Brain in Action.</u> Alexandria, VA: ASCD, 1999: 32-33; Sweeny, Michael S. <u>Brain: The Complete Mind.</u> Washington, D.C.: National Geographic, 2009: 69-70; 'Medina, John. <u>Brain Rules: 12 Principles for Surviving and Thriving at Work, Home, and School</u>. Seattle, WA: Pear Press, 2008: 40.

2. Begley's quote; Buonomano, Dean. <u>Brain Bugs: How the Brain's Flaws Shape Our Lives</u>. NY: Norton, 2011: 10.

3. Newquist, H. P. <u>The Great Brain Book</u>. New York: Scholastic, 2004: 48-49.

4. Armstrong, Sarah. <u>Teaching Smarter with the Brain in Focus</u>. New York, NY: Scholastic, Inc., 2008: 69.

5. Small, Gary, M.D. <u>iBrain: Surviving the Technological Alteration of the Modern Mind.</u> NY, NY: HarperCollins, 2008: 118.

6. Newquist, H. P. The Great Brain Book. New York: Scholastic, 2004: 32-36.

7. Amen, Daniel, M.D. Magnificent Mind At Any Age. NY, NY: Harmony Books, 2008: 13.

8. Sweeney, Michael, 2009: 20-21.

9. Pink, Daniel L. A Whole New Mind. NY: Riverhead Books., 2006.

10. Willis, Judy, MD, M.Ed. How Your Child Learns Best: Brain-Friendly Strategies You Can Use to Ignite Your Child's Learning and Increase School Success. Naperville, IL: Sourcebooks, Inc., 2008: 5.

11. Sousa, David A. Brainwork: The Neuroscience Behind How We Lead Others. Bloomington, IN: Triple Nickel Press, 2012: 13-17.

12. Goleman, Daniel. Emotional Intelligence: Why It Can Matter More Than IQ. New York, NY: Bantam Books, 1995: 14-15; Willis, Judy, 2008: 4.

13. Kotulak, Ronald. Inside the Brain: Revolutionary Discoveries of How the Mind Works. Kansas City, MI: Andrews McNeil Pub, 1997: 142.

14. Information about the brain's pleasure center comes from several sources: Small (2008): 48-49; Ratey, John J., M.D. with Eric Hagerman. (2008). Spark: The Revolutionary New Science of Exercise and the Brain. NY: Little, Brown and Company: 170; Amen, Daniel, 2008: 211; Sweeney, Michael, 2009: 48-49.

15. Medina, 2008: 41.

16. LeDoux, Joseph. (1996). The Emotional Brain. NY: Simon & Shuster. My summary is based on this book plus Daniel Goleman's conversations with Dr. Joseph LeDoux, a neuroscientist who studies the biological basis of emotion, which are detailed in Goleman's book, Emotional Intelligence.

17. Medina, 2008: 80.

18. Goleman, 1995: 16-17.

19. Medina, 2008: 93.

Chapter 4. Memory Matters

Quote. Kandel, Eric R. <u>In Search of Memory: The Emergence of a New Science of Mind</u>. NY: Norton, 2006, 10.

1. Foer, Joshua. (2007). "Why We Remember, Why We Forget", in <u>National Geographic</u>, Nov. 2007, 34.
2. Kandel, 2006: 127-131.
3. Howard, Pierce J. <u>The Owner's Manual for the Brain: Everyday Applications from Mind-Brain Research</u>. Austin, Texas: Bard Press, 2006: 61-66.
4. PubMed.Gov: PMID 18157658.
5. Willis, Judy, MD, M.Ed. <u>Brain-Friendly Strategies for the Inclusion Classroom</u>. Alexandria, VA: ASCD, 2007: 1-2.
6. Sousa, David A. <u>How the Brain Learns, 3rd ed.</u> Thousand Oaks, CA: Corwin Press, 2006: 80.
7. Sousa, 2006: 41-43.
8. Kandel, 2006: 255.
9. Sousa, 2006: 47.
10. Kandel, 2006: 274-276.
11. Medina, John. <u>Brain Rules: 12 Principles for Surviving and Thriving at Work, Home and School</u>. Seattle, WA: Pear Press, 2008: 104.
12. Memory pathways from: Sousa, 2006: 80-85 and Sprenger, Marilee. <u>Learning & Memory: The Brain in Action.</u> Alexandria, VA: ASCD, 1999: 49-55.
13. Medina, 2008: 127-129.
14. Medina, 2008: 110.
15. Medina, 2008: 133.
16. James, William. <u>The Principles of Psychology</u>. Retrieved from "Classics in the History of Psychology", an Internet resource developed by Christopher D. Green, York University: Toronto, Ontario, Canada., 1890.
17. Buonomano, Dean. <u>Brain Bugs: How the Brain's Flaws Shape Our Lives</u>. NY: Norton, 2011: 22.

Part Two: TRAIN YOUR BRAIN

Chapter 5. Common Sense Thinking

Quote. Smith, Frank. to think. NY: Teacher's College, Columbia University, 1990: 9.

1. Kahneman, Daniel. Thinking, Fast and Slow. NY: Farrar, Straus, and Giroux, 2011: 8-9.
2. Buonomano, Dean. Brain Bugs: How the Brain's Flaws Shape Our Lives. NY: Norton, 2011: 16-17.
3. Kahneman, 2011: 20-49.
4. Kahneman, 2011:79-88
5. Information about "Framing" came from Kahneman, 2011: 364-367 and Buonomano, 2011:147-152.
6. Information about "Priming" came from Kahneman, 2011: 52-56 and Buonomano, 2011:35-46.
7. Kahneman, 2011:53-54.
8. Kahneman, 2011: 6-7; 146-155.
9. Kahneman, 2011:137-145.
10. Kahneman, 2011: 115-125.
11. Kahneman, 2011: 35.
12. Kahneman, 2011: 44-45.
13. Buonomano, 2011: 99-102.
14. Kahneman, 2011: 23-24.
15. Kahneman, 2011: 14.
16. Argyris, C. "Teaching Smart People How to Learn". Harvard Business Review, 69 (3), 1991: 99-109.
17. Buonomano, 2011: 11.
18. Packard, Vance. The Hidden Persuaders, 1957. (Introduction copyright 2007 by Mark Crispin Miller). Brooklyn, NY: Ig Publishing.
19. Sousa, David A. Brainwork: The Neuroscience Behind How We Lead Others. Bloomington, IN: Triple Nickel Press, 2012.

Chapter 6. Critical Thinking

Quote. Ennis, Robert H. "A Taxonomy of Critical Thinking Dispositions and Abilities", pp. 9-26, in Baron, J.B. & Sternberg, R. (Eds.), <u>Teaching Thinking Skills: Theory & Practice,</u> NY: W.H. Freeman & Co., 1987: 10.

1. Dewey, John. <u>How We Think.</u> Boston, MA: D.C. Heath, 1910. This is the year I will cite throughout this book because that's when the ideas were written. I used an unabridged republication of the original Dewey, John. <u>How We Think</u>. Mineola, NY: Dover Pub., 1997.
2. Paul, Richard. <u>Critical Thinking: What Every Person needs to Survive in a Rapidly Changing World</u>. CA: Sonoma State University, Center for Critical Thinking and Moral Critique, 1990: 30-37 used in developing the chart.
3. Costa, A. & Kallick, B. <u>Discovering and Exploring Habits of Mind</u> .Alexandria, VA: ASCD, 2000.
4. Dewey, 1910: 30.
5. Raths, L. E., Wasserman, S., Jonas, A., & Rothstein, A. <u>Teaching for Thinking: Theory, Strategies, and Activities for the Classroom</u> (2nd ed.). New York: Teachers College, Columbia University, 1986.
6. Senge, Peter M. et al. <u>The Fifth Discipline Fieldbook</u>. NY: Doubleday. 1994: 108-112.
7. Paul, 1990: 276-277.
8. Dewey, 1910: 72-78.
9. Bloom. B. S., and Englehart, M. D., Furst, E. J., Hill, H. W., and Krathwohl, D. R. Taxonomy of Educational Objectives. IL: University of Chicago Press, 1956.
10. Sousa, David A. <u>How the Brain Learns, 3rd ed.</u> Thousand Oaks, CA: Corwin Press, 2006: 248-255.
11. Schrock, Kathy. (2014). Schrock Guide Website [http://www.schrockguide.net].
12. Medina, John. <u>Brain Rules: 12 Principles for Surviving and Thriving at Work, Home,and School</u>. Seattle, WA: Pear Press, 2008: 233.
13. Senge, Peter M., et al. <u>Schools That Learn: A Fifth Discipline Fieldbook forEducators, Parents, and Everyone Who Cares About Education</u>. NY: Doubleday, 2000: 59-65.

14. deBono, Edward. <u>Six Thinking Hats for Schools.</u> Logan Iowa: Perfection Learning, 1991.
15. deBono, 1991: 12-14.
16. Senge, 2000: 68-71.
17. Dewey, 1910: 26, italics in original.
18. Senge, Peter M. et al. <u>The Fifth Discipline Fieldbook</u>. NY: Doubleday, 1994: 242-246.
19. Sheikh Nahayan Mabarak Al Nahayan, 2007. Chancellor's message from the first "Festival of Thinkers [http://www.festivalofthinkers.com]".

Chapter 7. Creative Thinking

Quote. deBono, Dr. Edward. <u>Serious Creativity.</u> NY: Harper Business, 1992: xiv.

1. This chart is based on information from the following books: deBono, Edward. <u>DeBono's Thinking Course, revised edition</u>. NY: Facts on File, Inc., 1994; deBono, Edward. <u>Serious Creativity: Using the Power of Lateral Thinking to Create New Ideas</u>. NY: Harper Business, 1992; Michalko, Michael. <u>Creative Thinkering: Putting Your Imagination to Work.</u> Novato, CA: New World Library, 2011, and Michalko, Michael. <u>Thinkertoys: a handbook of creative-thinking techniques, 2nd ed</u>. Berkeley, CA: Ten Speed Press, 2006.
2. deBono, 1992: 7.
3. Michalko, 2011: 143-145.
4. Michalko, 2011: 81-85.
5. Michalko, 2006: 43-52.
6. Michalko, 2011: 161-171.
7. Michalko, 2006: 42; 199.
8. Osborn, Alex. <u>How to Think Up</u>. NY, NY: McGraw-Hill Book Company, Inc., 1942: 26-27.
9. Osborn, 1942: 34-35.
10. deBono, 1992: 52-56.
11. deBono, 1994: 62-63.
12. deBono, 1992: 150.

13. deBono, 1992: 165-168
14. deBono, 1992: 177-183.
15. Michalko, 2011: 203-212
16. deBono, 1992: 80; 208.
17. Michalko, 2006: 157-165.
18. Michalko, 2006: 72-108.
19. Michalko, 2006: 218-220.
20. Michalko, 2011: xiv-xviii; 14-17.

Chapter 8. Systems Thinking

Quote. Albert Einstein quotations.

1. Richmond, Barry. "Introduction. The Thinking in Systems Thinking: Eight Critical Skills". In Richmond, Joy, et al. Tracing Connections: Voices of Systems Thinkers. Lebanon, NH: isee systems, inc., 2010: 3.
2. Peterson, Steve. "Systems Thinking for Anyone: Practices to Consider". In Richmond, Joy, et al. Tracing Connections: Voices of Systems Thinkers. Lebanon, NH: isee systems, inc., 2010: 33.
3. Richmond, Barry. 2010: 5.
4. Richmond, Barry. 2010: 17.
5. Senge, Peter M. The Fifth Discipline: The Art and Practice of the Learning Organization. NY: Doubleday, 1990: xiv-xv.
6. Meadows, Donella H. edited by Diana Wright. Thinking in Systems: A Primer. White River Junction, VT: Chelsea Green Publishing. 2008: 172.
7. Source for Richmond's quote: Waters Foundation [http://www.watersfoundation.org/systems-thinking/definitions/%20]. (The emphasis in bold is mine.)
8. Peterson, Steve. 2010: 32-34.
9. Meadows, Donella. 2008: 2, 11-17.
10. Meadows. 2008: 14-16.
11. Senge, Peter M. The Fifth Discipline: The Art and Practice of the Learning Organization. NY: Doubleday, 1990: 42-44; Senge, Peter M. et al. The Fifth Discipline Fieldbook. NY: Doubleday. 1994: 90.
12. Senge, Peter. 1990: 40, 42-47, 52-54.

13. Senge, Peter. 1990: 114.

14. Senge, Peter. 1990: 64.

15. Meadows, Donella. 2008: 162-164.

16. Meadows, Donella. 2008: 91-92.

17. Meadows, Donella. 2008: 17.

18. Meadows, Donella. 2008: 18-19.

19. Meadows, Donella. 2008: 19-23.

20. Meadows, Donella. 2008: 24.

21. Senge, 2000: 75.

22. Senge, Peter M., et al. Schools That Learn: A Fifth Discipline Fieldbook for Educators, Parents, and Everyone Who Cares About Education. NY: Doubleday, 2000: 79.

23. Meadows, Donella. 2008: 25.

24. Senge, 1990: 83-88; Meadows, 2008: 27-30.

25. Senge, 1990: 79- 83: Meadows, 2008: 30-32.

26. Senge, 2000: 80-83.

27. Meadows, 2008: 88-89; Senge. 2000: 80-81.

28. Meadows, 2008: 89-90; Senge, Peter. 2000: 240-242.

29. Meadows, 2008: 88-90; Senge, Peter. 2000: 81-82.

30. Senge, 1990: 75.

31. Senge, 2000: 244-245.

32. Meadows, 2008: 163.

33. Senge, 2000: 79, 84.

34. Meadows, 2008: 164.

35. Meadows, 2008: 167-168.

For more information about Systems Thinking in K-12 schools, go to System Thinking in Schools at Waters Foundation [http://www.watersfoundation.org] and The Creative Learning Exchange [http://www.clexchange.org].

Chapter 9. Self-Control Thinking

Quote. Wooden, John and Jay Carty. Coach Wooden's Pyramid of Success. Ventura, CA: Regal Books, 2005: 50.

1. Wooden, John and Jay Carty. Coach Wooden's Pyramid of Success. Ventura, CA: Regal Books, 2005: 50.
2. Psychologist Margaret Chapman in Sousa, David A. Brainwork: The Neuroscience Behind How We Lead Others. Bloomington, IN: Triple Nickel Press, 2012: 49.
3. Goleman, Daniel. Working with Emotional Intelligence. New York, NY: Bantam Books, 1998: 82.
4. Mayer, John and Peter Salovey "Emotional Intelligence: Imagination, Cognition, and Personality". 1990: 9, 185-211. Lab oratory reprint: www.unh.edu/personalitylab [http://www.unh.edu/personalitylab].
5. Goleman, Daniel. Emotional Intelligence: Why It Can Matter More Than IQ. New York, NY: Bantam Books, 1995: 34.
6. Sousa, David A. Brainwork: The Neuroscience Behind How We Lead Others. Bloomington, IN: Triple Nickel Press, 2012: 49.
7. Sternberg, Robert. In Search of the Human Mind. New York: Harcourt Brace, 1994.
8. Amen, Daniel, M.D. Magnificent Mind At Any Age. NY, NY: Harmony Books, 2008: 173.
9. Chapman in Sousa, 2012: 51.
10. Sousa, 2012: 51.
11. New Haven's Social Competence Program and the "Stoplight" strategy in Goleman, Daniel. Emotional Intelligence: Why It Can Matter More Than IQ. New York, NY: Bantam Books, 1995: 269, 276.
12. New Haven's Social Competence Program and the "SOCS" strategy in Goleman, 1995: 281-282.
13. Amen, 2008:173.
14. "STARR" strategy in Hawkins, David J. and Richard F. Catalano. (2002). Guiding Good Choices. South Deerfield, MA: Channing Bete, Co., 2002: section 4, pp. 4-5.
15. ANT Therapy in Amen, 2008: 172-177.
16. "FEWW" Strategy in Hawkins, David J., 2002: section 4, pp. 4, 7.
17. Lehrer, Jonah. "Don't: The Secret of Self-Control" in The New Yorker, May 18, 2009.
18. Create a blueprint for your brain in Amen, 2008: 140.
19. One Page Miracle in Amen, 2008: 153-154.
20. Covey, Stephen. The 7 Habits of Highly Effective People. NY: Fireside Books, 1989: 89.

21. Brown, Jeff & Mark Fenske with Liz Neporent. <u>The Winner's Brain: 8 Strategies Great Minds Use to Achieve Success</u>. Philadelphia, PA: Da Capo Press, 2010.
22. Goleman, 1995: 286.
23. Dewey, J. <u>How We Think.</u> Boston, MA: D.C. Heath, 1910. Unabridged republication of the original in Dewey, John. <u>How We Think</u>. Mineola, NY: Dover Pub., 1997: 9.

Chapter 10. School Success Thinking

Quote. Medina, John. <u>Brain Rules: 12 Principles for Surviving and Thriving at Work, Home,and School</u>. Seattle, WA: Pear Press, 2008: 100.

1. Lorayne, Harry and Jerry Lucas. <u>The Memory Book: The Classic Guide to Improving Your Memory at Work, at School, and at Play</u>. NY: Ballantine Books, 1974: 24.
2. Foer, Joshua. <u>Moonwalking with Einstein: The Art and Science of Remembering Everything</u>. New York: The Penguin Press, 2011.
3. Lorayne, 1974: 32.
4. Lorayne, 1974: 25-28.
5. Lorayne, 1974:22.
6. Sousa, David A. <u>How the Brain Learns, 3<u>rd</u> ed.</u> Thousand Oaks, CA: Corwin Press, 2006: 89-94; 121-122.
7. Covey, Stephen. <u>The 7 Habits of Highly Effective People</u>. NY: Fireside Books, 1989: 151.

Part Three: MAINTAIN YOUR BRAIN

Chapter 11. Brain Care: Eat, Play, Sleep

Quote. Medina, John. <u>Brain Rules: 12 Principles for Surviving and Thriving at Work, Home,and School</u>. Seattle, WA: Pear Press, 2008: 28.

1. Restak, Richard, M.D. <u>Think Smart: A Neuroscientist's Prescription for Improving Your Brain's Performance</u>. NY, NY: Riverhead Books, 2009.
2. Amen, Daniel, M.D. <u>Magnificent Mind At Any Age.</u> NY, NY: Harmony Books, 2008: 11.
3. Restak, 2009: 25-45.
4. Kotulak, Ronald. <u>Inside the Brain: Revolutionary Discoveries of How the Mind Works</u>. Kansas City, MI: Andrews McNeil Pub., 1997: 106.
5. Medina, John. <u>Brain Rules: 12 Principles for Surviving and Thriving at Work, Home, and School</u>. Seattle, WA: Pear Press, 2008: 22.
6. Amen, 2008: 14-16.
7. Medina, 2008: 21.
8. Ratey, John J., M.D. with Eric Hagerman. <u>Spark: The Revolutionary New Science of Exercise and the Brain.</u> NY: Little, Brown and Company, 2008: 245.
9. Ratey, 2008: 269.
10. Ratey, 2008: 19.
11. Willis, Judy, MD, M.Ed. <u>How Your Child Learns Best: Brain-Friendly Strategies You Can Use to Ignite Your Child's Learning and Increase School Success</u>. Naperville, IL: Sourcebooks, Inc., 2008:23.
12. Willis, 2008: 52-54.
13. McGonigal, Kelly. TED Talk, "How to Make Stress Your Friend [http://www.ted.com/talks/kelly_mcgo-nigal_how_to_make_stress_your_friend.]", 2013.
14. Ratey, 2008: 61.
15. Fernandez, Alvaro and Elkhonon Goldberg with Pascale Michelon. <u>The SharpBrains Guide to Brain Fitness</u>, 2nd ed. SharpBrains, 2013: 141-147.

16. Montagu, Ashley. <u>Growing Young</u>, 2nd ed. Westport, CT: Bergin & Garvey, 1989.

17. Armstrong, Thomas. <u>Awakening Genius in the Classroom</u>. Alexandria, VA: ASCD, 1998.

18. Dewey, J. <u>How We Think.</u> Boston, MA: D.C. Heath, 1910: vii.

19. Dewey, 1910: 218.

20. Fernandez, et al. 2013: 201.

Chapter 12. Technology and Your Brain

Quote. Small, Gary, M.D. <u>iBrain: Surviving the Technological Alteration of the Modern Mind.</u> NY, NY: HarperCollins, 2008, 1.

1. Small, 2008: 24.

2. Small, 2008: 14-17.

3. Prensky, Marc. Digital Natives, Digital Immigrants". From *On the Horizon* (MCB University Press, Vol. 9 No. 5), 2001.

4. Sousa, David A. <u>Brainwork: The Neuroscience Behind How We Lead Others</u>. Bloomington, IN: Triple Nickel Press, 2012: 25.

5. Small, 2008: 29.

6. Hallowell, Edward. Keynote address, "Crazy Busy: Dealing with an Overstretched, Overbooked, Distracted Life", 24th Learning and the Brain Conference, on Nov. 21, 2009.

7. Small, 2008: 48-53.

8. Small, 2008: 35-37.

9. Sousa, 2012: 23-24.

10. Sousa, 2012, 27-29.

11. The information on cell phone use and driving came from Small, 2008, 161-163 and Sousa, 2012: 25-27.

12. Medina, John. <u>Brain Rules: 12 Principles for Surviving and Thriving at Work, Home, and School</u>. Seattle, WA: Pear Press, 2008: 84-85, 93.

13. Small, pp. 17-19.

Chapter 13. Putting It All Together

Quote. Internet search for quotations about success. Vince Lombardi quotation.

1. Kahneman, Daniel. Thinking, Fast and Slow. NY: Farrar, Straus, and Giroux, 2011: 418.
2. Toffler, Alvin and Heidi. Revolutionary Wealth. NY: Currency Books, 2006: 104-106.

Bibliography

Amen, Daniel, M.D. (2008). <u>Magnificent Mind At Any Age.</u> NY, NY: Harmony Books.

Argyris, C. (1991). "Teaching Smart People How to Learn". <u>Harvard Business Review, 69</u> (3), 99-109.

Armstrong, Thomas. (1998). <u>Awakening Genius in the Classroom</u>. Alexandria, VA: ASCD.

Armstrong, Sarah. (2008). <u>Teaching Smarter with the Brain in Focus</u>. New York, NY: Scholastic, Inc.

Begley, Sharon. (2010). "The Human Brain: Marvel or Mess? [http://www.newsweek.com/human-brain-marvel-or-mess-97675]" 2010.

Bloom. B. S., and Englehart, M. D., Furst, E. J., Hill, H. W., and Krathwohl, D. R. (1956). <u>Taxonomy of Educational Objective</u>s. IL: University of Chicago Press.

Brooks, David. (2011). <u>The Social Animal: The Hidden Sources of Love, Character, and Achievement</u>. New York, NY: Random House.

Brown, Jeff & Mark Fenske with Liz Neporent. (2010). <u>The Winner's Brain: 8 Strategies Great Minds Use to Achieve Success</u>. Philadelphia, PA: Da Capo Press.

Buonomano, Dean. (2011). <u>Brain Bugs: How the Brain's Flaws Shape Our Lives</u>. NY: Norton.

Caine, R. N. & Caine, G. (1991). <u>Making Connections: Teaching and the Human Brain.</u> Alexandria, VA: ASCD.

Connell, J. Diane. (2005). <u>Brain-Based Strategies to Reach Every Learner</u>. NY: Scholastic.

Costa, Arthur L. and Lawrence F. Lowery. (1989). <u>Techniques for Teaching Thinking</u>. Pacific Grove, CA: Midwest Publications.

Costa, A. & Kallick, B. (2000). <u>Discovering and Exploring Habits of Mind</u>. Alexandria, VA: ASCD.

Covey, Stephen. (1989). <u>The 7 Habits of Highly Effective People</u>. NY: Fireside Books.

deBono, Edward. (1991). <u>Six Thinking Hats for Schools.</u> Logan Iowa: Perfection Learning.

deBono, Edward. (1992). <u>Serious Creativity: Using the Power of Lateral Thinking to Create NewIdeas</u>. NY: Harper Business.

deBono, Edward. (1994). <u>DeBono's Thinking Course, revised edition</u>. NY: Facts on File, Inc.

Dewey, J. (1910). <u>How We Think.</u> Boston, MA: D.C. Heath. Unabridged republication of the original in Dewey, John. (1997). <u>How We Think</u>. Mineola, NY: Dover Pub.

Ennis, Robert H. (1962). "A Concept of Critical Thinking" in Harvard Educational Review, vol. 32, no.1, winter 1962, pp. 81-111.

Ennis, Robert H. (1987). A Taxonomy of Critical Thinking Dispositions and Abilities. In Baron, J.B. & Sternberg, R. (Eds.), Teaching Thinking Skills: Theory & Practice (pp. 9-26). NY: W.H. Freeman & Co.

Fernandez, Alvaro and Elkhonon Goldberg with Pascale Michelon. (2013). The SharpBrains Guide to Brain Fitness, 2nd ed. SharpBrains.

Ferron, Mary Fennessey (1994). Creating a Community of Thinkers: A Case Study of the Implementation of a Program to Teach Thinking in a Middle School. Unpublished Doctoral Dissertation, School of Education, University of Connecticut, Storrs, CT.

Foer, Joshua. (2011). Moonwalking with Einstein: The Art and Science of Remembering Everything. New York: The Penguin Press.

Foer, Joshua. (2007). "Why We Remember, Why We Forget", in National Geographic, Nov. 2007, pp. 32-55.

Forrester, Jay. (2000)."Systems Study for the Long Term" pp. 232-238 in Senge, Peter M., et al. (2000). In Schools That Learn. NY: Doubleday.

Forrester, Jay. (2013). An interview with Jay Forrester on the nature of the problems we face [http://http//thefrogthatjumpedout.blogspot.com/2013/06/jay-forrester-on-nature-of-problems-we.html]. Conducted by Anupam Saraph in April 2013 and posted on YouTube June 18, 2013 by Ugo Bardi.

Fullan, M. (2007). The New Meaning of Educational Change, 4th ed. NY: TeachersCollege Press, Columbia Univ.

Gardner, Howard. (2011). Frames of Mind: The Theory of Multiple Intelligences, 3rd. ed. New York, NY: Basic Books.

Goleman, Daniel. (1995). Emotional Intelligence: Why It Can Matter More Than IQ. New York, NY: Bantam Books.

Goleman, Daniel. (1998). Working with Emotional Intelligence. New York, NY: Bantam Books.

Greenfield, Patricia M., PhD. (2009). "Technology and Informal Education: What is Taught, What is Learned". Science Magazine, 55- Vol. 323, pp. 69-71.

Hallowell, Edward, MD. "Crazy Busy: Dealing with an Overstretched, Overbooked, Distracted Life." Keynote address at the 24th Learning and the Brain Conference, Nov. 21, 2009.

Hawkins, David J. and Richard F. Catalano. (2002). Guiding Good Choices. South Deerfield, MA: Channing Bete, Co.

Howard, Pierce J. (2006). The Owner's Manual for the Brain: Everyday Applications from Mind-Brain Research. Austin, Texas: Bard Press.

Hyerle, David. (1996). Visual Tools for Constructing Knowledge. Alexandria, VA: ASCD.

James, William. (1890). The Principles of Psychology. Retrieved from "Classics in the History of Psychology", an Internet resource developed by Christopher D. Green, York University: Toronto, Ontario, Canada.

Jenson, Eric. (2008). "A Fresh Look at Brain-Based Education", in Phi Delta Kappan, v 89, n 6, pp. 408-417.

Kahneman, Daniel. (2011). Thinking, Fast and Slow. NY: Farrar, Straus, and Giroux.

Kandel, Eric R. (2006). In Search of Memory: The Emergence of a New Science of Mind. NY: Norton.

Kotulak, Ronald. (1997). Inside the Brain: Revolutionary Discoveries of How the Mind Works. Kansas City, MI: Andrews McNeil Pub.

LeDoux, Joseph. (1996). The Emotional Brain. NY: Simon & Shuster.

Lehrer, Jonah. (2009). "Don't: The Secret of Self-Control" in The New Yorker, May 18, 2009,pp. 6 pgs.

Lorayne, Harry and Jerry Lucas. (1974). <u>The Memory Book: The Classic Guide to Improving Your Memory at Work, at School, and at Play</u>. NY: Ballantine Books.

Mayer, John and Peter Salovey (1990). "Emotional Intelligence: Imagination, Cognition, and Personality [http://www.unh.edu/personalitylab]". 9, 185-211. Lab oratory reprint.

Meadows, Donella H. edited by Diana Wright (2008). <u>Thinking in Systems: A Primer</u>. White River Junction, VT: Chelsea Green Publishing.

Medina, John. (2008). <u>Brain Rules: 12 Principles for Surviving and Thriving at Work, Home, and School</u>. Seattle, WA: Pear Press.

Michalko, Michael. (2011). <u>Creative Thinkering: Putting Your Imagination to Work</u>. Novato, CA: New World Library.

Michalko, Michael. (2006). <u>Thinkertoys: a handbook of creative-thinking techniques, 2nd ed</u>. Berkeley, CA: Ten Speed Press.

Montagu, Ashley. (1989). <u>Growing Young</u>, 2nd ed. Westport, CT: Bergin & Garvey.

Nahayan Mabarak Al Nahayan, Sheikh. (2013; 2007). Chancellor's Messages at the Festival of Thinkers, [http://www.festivalof thinkers.com].

Nelis, Delphine, et al. (2011). "Increasing Emotional Competence Improves psychological and Physical Well-Being, Social Relationships, and Employability" in <u>Emotion</u>, Vol. 11, No. 2, pp. 354-366.

Newquist, H. P. (2004). <u>The Great Brain Book</u>. New York: Scholastic.

Osborn, Alex. (1942). <u>How to Think Up</u>. NY, NY: McGraw-Hill Book Company, Inc.

Packard, Vance. (1957, 2007). <u>The Hidden Persuaders</u>. (Introduction copyright 2007 by Mark Crispin Miller). Brooklyn, NY: Ig Publishing.

Paul, R., Binker, A., Martin, D., Vetrano, C. & Kreklau, H. (1989). Critical Thinking Handbook. CA: Sonoma State University, Center for Critical Thinking.

Paul, Richard. (1990). Critical Thinking: What Every Person needs to Survive in a Rapidly Changing World. CA: Sonoma State University, Center for Critical Thinking and Moral Critique.

Payton, John et al. (2008). The Positive Impact of Social and Emotional Learning for Kindergarten to Eighth-Grade Students: Executive Summary. IL: Collaboration for Academic, Social, and Emotional Learning, 12 p.

Peters, Tom. (1994). The Tom Peters Seminar: Crazy Times Call for Crazy Organizations. NY: Vintage Books.

Peterson, Steve. (2010). "Systems Thinking for Anyone: Practices to Consider". In Richmond, Joy, et al. Tracing Connections: Voices of Systems Thinkers. Lebanon, NH: isee systems, inc., 2010: 31-51.

Pink, Daniel L. (2006). A Whole New Mind. NY: Riverhead Books.

Prensky, Marc. (2001)."Digital Natives, Digital Immigrants". From *On the Horizon* (MCB University Press, Vol. 9 No.5).

Project Zero [http://www.pz.harvard.edu./]. (2013). VisibleThinking. MA: Harvard University.

Raths, L. E., Wasserman, S., Jonas, A., & Rothstein, A. (1986) Teaching for Thinking: Theory,Strategies, and Activities for the Classroom (2nd ed.). New York: Teachers College, Columbia University.

Ratey, John J., M.D. with Eric Hagerman. (2008). Spark: The Revolutionary New Science of Exercise and the Brain. NY: Little, Brown and Company.

Restak, Richard, M.D (2009). Think Smart: A Neuroscientist's Prescription for Improving Your Brain'sPerformance. NY, NY: Riverhead Books.

Richmond, Barry. "Introduction. The Thinking in Systems Thinking: Eight Critical Skills". In Richmond, Joy, et al. <u>Tracing Connections: Voices of Systems Thinkers.</u> Lebanon, NH: isee systems, inc., 2010: 3-21.

Schenck, Jeb, ed. (2008). <u>Teaching to the Brain: Best Practices and Best Ideas.</u> Thermopolis, WY: Knowa Pub.

Schrock, Kathy. (2014). Kathy Schrock's Guide to Everything [http://www.schrockguide.net].

Senge, Peter M. (1990). <u>The Fifth Discipline: The Art and Practice of the Learning Organization</u>. NY: Doubleday.

Senge, Peter M. et al. (1994). <u>The Fifth Discipline Fieldbook</u>. NY: Doubleday.

Senge, Peter M., et al. (2000). <u>Schools That Learn: A Fifth Discipline Fieldbook for Educators, Parents, and Everyone Who Cares About Education</u>. NY: Doubleday.

Small, Gary, M.D. and Gigi Vorgan. (2008). <u>iBrain: Surviving the Technological Alteration of the Modern Mind.</u> NY, NY: HarperCollins.

Smith, Frank. (1990). <u>to think</u>. NY: Teacher's College, Columbia University.

Sousa, David A. (2006). <u>How the Brain Learns, 3rd ed.</u> Thousand Oaks, CA: Corwin Press.

Sousa, David A., ed. (2010). <u>Mind, Brain, & Education: Neuroscience Implications for the Classroom.</u> Bloomington, IN: Solution Press.

Sousa, David A. (2012). <u>Brainwork: The Neuroscience Behind How We Lead Others</u>. Bloomington, IN: Triple Nickel Press.

Sprenger, Marilee. (1999). <u>Learning & Memory: The Brain in Action.</u> Alexandria, VA: ASCD.

Sternberg, Robert. (1994). In Search of the Human Mind. New York: Harcourt Brace.

Sylwester, Robert. (1995). A Celebration of Neurons: An Educator's Guide to the Human Brain. Alexandria, VA: ASCD.

Swartz, R. & Parks, S. (1994). Infusing Critical and Creative Thinking Into Content Instruction. Pacific Grove, CA: Critical Thinking Press & Software.

Sweeny, Michael S. (2009). Brain: The Complete Mind. Washington, D.C.: National Geographic.

Toffler, Alvin and Heidi. (2006). Revolutionary Wealth. NY: Currency Books.

Trilling, Bernie & Charles Fadel. (2009). 21st Century Skills: Learning for Life in Our Times. SanFrancisco, CA: Jossey-Bass.

Willis, Judy, MD, MEd. (2007). Brain-Friendly Strategies for the Inclusion Classroom. Alexandria, VA: ASCD.

Willis, Judy, MD, MEd. (2008). How Your Child Learns Best: Brain-Friendly Strategies You Can Use to Ignite Your Child's Learning and Increase School Success. Naperville, IL: Sourcebooks, Inc.

Wooden, John and Jay Carty. (2005). Coach Wooden's Pyramid of Success. Ventura, CA: Regal Books.

Index

Format:

1. SEARCH WORD(S)
2. **CHAPTER(S) (in bold)**
3. PAGE(S) (pages are precise in print format only)